The Coming Christian Persecution

Thomas D. Williams

The Coming
Christian Persecution
Why Things Are Getting Worse
and How to Prepare for What Is to Come

Manchester, New Hampshire

Crisis Publications

Box 5284, Manchester, NH 03108

1-800-888-9344

www.CrisisMagazine.com

Sophia Institute Press® is a registered trademark of Sophia Institute.

paperback ISBN 978-1-64413-445-0

ebook ISBN 978-1-64413-446-7

Library of Congress Control Number: 2022950965

First printing

This is the victory that overcomes the world, our faith. Who is it that overcomes the world but he who believes that Jesus is the Son of God? This is he who came by water and blood, Jesus Christ, not with the water only but with the water and the blood.

−1 John 5:4–6

Contents

The Coming Christian Persecution

Introduction

At 9:00 a.m. on Thursday, October 29, 2020, Brahim Issaoui walked into the Basilica of Notre Dame in Nice, France, brandishing a knife with a six-inch blade along with a copy of the Quran. Shouting "Allahu Akbar!" the twenty-one-year-old Tunisian stabbed the sacristan and two women to death and was attempting to decapitate them when he was apprehended. A month earlier, Issaoui had traveled across the Strait of Sicily from Tunisia to the Italian island of Lampedusa before making his way north to France, where he carried out his attack.

That same week, pro-abortion activists stormed into Catholic churches across Poland, interrupting Sunday Masses and hurling insults at priests and faithful. They were protesting a high court decision to ban eugenic abortions of children with Down syndrome and other disabilities. Meanwhile, on October 18, in Chile, radical secularists burned to the ground two Christian churches—San Francisco de Borja and the Church of the Ascension.

As a journalist following countless such incidents on a daily basis for years on end, I have been horrified and alarmed by the intensity, relentlessness, and acceleration of Christian persecution around the world. And I have been dismayed by the relative silence of the world's opinion leaders as the tragedy unfolds in plain sight. My own contacts with heartbreaking personal stories of violence, discrimination, abuse, and harassment eventually moved me to put pen to paper to sound the alarm about the magnitude of the problem, to help people understand how it resembles and differs from Christian persecutions in times past, and to suggest how men and women of goodwill might effectively address the problem.

When we hear of Christian persecution, most of us think of the early disciples huddled in catacombs, waiting to be rounded up and brutally executed by a hostile Roman Empire. Those were the days when followers of Jesus worshipped in private "house churches," since they were not permitted to build their own temples or worship publicly. They were the times when two young women—an aristocrat and her servant—were sentenced to be gored to death by a wild cow in Carthage, when the eighty-six-year-old bishop of Smyrna was burned alive in a stadium, when a Roman deacon was grilled to death on a gridiron for having proclaimed the poor of the Church to be her greatest treasure. Tyrannical emperors such as Nero, Domitian, Decius, and Diocletian hunted down and executed countless Christians for the simple crime of belonging to an illegal religion, and the early-Church historian Eusebius wrote that "great multitudes" perished during their reigns.

Many of us learned in school that when the emperor Constantine issued the Edict of Milan in 313 and Christianity was finally legalized in the empire, this all came to an end: the age of martyrs, the era of Christian persecution, was over and done with.

Even today, many Christians and casual observers sincerely believe that the age of Christian persecution ended long ago, that the world has come to accept and respect followers of Christ, and that discipleship now entails little fear of intimidation, hostility, persecution, or violence. The numbers tell a different story. Though largely ignored by the secular media, Christian persecution has not only continued unabated: it has now reached unprecedented levels. A major human-rights watchdog group recently announced the "worst year yet" for Christian persecution, noting that "Christians throughout the world continue to risk imprisonment, loss of home and assets, torture … rape and even death as a result of their faith."[1]

But given the severity of anti-Christian persecution today, this makes a comparison to the early Church even more apt. For us, the blood of those martyred under the Roman Empire cry out louder than ever. And we cannot understand our own time without making a careful study of that bloody age, its villains, and its heroes.

In exploring the plight of countless Christians around the world who are facing persecution for their faith, I do not wish to downplay the real persecution suffered by the followers of other religions. Many Jews, Muslims, Hindus, and Buddhists suffer for their faith, and activists fighting to defend people's most basic human rights may also face hostility for their deeply held beliefs. Yet Christians face an unmatched level of persecution in the world, and the unique status of anti-Christian hatred deserves to be examined as a phenomenon unto itself.

As the end of the second millennium approached, Pope John Paul II noted that the global Christian community was *increasingly* becoming a Church of martyrs, similar to the early Church. "The Church of the first millennium was born of the blood of

---

[1] RNS Press Release Distribution Service, "Persecution in World's Two Most-Populous Countries Escalates to Troubling Levels," Religion News Service, January 16, 2019, https://religionnews.com/2019/01/16/persecution-in-worlds-two-most-populous-countries-escalates-to-troubling-levels/.

the martyrs," the saintly pope wrote. "The historical events linked to the figure of Constantine the Great could never have ensured the development of the Church as it occurred during the first millennium if it had not been for the *seeds sown by the martyrs and the heritage of sanctity which marked the first Christian generations.*"

"At the end of the second millennium," he continued, "*the Church has once again become a Church of martyrs.* The persecution of believers — priests, Religious and laity — has caused a great sowing of martyrdom in different parts of the world."[2]

Seven years later, at the close of the Jubilee 2000, John Paul again called attention to the crisis. The intervening years had served only to confirm his earlier observation. And yet his reflection was hopeful, because it flowed from his conviction that persecution and martyrdom are the conditions of the fruitfulness of the Church's apostolic mission. "Perhaps we were too used to thinking of the martyrs in rather distant terms, as though they were a category of the past, associated especially with the first centuries of the Christian era," he reflected.[3] "The Jubilee remembrance has presented us with a surprising vista, showing us that our own time is particularly prolific in witnesses, who in different ways were able to live the Gospel in the midst of hostility and persecution, often to the point of the supreme test of shedding their blood." As promised by Jesus in the Gospel, the pope noted, in these witnesses, the word of God, sown in good soil, yielded a hundredfold (see Matt. 13:8, 23). "By their example they have shown us, and made smooth for us, so to

---

[2] Pope John Paul II, apostolic letter *Tertio Millennio Adveniente* on preparation for the Jubilee of the Year 2000 (November 10, 1994), no. 37.

[3] Pope John Paul II, apostolic letter *Novo Millennio Ineunte* at the beginning of the new millennium and the close of the great jubilee of the year 2000. No. 41.

speak, the path to the future," he added. "All that remains for us is, with God's grace, to follow in their footsteps."[4]

Today, twenty years later, the trend not only continues undiminished but is accelerating. "In terms of the number of people involved, the gravity of the acts committed, and their impact, it is clear that the persecution of Christians is worse today than at any time in history," declared Aid to the Church in Need in late 2017. "Not only are Christians more persecuted than any other faith group, but ever-increasing numbers are experiencing the worst forms of persecution."[5]

In January 2021, the U.S.-based Christian charity Open Doors published its World Watch List 2021, revealing that Christian persecution around the globe had reached a new acme in 2020, with an incredible 340 million Christians facing "high levels of persecution."[6] Open Doors publishes its World Watch List every January, chronicling how many followers of Jesus are targeted, discriminated against, persecuted, and attacked around the globe for their faith. Every single day around the world, some thirteen Christians are killed for their faith, twelve are illegally arrested or imprisoned, five are abducted, and twelve churches or other Christian buildings are attacked, Open Doors revealed.

---

[4] Pope John Paul II, apostolic letter *Novo Millennio Ineunte* at the beginning of the new millennium and the close of the great jubilee of the year 2000 (January 6, 2001), no. 41.

[5] Aid to the Church in Need, *Persecuted and Forgotten?: A Report on Christians Oppressed for Their Faith, 2015–17*, 10, 12, https://www.churchinneed.org/wp-content/uploads/2017/10/persecution-1-1.pdf.

[6] Open Doors, *World Watch List 2021: The Top 50 Countries Where It's Most Difficult to Follow Jesus* (January 2021), Open Doors, https://odusa-media.com/2021/01/WWL2021_Booklet-digital.pdf

The Coming Christian Persecution

Clearly, not everyone is called to martyrdom, but we should be ready for the crosses that come from following Christ. We are also called to come to the aid of our suffering brothers and sisters and to promote religious liberty so that Christians can worship in peace.

Persecution takes many forms. The most emblematic form is *martyrdom*, the suffering of death because of one's faith in Jesus Christ. The word *martyr* comes directly from the Greek word for "witness." But martyrdom is far from the only type of persecution. Persecution can also involve actions intent on making it unpleasant, difficult, uncomfortable, or unprofitable to be a committed Christian. Dictionaries define *persecution* as subjection to hostility and ill-treatment, noting its similarity to oppression, abuse, ill-treatment, discrimination, intimidation, torment, and harassment.

Christian persecution in today's world also wears many faces, whether the religiously motivated attacks on Christians as infidels by radical Islamists, the sufferings of believers under the institutional atheism of China and North Korea, the Hindu nationalism in India that treats Christians as second-class citizens, or the prejudice, ostracization, and discrimination against Christians and their beliefs among academics, media, and Big Tech in the West.

In the following pages, we will explore the phenomenon of Christian persecution and its modern-day expressions. To do this, I will begin by offering a sharp portrayal of the reality of anti-Christian hostility and violence around the globe today. Using hard data provided by human rights groups that monitor Christian persecution around the globe, we will examine some of the anti-Christian hot spots where it is most dangerous to be a committed follower of Jesus.

Chapter 1 will furnish us with the *facts*, *stories*, and *statistics* of anti-Christian aggression, providing the raw material for an in-depth analysis of the problem and a realistic understanding of its nature and scale.

Chapters 2 through 4 will situate today's problem in its historical and theological context, beginning by recalling the hatred directed at Jesus Christ Himself as well as His prophecies of what sort of welcome His disciples could expect in the world. If the vehemence of anti-Christian hatred in today's world surprises us, it is often because we forget how Jesus was received and His explicit promise that His followers would be treated in the same way.

Chapter 3 recounts the persecution in the early Church, examining the emblematic "Age of the Martyrs" in the increasingly hostile Roman Empire—the age that laid the groundwork for the future of the Church. The first three hundred years of Christianity offer us numerous examples of heroic Christian witness at the hands of an empire that often sought to stamp out all vestiges of the new religion. While this period does not nearly exhaust the historical, systematic persecution of Christians, it warrants particular attention because of its unique place in the history of the Church.

Chapter 4 will explore possible causes of the special antipathy and aggression to which Christianity has been subjected down through the ages. To this end, I will first examine the theories of those who have historically tried to minimize the reality of Christian persecution—men such as Voltaire and Edward Gibbon, who blamed the Christians themselves for their sufferings. I will then investigate other theories that are more sympathetic to the plight of Christians and that offer a deeper and more convincing explanation for anti-Christian hatred.

Against that background, chapter 5 will examine the primary drivers of Christian persecution in the world today, drawing on studies of the groups and ideologies behind much of the hostility experienced by Christians in the twenty-first century. While the geopolitical component of this aggression is noteworthy, the spiritual dimension is more central still, as the age-old spiritual battle between good and evil works itself out in history. This chapter's analysis of the drivers of anti-Christian aggression in today's world leads to a core thesis of this book—namely, that in coming years, Christian persecution is destined to grow more widespread and acute rather than to diminish.

Chapter 6 will then take a sobering look at Christian persecution in the post-Christian West, where the gospel was embraced for a period but then progressively marginalized and rejected. While a good percentage of Westerners still identify as Christians, the environment in occidental nations is growing more and more unfriendly to Christian belief and practice as what began as disdain and mockery easily descends into active aggression and violence.

Chapter 7 will summarize the causes for the declining tolerance toward Christianity in the world today and explain why Christians can expect to face more and more hostility in the coming years. We will see that the powerful and enduring drivers of persecution are abetted by ignorance, silence, and indifference among those who should be coming to the defense of persecuted Christians. Persecution will continue to increase for the foreseeable future due to a confluence of factors that have created a perfect storm of anti-Christian fury in the contemporary world.

In conclusion, chapter 8 will reflect on what persecution means for followers of Christ and how we are called to respond to it at personal and institutional levels. The Christian response to persecution, from the first centuries to the present day, has been marked by the practice of heroic virtues that have inspired generations of believers and nonbelievers alike. In fact, the admirable behavior of Christians in the face of aggression has often been the catalyst behind conversion to the Christian faith.

Although this study focuses on the ugly reality of persecution in the world today, it is meant not to discourage but to embolden. Jesus never told His disciples to expect acceptance and welcome in the world; rather, He assured them that persecution was part and parcel of the Christian vocation. The disciples, in turn, *rejoiced* when they were found worthy to suffer for their Savior (see Acts 5:41). We, too, share in that privilege. On the other hand, coming face-to-face with the reality of Christian persecution in the world should also spur us on to action. Praying for our suffering brethren around the world, supporting those who actively assist them, providing a voice for the voiceless and making known their plight, and committing ourselves to the pursuit of true religious freedom are just some of the ways in which we can join together in meeting this tremendous challenge.

1

Persecution by Numbers
The Global State of Christian Persecution

Statistics can never convey the grim reality of the personal experiences of victims of Christian persecution. Those who undergo persecution are not *numbers* but real individuals of flesh and blood, each with his or her own name, background, and history. But statistics are needed to grasp the enormity of the situation and to put the reality of Christian persecution into perspective. Sadly, the vast majority of people, Christians included, have little understanding of the seriousness, magnitude, and acceleration of the problem in today's world.

Fortunately, a number of organizations and institutions have taken it upon themselves to monitor and document in startling detail the persecution of Christians in the contemporary world. Groups such as Aid to the Church in Need, Open Doors, the Observatory on Intolerance and Discrimination against Christians in Europe, the U.S. Commission on International Religious Freedom, International Christian Concern, *L'Observatoire de la Christianophobie*, Voice of the Martyrs, Christian Solidarity Worldwide, and Release International provide invaluable research and reporting on the abuse currently being inflicted on followers of Jesus. While their voices often fall on deaf ears, their research is a treasure trove for those hoping to train a spotlight on this disturbing reality and to arouse the consciences of people of goodwill.

Although not limited to *Christian* persecution, the U.S. State Department also submits to Congress an annual report on international religious freedom in compliance with the International Religious Freedom Act of 1998. This report describes the status of religious freedom around the world and designates certain nations as "Countries of Particular Concern" (CPCs) for having "engaged in or tolerated particularly severe violations of religious freedom" during the reporting period. According to the International Religious Freedom Act, "particularly severe" refers to "systematic, ongoing, egregious violations of religious freedom," including torture, degrading treatment or punishment, prolonged detention without charges, abduction or clandestine detention, and other flagrant denials of the right to life, liberty, or the security of persons. For its part, the independent, bipartisan U.S. Commission on International Religious Freedom (USCIRF) also publishes a yearly report in which it recommends that the State Department designate certain countries as CPCs.

According to multiple sources, Christian persecution around the globe reached an unprecedented level at the end of 2020. Open Doors' *World Watch List 2021*, for example, chronicles how, around the globe, followers of Jesus are targeted, discriminated against, persecuted, and attacked for their faith,[7] stated that 1 in 8 Christians worldwide experiences high levels of persecution and discrimination—far more than members of any other religion. The list also provided an in-depth look at the fifty countries where it

---

[7] Open Doors, *World Watch List 2021: The Top 50 Countries Where It's Most Difficult to Follow Jesus*, https://www.opendoorsusa.org/wp-content/uploads/2021/01/WWL2021_Booklet-digital.pdf.

is most difficult and dangerous to be a Christian. Countries are ranked by the severity of persecution of Christians, calculated by analyzing the level of violent persecution plus the pressure experienced in five spheres of life. In 2020, some 4,761 Christians were killed around the world (an average of 13 every day), 4,277 were arrested without trial and imprisoned (11 each day), and 1,710 were abducted (4 per day).

Similarly, a 2019 report by Aid to the Church in Need, titled *Persecuted and Forgotten?*, related that Christians are the victims of at least 75 percent of all religiously motivated violence and oppression in the world.[8] In recent years, in the thirteen countries where Christians suffer the most intense persecution, the situation has worsened in all but one—Saudi Arabia. "In almost all the countries reviewed," the report said, "the oppression and violence against Christians have increased since 2015—a development especially significant given the rate of decline in the immediate run-up to the reporting period."

In 2019, Open Doors revealed that, on average, some 345 Christians are murdered around the globe *each month* because of their beliefs.[9] On a monthly basis, at least 105 churches or places of worship are vandalized or set on fire, and 219 Christians are put on trial or sent to prison for expressing their faith in the Christian Gospels.

---

[8] Aid to the Church in Need (ACN), *Persecuted and Forgotten? A Report on Christians Oppressed for their Faith 2017–19*, https://www.churchinneed.org/wp-content/uploads/2019/10/Persecuted-Forgotten_digital.pdf.

[9] Chris Tomlinson. "Christian Charity: Average of 345 Christians Killed Per Month Globally" Breitbart, April 23, 2019, https://www.breitbart.com/europe/2019/04/23/christian-charity-average-of-345-christians-killed-per-month-globally/.

The Coming Christian Persecution

The nonpartisan Pew Research Center confirmed that Christians continue to be harassed in more countries than members of any other faith. Pew found that Christians undergo harassment in 145 out of 198 countries in the world, a significantly higher number than for any other single religion. In the ten years from 2009 to 2018, the number of countries in which Christians suffer persecution from governments, groups, or individuals rose by 50.[10]

In its definition of *harassment*, Pew included a wide range of actions—"from verbal abuse to physical violence and killings"—motivated at least in part by the target's religious identity. According to the study, Christians face governmental harassment in 124 countries worldwide, while undergoing "social harassment" in 104 countries. Christians experience concentrated harassment in the Middle East–North Africa region, Pew noted, with harassment targeting Christians (either by governments or social groups) occurring in 19 of the 20 countries in the region. While social harassment of Christians occurred in 15 of the 20 countries in the region, governmental harassment of Christians was reported in 19 of the countries. Pew's findings match reports from other groups that have found Christian persecution to be the most common form of religious persecution in the world.

Hungary's state secretary for the Aid of Persecuted Christians, Tristan Azbej, speaking for a November 2020 conference organized by International Christian Concern, underscored the startling increase in the number of Christians facing persecution

---

[10] "In 2018, Government Restrictions on Religion Reach Highest Level Globally in More Than a Decade," Pew Research Center, November 10, 2020, https://www.pewforum.org/2020/11/10/in-2018-government-restrictions-on-religion-reach-highest-level-globally-in-more-than-a-decade/.

for their faith, insisting that the international community "must hear their cry for help." Azbej stated that according to the most recent statistics, the number of Christians facing persecution globally has risen from 245 million to 260 million in just one year, and during this period nearly 3,000 Christians have been murdered and 3,700 arrested for their beliefs. Approximately one-third of the world's population faces some form of religious persecution, he said, with Christians being the most persecuted community.[11]

Taking note of the situation in 2020, Pope Francis called the numbers "chilling" and said that they provide a sobering reminder of the cost of following Christ. "It is painful to remember that, at this moment, there are many Christians who suffer persecution in various areas of the world," he said, "and we must hope and pray that their tribulation will be stopped as soon as possible. There are so many; today's martyrs are more numerous than the martyrs of the first centuries.... These Christians are the bleeding members of the Body of Christ, which is the Church."[12]

And yet, Francis asserted, Christians are able to rejoice in the midst of persecution because they have "found something worth more than the whole world." Moreover, he added, Christians can find peace knowing that "enduring persecution and hostility is part of the Christian vocation."[13] Clearly, not everyone is called to martyrdom, but we should be ready for the crosses that come from following Christ. We are also called to come to the aid of

---

[11] "Government Official Urges Greater INTL Efforts to Aid Persecuted Christians," *Debrecen Sun*, November 17, 2020, https://www.debrecensun.hu/national/2020/11/17/government-official-urges-greater-intl-efforts-to-aid-persecuted-christians/.

[12] Pope Francis, General Audience, April 29, 2020.

[13] Pope Francis, Angelus message, July 19, 2020.

our suffering brothers and sisters and to promote religious liberty so that Christians can worship in peace.

Christian persecution is so widespread in the third millennium that it is impossible to narrow it down to a handful of nations or even specific continents, but there are a number of hot spots where persecution is especially acute and bloody, rendering it particularly dangerous to be a Christian in those places. The following brief survey will examine the manifestations of anti-Christian hostility in eight nations, singled out here both for their diversity and for the especially aggressive nature of the phenomenon. Although many other regions could be mentioned, the purpose here is not to provide an exhaustive look at Christian persecution around the globe—a task done exceptionally well by others—but rather to explore the deeper meaning of these trends and how Christians are to understand and react to them.

North Korea

Topping the World Watch List every single year since the publication began in 1992 is the Democratic People's Republic of Korea, or North Korea, where, at the hands of the officially atheist, Marxist state, Christians undergo "unspeakable atrocities including extrajudicial killings, forced labour, torture, persecution, starvation, rape, forced abortion and sexual violence."[14] Documented incidents against Christians include being hung on a cross over a fire, crushed under a steamroller, herded off bridges, and trampled underfoot.

In 2018, U.S. vice president Mike Pence castigated North Korea's record of human-rights violations, insisting that the nation's persecution of Christians is the worst on the planet. "North Korea's persecution of Christians has no rival on the Earth," Pence told

---

[14] ACN, *Persecuted and Forgotten? 2015–17*, 28.

leaders gathered in Washington, DC, for the State Department's Ministerial to Advance Religious Freedom. "It is unforgiving, systematic, unyielding and often fatal."[15]

Prior to the Korean War (1950–1953), North Korea had long been home to an extensive Christian community, as South Korea is today. The capital, Pyongyang, was once referred to as the "Jerusalem of the East," and regime founder Kim Il-sung himself came from a Christian family.[16] Ever since its fall to communism, however, North Korea has become more fiercely anti-Christian than any country on earth.

North Korea's 1972 constitution purports to guarantee "freedom of religious belief," which includes "approval of the construction of religious buildings and the holding of religious ceremonies." But as Aid to the Church in Need points out, "every single article of the Universal Declaration of Human Rights is, in some manner or another, denied to the people of North Korea."[17] In 2019, the United Nations special rapporteur Tomás Ojea Quintana reported to the UN General Assembly on the situation of human rights in North Korea: "There is no freedom of expression and citizens are

---

[15] Remarks by Vice President Pence at Ministerial to Advance Religious Freedom, July 26, 2018, https://trumpwhitehouse.archives.gov/briefings-statements/remarks-vice-president-pence-ministerial-advance-religious-freedom/.

[16] See Frances Martel, "North Korean Christians Face Beatings, Rape, Torture for Professing Faith," Breitbart, October 25, 2017, https://www.breitbart.com/national-security/2017/10/25/north-korea-christians-beaten-raped-tortured/.

[17] Aid to the Church in Need (ACN), *Religious Freedom in the World Report 2021* (released April 20, 2021), 528, https://acninternational.org/religiousfreedomreport/wp-content/uploads/2021/04/Executive-Summary-2021-EN-single-pages-small.pdf.

subject to a system of control, surveillance and punishment that violates their human rights."[18]

In this officially atheist state, being a Christian is a political crime because the ruling Workers' Party considers Christians to be foreign agents. As USCIRF noted in its 2021 annual report, North Korea's ruling ideology, known as *Juche*, divinizes North Korean leaders and forbids competing ideologies—including religious ones—and "treats religion as an existential threat."[19] The very definition of totalitarian, *Juche* demands unconditional loyalty and obedience to the North Korean leader, overriding the rights and freedoms enshrined in international and North Korean law, including the country's constitution.

If North Korean Christians are discovered, they are deported to labor camps as political criminals or even killed on the spot. Meeting other Christians to worship is nearly impossible and is punishable by death. One estimate suggests that three-quarters of Christians in labor camps die from the harsh punishments inflicted on them. Despite an increase in diplomatic activity, starting with the 2018 Winter Olympics in South Korea, observers insist that little has changed for Christians in the country.

"The State considers the spread of Christianity a particularly serious threat, since it challenges ideologically the official personality cult and provides a platform for social and political organization

---

[18] Tomás Ojea Quintana, "Situation of Human Rights in the Democratic People's Republic of Korea," United Nations General Assembly, September 20, 2019, https://reliefweb.int/report/democratic-peoples-republic-korea/report-special-rapporteur-situation-human-rights-4.

[19] U.S. Commission on International Religious Freedom (USCIRF), *Annual Report 2021*, April 2021, 34, https://www.uscirf.gov/sites/default/files/2021-04/2021%20Annual%20Report.pdf.

and interaction outside the realm of the State," the United Nations Commission of Inquiry on the human-rights situation of North Korea declared in 2014. "Apart from the few organized State-controlled churches, Christians are prohibited from practising their religion and are persecuted. People caught practising Christianity are subject to severe punishments in violation of the right to freedom of religion and the prohibition of religious discrimination."[20]

North Korean authorities persecute believers on a variety of charges, including religious practice, possessing religious items, contact with known Christians, attending worship services, and sharing Christian beliefs. The mere possession of a Christian Bible in North Korea is grounds for arrest, torture, and life imprisonment in a labor camp, which equates to a death sentence. Currently, some fifty thousand to seventy-five thousand Christians live inside North Korea's massive prison system, where starvation as well as physical and mental abuse are part and parcel of their sentences. Christian Solidarity Worldwide has noted that a policy of guilt by association is often applied in cases of detentions of Christians, meaning that the relatives of Christians are also detained, regardless of their beliefs.[21]

Remarkably, in spite of terrifying persecution, the Christian population in North Korea is growing. Between two hundred thousand and four hundred thousand Christians are believed to

---

[20] *Report of the Commission of Inquiry on Human Rights in the Democratic People's Republic of Korea*, United Nations Human Rights Council (February 7, 2014), 7. http://www.ohchr.org/EN/HRBodies/HRC/CoIDPRK/Pages/ReportoftheCommissionofInquiryD-PRK.aspx.

[21] See Edwin Mora, "Defector: Christianity Thrives in North Korea as Citizens 'No Longer Respect' Kim Jong-Un," Breitbart, August 16, 2017, https://www.breitbart.com/national-security/2017/08/16/defector-christianity-thrives-north-korea-citizens-no-longer-respect-kim-jong-un/.

belong to the massive underground Church, though numbers are understandably difficult to ascertain with precision.

As USCIRF has revealed, most North Korean Christians "are unable to meet for collective worship due to severe repression, and they suffer from harsh abuses such as long-term imprisonment in various prisons or prison-like facilities, severe beatings that result in broken bones and ruptured skin, strangulation, starvation, sexual violence, forced abortion, and execution." Principally responsible for the persecution against Christians is North Korea's Ministry of State Security, "which operates internment camps, holding centers, political prison camps, and pretrial detention centers."

Afghanistan

In the Islamic Republic of Afghanistan, Christians are also seen as traitors—but traitors to Islam rather than to an atheist state. The country is 99 percent Muslim, with some 90 percent Sunni and 9.7 percent Shia. USCIRF reported in October 2021 that religious-freedom conditions in Afghanistan—which were already horrific—have deteriorated since the Taliban seized control of the country on August 15, 2021.[22] Many religious-minority community members, including Christians, practice their faith in hiding due to fear of reprisal. The ruling Taliban consider conversion from Islam to another religion apostasy, which could be punishable by death according to their interpretation of Sharia, or Islamic law.

Prior to the Taliban takeover, the United Nations documented 8,820 civilian casualties in Afghanistan in 2020, including 3,035

---

[22] Niala Mohammad and Zack Udin, "Factsheet Afghanistan," USCIRF, October 2021, https://www.uscirf.gov/sites/default/files/2021-10/2021%20Factsheet%20-%20Religious%20Minorities%20in%20Afghanistan.pdf.

deaths, with some of the most brutal attacks targeting religious minorities. Anti-government, non-state actors, including the Taliban and a local branch of the Islamic State (ISIS-K), were blamed for the violence, and jihadists claimed responsibility for many of the deadliest attacks. As a point of reference, the UN reported that the Taliban were responsible for 45 percent of civilian casualties.[23]

According to USCIRF, fear among religious minorities "markedly increased" in 2020 due to a variety of factors, including "the downsizing of the U.S. troop presence, continued violence, and the government's lack of control over the entirety of the country's territory."

The preamble to the Afghan constitution declares that the people of Afghanistan believe "firmly in Almighty God, relying on His divine will and adhering to the Holy religion of Islam," and appreciate "the sacrifices, historical struggles, jihad and just resistance of all the peoples of Afghanistan, admiring the supreme position of the martyrs of the country's freedom." Article 1 of the constitution states that "Afghanistan shall be an Islamic Republic, independent, unitary and indivisible state," and article 2 adds that the "sacred religion of Islam is the religion of the Islamic Republic of Afghanistan." No law shall "contravene the tenets and provisions of the Holy religion of Islam in Afghanistan," the constitution stipulates, and the president of the country must be a Muslim.

Although the text goes on to say, "Followers of other faiths shall be free within the bounds of law in the exercise and performance

---

[23] "Nearly 6,000 Afghan Civilians Killed or Wounded in 2020: U.N.," Reuters, October 27, 2020, https://www.reuters.com/article/us-afghanistan-casualties/nearly-6000-afghan-civilians-killed-or-wounded-in-2020-u-n-idUSKBN27C1FL.

of their religious rituals," the actual freedom of minority religions is restricted by a number of laws as well as local traditions, since Islamic law (Sharia) is recognized as a source of civil law.[24]

Afghanistan's 2004 constitution requires all parliamentary laws to respect Islamic principles and requires the courts to rely on Sharia jurisprudence in the absence of governing constitutional or legal provisions. Because Afghanistan is an Islamic state, Afghan law imposes the death penalty for both apostasy and blasphemy, following Sharia, and proselytizing by non-Muslims is also a criminal offense. According to that law, male apostates must be killed, and females must be held in solitary confinement and beaten every three days until they recant and return to Islam. The crime of blasphemy includes anti-Islamic writings or speech and can be punished with the death penalty unless the accused recants within three days. Islamic religious education is also mandatory in state-run and private schools, even for non-Muslims.

In Afghanistan, "living openly as a Christian is impossible," the Watch List states, and Christian converts face dire consequences if their new faith is discovered. As a result, converts to Christianity have two options: flee the country or risk being killed. According to Afghan law, citizens are not permitted to become Christians, and conversion is seen as apostasy as well as treason. Converts are often killed by their own families, clans, or tribes. Christians from a Muslim background have also been sent to a psychiatric hospital, because leaving Islam is deemed a sign of insanity.[25]

In 2018, the United Nations Assistance Mission in Afghanistan documented 22 attacks against places of worship, religious leaders, and worshippers, which brought about 453 civilian casualties (156

---

[24] ACN, *Religious Freedom in the World Report 2021*, 24.
[25] See Open Doors, *World Watch List 2021*.

deaths and 297 injured). While the situation improved slightly in 2019, there were still 20 such attacks that resulted in 236 civilian casualties (80 deaths and 156 injured).[26] Attacks continued apace in 2020, although no official data were yet available at the time of this writing. The vast bulk of the violence against religious minorities and religious leaders were carried out by radical Islamists, especially the Taliban and ISIS-K.

Simply put, there is no safety for Christians in Afghanistan, and all are extremely vulnerable to persecution. "Areas controlled by the Taliban are particularly oppressive," Open Doors notes, "but there is no safe way to express any form of Christian faith in the country."[27]

Iraq

The violent extremism of the Islamic State, which invaded Mosul and the Nineveh Plains in 2014, resulted in the decimation of Iraq's Christian community. As much as 99 percent of the Christian population of Mosul has vanished in less than two decades, and Iraq has lost more than 90 percent of its Christian population nationwide.[28] Persecution in Iraq has decreased somewhat in the aftermath of the fall of the Islamic State, principally because the affected areas have been mostly stripped of their Christian populations. Exact figures

---

[26] United Nations Assistance Mission in Afghanistan (UNAMA), *Afghanistan: Protection of Civilians in Armed Conflict: Annual Report 2018* (Kabul: UNAMA, 2019), https://unama.unmissions.org/sites/default/files/unama_annual_protection_of_civilians_report_2018_-_23_feb_2019_-_english.pdf.

[27] "2021 World Watch List #2," Open Doors, https://cdn.open-doors.ph/en/worldwatchlist/afghanistan/.

[28] Frances Martel, "Report: Persecution in Iraq Down after Loss of over 90% of Nation's Christians," Breitbart, October 24, 2019, https://www.breitbart.com/faith/2019/10/24/report-persecution-in-iraq-down-after-loss-of-over-90-of-nations-christians/.

are unavailable, but estimates suggest that there are only 200,000 to 250,000 Christians left in Iraq, a massive drop from the 1.4 to 2 million Christians in the 1990s. Many of the Christians remaining in Iraq have been displaced internally.

As Open Doors has revealed, the Assyrian Church of the East, the Syrian Orthodox Church, the Syrian Catholic Church, the Chaldean Catholic Church, and the Armenian Orthodox Church are all still seriously affected by persecution in Iraq, especially from Islamic extremist movements and non-Christian leaders.[29] Christians also face discrimination from government authorities, and in central and southern Iraq, Christians rarely display crosses or other Christian symbols in public since this can lead to harassment or discrimination at checkpoints, at universities, in government buildings, and in the workplace. Christians who have remained in Iraq fear a systematic campaign against them that aims to change the area's demographic composition.[30]

In late 2018, the media reported a number of real-estate scams at the expense of Christians, and an Iraqi TV network revealed that at "least 350 homes belonging to Christians ... have been illegally taken away from their legitimate owners, taking advantage of their absence and through the creation of false legal documents, which make their recovery very difficult."[31]

---

[29] Open Doors, *World Watch List 2019*.

[30] "Iraq: Intimidation of Nineveh Plain Christians," Middle East Concern, August 8, 2019, https://www.meconcern.org/2019/08/08/iraq-intimidation-of-nineveh-plain-christians/.

[31] Agenzia Fides, "Hundreds of Houses Illegally Taken Away from Christians in the Nineveh Province," November 16, 2018. http://www.fides.org/en/news/65099-ASIA_IRAQ_Hundreds_of_houses_illegally_taken_away_from_Christians_in_the_Nineveh_province.

The Fides News Service noted that the phenomenon of illegal theft of real estate from Christian owners "has been able to take hold thanks to the connivance and coverage of corrupt and dishonest officials, who put themselves at the service of individual impostors and organized groups of scammers." Moreover, the theft of the properties of Christian families "is closely linked to the mass exodus of Iraqi Christians," Fides said. "The scammers take possession of empty houses and buildings, counting on the easy prediction that none of the owners will return to claim their property."[32]

More than 98 percent of Iraq's population are Muslims; about two-thirds of these are Shiites living in the south, and a third are Sunnis in the center and in the north. The 2005 Iraqi constitution establishes Islam as the official state religion and a "source of legislation." Though formally providing for freedom of religion, the constitution specifies that no law may conflict with Islam; in practice, this often leads to discrimination against minorities, so that Christians and other religious minorities describe their situation as that of "second-class citizens." Iraq's 1969 penal code criminalizes insulting religious beliefs, practices, symbols, or individuals seen as holy, worshipped, or revered, stipulating a punishment of imprisonment of up to three years or fines.[33]

Especially affected are Christian converts from Islam, who often have to keep their faith secret from neighbors and family members to avoid threats of violence or risk losing their inheritance rights and the possibility of marrying. The constitution prohibits Muslims from converting to other religions, and openly leaving Islam leads to difficult situations throughout the country.

---

[32] Ibid.
[33] ACN, *Religious Freedom in the World Report 2021*.

The Coming Christian Persecution

In 2019, Chaldean archbishop Bashar Warda of Erbil offered a grim prediction for the future of Christianity in the Middle East, saying that cyclical Islamic purges will inevitably lead to the extinction of Christians.[34] The Islamic State invasion of Iraq in 2014 led to the displacement of more than 125,000 Christians from their historical homelands and left the Christian community bereft of homes, employment, and churches. And yet, as terrible as it was, this event was far from unique. "This was an exceptional situation, but it's not an isolated one," Archbishop Warda said. "It was part of the recurring cycle of violence in the Middle East over more than 1,400 years," and this cycle is leading to the gradual eradication of Christians from the area.

"With each successive cycle the number of Christians drops, till today we are at the point of extinction," Warda said. "Argue as you will, but extinction is coming, and then what will anyone say? That we were made extinct by natural disaster, or gentle migration? That the ISIS attacks were unexpected, and that we were taken by surprise? That is what the media will say."

"Or will the truth emerge after our disappearance: that we were persistently and steadily eliminated over the course of 1,400 years by a belief system which allowed for recurring cycles of violence against Christians, like the Ottoman genocide of 1916–1922?" he asked.

The interview with Archbishop Warda marked the fifth anniversary of the Islamic State invasion of the Nineveh Plains on August 6, 2014. Christians were driven from the area and were able to return only in the fall of 2016. Christianity has been present in

---

[34] See "Iraqi Archbishop: 'Extinction Is Coming' for Christians in Middle East," Breitbart, August 8, 2019, https://www.breitbart.com/middle-east/2019/08/08/iraqi-archbishop-extinction-is-coming-for-christians-in-middle-east/. All quotations from Archbishop Warda in this section are taken from this article.

the Nineveh Plains in Iraq since the first century, and the arrival of Islam came centuries later. There have indeed been periods of Muslim tolerance of Christians in the area, Warda noted, but violent persecution has always returned.

These moments of toleration "have been a one-way experience: Islamic rulers decide, according to their own judgment and whim, whether Christians and other non-Muslims are to be tolerated and to what degree," the archbishop said. "It is not, and has never, ever been a question of equality."

"Fundamentally, in the eyes of Islam, Christians are not equal," he said. "We are not to be treated as equal; we are only to be tolerated or not tolerated, depending upon the intensity of the prevailing jihadi spirit."

"The root of all of this is the teachings of jihad, the justification of acts of violence," he said.

It should be noted that there once was a time of peace when this violence waned, at least for a while. Muslims engaged with Christians and Jews in respectful dialogue from the eighth century until the fourteenth century, helping to create the Arab Golden Age, with its flowering of science, mathematics, and medicine. But the imposition of Sharia law put an end to all that. "The imposition of Sharia law saw the decline of great learning, and the end of the Golden Age of Arab culture," Warda said. "A style of scholastic dialogue had developed, and this could only occur because a succession of caliphs tolerated minorities. As toleration ended, so did the culture and wealth which flowed from it."

"The truth is that there is a foundational crisis within Islam itself, and if this crisis is not acknowledged, addressed and fixed then there can be no future for civil society in the Middle East, or indeed anywhere Islam brings itself to bear upon a host nation," he said.

The Coming Christian Persecution

The archbishop's view of the future for Christians in the Middle East is not a hopeful one, unless Islam undergoes major internal changes. And in his mind, the West is complicit because of its failure to take Christian persecution seriously. "When the next wave of violence begins to hit us, will anyone on your campuses hold demonstrations and carry signs that say, 'We are all Christians?'" he asked. "And yes I do say, the 'next wave of violence,' for this is simply the natural result of a ruling system that preaches inequality and justifies persecution."

Cardinal Louis Raphaël Sako, the Chaldean patriarch of Baghdad, has called on Iraqi leaders to make of Iraq a secular state that gives equal standing to all citizens, regardless of their religion. "I think the only future for countries in the Middle East is to set up a secular regime, and to respect religion," Cardinal Sako said in April 2021. He issued this proposal on the one-month anniversary of Pope Francis's visit, urging Iraq to separate religion from government, "as the Christian West has done for a long time."

What we need is an end to "this mentality that Christians are infidels," Sako said, "this mentality of sectarianism, and this bad mentality of a lack of respect for non-Muslims." The cardinal said Pope Francis's visit to Iraq seemed to have an impact on Iraqi's sympathy toward Christians and effected a change of the people's mentality. "Christians are accustomed to the pope," he said, but this was "the first time that Muslims can see the pope, hear the pope."

"A civil or secular state is not hostile to religion and respects all faiths, but does not include it in politics," Sako said, proposing that Iraq adopt a model "that guarantees freedom of religion and worship for all Iraqis equally and protects the human rights contained in all international treaties." All Iraqis, "by principle and by constitution, are fully citizens with the same rights and duties," he said. "Citizenship cannot be limited to religion, creed, region, race, or number. Citizenship is a universal right for all."

"Every individual can follow his own religion and traditions," he said, "provided that he respects the religion of his brother, not treating him as a non-believer, or betraying him, or excluding or eliminating him. Such diversity flows from the will of God."

Syria

Syria is another Middle Eastern country where the Christian population has been devastated by Islamic extremism. A 2017 report revealed that more than half the Christians living in Syria had been killed or had fled the country since 2011, mostly because of targeted persecution from the Islamic State. The report said that since 2011, Christians living in much of the Middle East had experienced an "overall loss of hope for a safe and secure future," and this has driven the majority to flee their homeland in search of safety for themselves and their families.[35]

Estimates suggest that prior to 2011, approximately 8 to 10 percent of the Syrian population was Christian, meaning between 1.7 and 2.2 million people. Currently, estimates of the Christian population in Syria range from 1.4 million all the way down to 800,000, meaning that somewhere between 300,000 and 1.4

---

[35] Open Doors, Served, and Middle East Concerns, *Understanding Recent Movements of Christians from Syria and Iraq to Other Countries across the Middle East and Europe* (June 2017), https:// www.worldwatchmonitor.org/wp-content/uploads/2017/06/ Understanding-the-recent-movements-of-Christians-leaving-Syria-and-Iraq.-Hope-for-the-Middle-East.pdf. "Half of Syria and Iraq's Christians Have Left since 2011, Says Report," World Watch Monitor, June 6, 2017, https://www.worldwatchmonitor.org/2017/06/ half-syria-iraqs-christians-left-since-2011-says-report/.

million have left the country. In 2016, the Chaldean bishop of Aleppo, Antoine Audo, reported that in just five years of conflict and persecution, the Christian population in Syria had been reduced by two-thirds, from 1.5 million to only 500,000.[36]

The Syrian province of Al-Hasakeh, home to a historical Christian population, lost about half of its Christians (some 75,000 people) due to pressure from the Islamic State. When asked their reasons for leaving, Christians cited "the violence of conflict, the near complete destruction of some historically Christian towns, the emigration of others and consequent loss of community, the rate of inflation and loss of employment opportunities, and the lack of educational opportunities."

In the Syrian city of Aleppo, the Christian population fell by more than 75 percent in less than a decade, thanks in large part to militants of the Islamic State. Until 2011, Aleppo was home to Syria's largest Christian community, but in just six years, numbers dropped from 150,000 to just over 35,000.[37] Aleppo's Bishop Audo said in 2016 that the city's three cathedrals had been almost completely destroyed, and hundreds of people were carried off and later released in Chaldean villages. "You cannot imagine the dangers that we face every day," he said. Wealthy Christians have all left, while "the middle classes have become poor and the poor have become miserable."[38]

In parts of Syria under the control of radical Islamic groups, most historic churches have been demolished or repurposed as

---

[36] "Les deux-tiers des chrétiens ont quitté la Syrie, selon l'évêque d'Alep," *L'Orient-Le Jour*, March 16, 2016.

[37] ACN, *Persecuted and Forgotten?*

[38] "SYRIA – 66 % of Syrian Christians Gone, Chaldean Catholic Bishop Says," Aid to the Church in Need–Malta, https://www.acnmalta.org/syria-66-of-syrian-christians-gone-chaldean-catholic-bishop-says-acn-malta/.

Islamic centers. Authorities in these regions have outlawed public expressions of Christian faith, and Christians are forbidden from repairing or restoring church buildings or monasteries.

Jihadists bombed the Christian village of Al-Sekelbiya (Suqaylabiyah) in northwestern Syria on May 12, 2019, killing at least five young children along with their teacher during a catechism lesson and leaving six children injured.[39] The Islamists who launched the missiles belong to the terror group Hayat Tahrir al-Sham, which was previously affiliated with al-Qaeda. Two months later, on July 11, Islamists targeted the Syrian Orthodox Church of the Virgin Mary in Qamishli, in northeastern Syria, in a car-bomb attack that injured eleven civilians and damaged the church and nearby shops. Qamishli has an ancient Christian population. "They are targeting residential areas in Qamishli, where people of all religious backgrounds live," said Bassam Ishak, a Syriac Christian leader. "We think this is a message to the Kurds and Christians there to leave, so Turkey can move refugees there. We think it's a form of ethnic cleansing."[40]

Nigeria

Nigeria, an African nation split nearly fifty-fifty between Muslims and Christians, has become a theater for some of the worst

---

[39] Thomas D. Williams. "Jihadists Bomb Christian School in Syria, Killing Four Children," Breitbart, May 14, 2019, https://www. breitbart.com/middle-east/2019/05/14/jihadists-bomb-christian-school-in-syria-killing-four-children/. The number of children killed was later adjusted to five.

[40] Frances Martel, "Expert: Turkish Invasion Threatens Syrian Christian Communities in 'Renaissance,'" Breitbart, October 30, 2019, https://www.breitbart.com/faith/2019/10/30/expert-turkish-invasion-threatens-syrian-christian-communities-in-renaissance/.

anti-Christian violence in the world, with reports of massacres, kidnappings, assaults, rape, sexual enslavement, forced conversions, and destructions of homes and property arriving with alarming regularity. "More Christians are murdered for their faith in Nigeria than in any other country," declared the 2021 World Watch List.

Nigeria is the most populous country in Africa, with nearly 219 million people, of whom about 53.5 percent identify as Muslim and 45.9 percent identify as Christian. The remaining 0.6 percent identify with other religious beliefs, including atheism, the Baha'i faith, Judaism, Hinduism, Buddhism, and African traditional religions.

On December 7, 2020, the U.S. State Department designated Nigeria for the first time as a Country of Particular Concern (CPC), the short list of the world's worst violators of religious freedom. Under the International Religious Freedom Act of 1998, countries are designated as CPCs for engaging in or tolerating "systematic, ongoing egregious violations of religious freedom."[41] USCIRF had been urging the State Department to make this designation every year since 2009.[42]

Three weeks later, on December 29, 2020, Islamic terrorists released a video showing the execution of five Christians. The footage showed five armed members of the local branch of the Islamic State (ISWAP) standing behind five kneeling men dressed in orange suits and with their arms tied behind their backs. The terrorists ordered each of the men to say their names aloud, and the hostages did so, each one adding, "I am a Christian." One of

---

[41] Mike Pompeo, "United States Takes Action against Violators of Religious Freedom," U.S. Department of State, December 7, 2020, https://2017-2021.state.gov/united-states-takes-action-against-violators-of-religious-freedom-2/index.html.

[42] USCIRF, *Annual Report 2021*, 7.

the terrorists then said, "This is a warning to Christians in all parts of the world and those in Nigeria.... Use the heads of these five of your brethren to continue with your ungodly celebrations," referring to Christmas festivities. The five Muslims then executed the Christians in cold blood, shooting them in the back of the head.

According to the USCIRF annual report for 2021, conditions of religious freedom in Nigeria deteriorated significantly during 2020, "with both state and nonstate actors committing egregious violations of the right to freedom of religion or belief." Nigeria's constitution protects freedom of religion in theory, but Nigerians faced violence by "militant Islamists and other nonstate armed actors, as well as discrimination, arbitrary detentions, and capital blasphemy sentences by state authorities."

In July 2020, the president of the Commission of the Bishops' Conferences of the European Union (COMECE) denounced the ongoing violence and the targeted persecution of Christians in Nigeria by Islamist militants. In a letter to the Catholic Bishops' Conference of Nigeria, Cardinal Jean-Claude Hollerich said that the Christian communities in Nigeria are "living a situation of continuous attacks by terrorists, insurgents and militias, that in some cases reaches levels of genuine criminal persecution." In his letter, Cardinal Hollerich said that his heart goes out in a special way to "the many young people who are forced to leave the country because of violence and lack of socio-economic prospects."[43]

Already in May 2020, COMECE had appealed to the international community to increase efforts to put a halt to the violence in Nigeria, bring criminals to justice, support victims, and promote dialogue and peace. Along with urging assistance to stop the religiously motivated violence in the country, COMECE called for the

---

[43]   Ibid.

inclusion of Christians, who make up 47 percent of the national population, in all state structures and levels of administrations, including the police and the armed forces.

The extreme anti-Christian violence in Nigeria is driven primarily by two groups: (1) Boko Haram and the Islamic State in West Africa Province (ISWAP), primarily in the Northeast, and (2) Muslim Fulani militants in the Middle Belt and elsewhere in the nation. Boko Haram—a name that means "Western education is forbidden"—began its bloody insurgency in Northeast Nigeria in 2009 and, since then, has been responsible for more than thirty-six thousand violent deaths, mostly of Nigerian Christians, and three million people have been forced from their homes.

The archbishop of Kaduna, Matthew Man-oso Ndagoso, has decried the slaughter of Christians in his country and the media silence surrounding it, declaring that "Christians are being killed like chickens." In the Muslim-dominated Northwest of the country, people live in constant fear, especially in the state of Kaduna, the archbishop said in April 2019. "It is one of the states where everybody walks around afraid. There are kidnappers and bandits and they are killing people. Villages are being burned down," Archbishop Ndagoso said. "In other parts of the country if something happens, the president shows up. But here people are being killed and nothing is being done about it," he added. There is "a systemic persecution of Christians in these states," but the nation's leaders "do not have the political will to address the issues, to enforce the provisions of the constitution regarding the equality of religions and the equality of citizens before the law."[44]

---

[44] Thomas D. Williams, "Archbishop Says Christians Slaughtered 'Like Chickens' in Nigeria," Breitbart, April 30, 2019, https://

While mainstream media have insisted that much of the anti-Christian violence in Nigeria, especially that in the Middle Belt, is not religiously motivated, that is not the experience of people on the ground. The secular media in particular have attempted to downplay the religious nature of killings by Muslim Fulani militants in Nigeria's Middle Belt, preferring to attribute the violence to "ethnic tensions," a "battle for land and resources," or even "climate change," and Nigeria's president Muhammadu Buhari, who is himself of the Fulani ethnic group, has encouraged this narrative, minimizing the importance of religion in the conflict.[45]

As renowned human-rights advocate Nina Shea observed in late 2020: "A recent Nigerian news report was headlined that two sisters were released after kidnapping by 'bandits.' Deep into the article the freed girls are quoted saying that their captors forcibly converted them to Islam. Clearly more was involved than simply banditry but no doubt the case was dutifully recorded as 'banditry' in government databases."[46] In this way, much religiously motivated violence continues to be attributed simply to land disputes, ethnic rivalries, and banditry.

www.breitbart.com/africa/2019/04/30/archbishop-decries-slaughter-of-christians-like-chickens-in-nigeria/.

[45] Edwin Mora, "Nigerian President Blames 'Climate Change' for 'Genocide' of Christians by Fulani Terrorists," Breitbart, July 19, 2018, https://www.breitbart.com/national-security/2018/07/09/nigerian-president-blames-climate-change-for-genocide-of-christians-by-fulani-terrorists/.

[46] Nina Shea, "Hearing on Conflict and Killings in Nigeria's Middle Belt," House Foreign Affairs Committee, Tom Lantos Human Rights Commission Hearing on Conflict and Killings in Nigeria's Middle Belt, December 17, 2020, Hudson Institute, December 19, 2020, https://www.hudson.org/research/16578-hearing-on-conflict-and-killings-in-nigeria-s-middle-belt.

Nigeria's Christians disagree. The ongoing slaughter of Christians in Nigeria is part of a "hidden agenda" to convert the nation to Islam, an agenda that reaches to the highest echelons of the nation's leadership, according to local prelates. Fr. Valentine Obinna, a priest of the Aba Diocese in Nigeria, said in 2019 that the ongoing murders of priests and other Christians in the region are not isolated events but are tied to a long-term program of the "Islamization of Nigeria." "It's obvious. It's underground. It's trying to make the whole country a Muslim country," Father Obinna said. "But they are trying to do that in a context with a strong presence of Christians, and that's why it becomes very difficult for him," he said, in reference to Nigerian president Buhari.[47]

The reason Christians have become targets is that Buhari and others in power "want to make sure the whole country becomes a Muslim country," and they are using Boko Haram and the Fulani to achieve that objective, Father Obinna said. "People read the handwriting on the wall." During Buhari's first four-year term in office (2015–2019), in fact, more than 23,000 people died violently, primarily at the hands of Boko Haram.[48]

The Nigeria-based International Society for Civil Liberties and Rule of Law declared that some 2,400 Christians were killed by the Fulani raiders in 2018 alone. And Nigeria's *Daily Post* reported

---

[47] Elise Harris, "Slain Nigerian Clerics Are Victims of a 'Hidden Agenda', Priest Says," *Crux*, September 4, 2019, https://cruxnow.com/church-in-africa/2019/09/04/slain-nigerian-clerics-are-victims-of-a-hidden-agenda-priest-says.

[48] Edwin Mora, "Report: Jihadis, State Security Killed over 20,000 in Nigeria under President Buhari," Breitbart, June 24, 2019, https://www.breitbart.com/national-security/2019/06/24/report-jihadis-state-security-killed-over-20000-in-nigeria-under-president-buhari/.

that from June 2015 to June 2018, Fulani militants "killed 8,800 Christians and other non-Muslims," torching "no less than 1,000 churches and other places of worship during the same period." Meanwhile, a report by the Jubilee Campaign asserted that 52 lethal anti-Christian attacks took place in Nigeria during the first six months of 2019.

"It's tough to tell Nigerian Christians this isn't a religious conflict since what they see are Fulani fighters clad entirely in black, chanting 'Allahu Akbar!' and screaming 'Death to Christians,'" said Sr. Monica Chikwe of the Hospitaller Sisters of Mercy at a 2019 Rome conference on Christian persecution.[49]

Two local Catholic bishops have also insisted that the use of armed Fulani jihadists as weapons indicates that the violence represents a "clear agenda for Islamizing the Nigerian Middle Belt." One of the bishops, Matthew Ishaya Audu of Lafia, said in 2018 that the ongoing attacks are not random or economically motivated but purposefully target Christians. "They want to strike Christians," Bishop Audu said, "and the government does nothing to stop them, because President Buhari is also of the Fulani ethnic group."[50]

Christian pastors are not the only ones who recognize the religiously motivated anti-Christian violence prevalent in Nigeria's Middle Belt. According to a disturbing December 2019 *Wall Street Journal* essay titled "The New War against Africa's Christians,"

---

[49] John L. Allen Jr., "Anti-Christian Carnage in Nigeria Could Be Global Security Nightmare," *Crux*, August 4, 2019, https://cruxnow.com/news-analysis/2019/08/anti-christian-carnage-in-nigeria-could-be-global-security-nightmare.

[50] Thomas D. Williams, "Prelates: Nation's Leaders Seek 'Islamization of Nigeria,'" Breitbart, September 4, 2019, https://www.breitbart.com/africa/2019/09/04/nations-leaders-seek-islamization-nigeria-prelates-say/.

The Coming Christian Persecution

Islamist Fulani militants are waging a brutal war on Nigeria's Christians in a crusade to rid the country's Middle Belt of non-Muslims.[51] In his firsthand account of the atrocities in the former British colony, Bernard-Henri Lévy wrote that Fulani extremists now pose a greater threat than Boko Haram, and they carry out systematic jihadist attacks involving burning, raping, maiming, pillaging, and killing.

This "slow-motion war" against Nigeria's Christians is "massive in scale and horrific in brutality," wrote Lévy, and yet "the world has hardly noticed." While mainstream media normally describe the attacks on Christians as ethnically motivated, this description is false, Lévy insisted, the work of "professional disinformers."

"They are Islamic extremists of a new stripe," said a Nigerian NGO director interviewed by Lévy, "more or less linked with Boko Haram." According to the 2019 Global Terrorism Index, the Fulani militants are now deadlier than Boko Haram and carried out the majority of Nigeria's 2,040 documented terrorist fatalities in 2018.

In his account, Lévy chronicles a series of atrocities: "The mutilated cadavers of women. A mute man commanded to deny his faith, then cut up with a machete until he screams. A girl strangled with the chain of her crucifix." There are "too many Christians in Lagos," one of the Fulani told Lévy. "The Christians are dogs and children of dogs. You say Christians. To us they are traitors. They adopted the religion of the whites. There is no place here for friends of the whites, who are impure."

According to the Anglican bishop of Jos, Benjamin Kwashi, the Fulani raiders are trying to spread fear throughout the region

---

[51] Bernard-Henri Lévy, "The New War against Africa's Christians," *Wall Street Journal*, December 20, 2019, https://www.wsj.com/articles/the-new-war-against-africas-christians-11576880200.

so that the survivors of their attacks will convince others to leave. Their brutality is essential to creating an atmosphere of terror among local Christians. Whereas Boko Haram is confined to as little as 5 percent of Nigerian territory, Lévy notes, "the Fulani terrorists operate across the country."

As USCIRF noted in 2021, Fulani-affiliated armed groups "used religious rhetoric while conducting myriad attacks on predominantly Christian villages in Kaduna State," and kidnappers "deliberately targeted Christians for abduction and execution." Meanwhile, the Nigerian government "has routinely failed to investigate these attacks and prosecute those responsible, demonstrating a problematic level of apathy on the part of state officials."[52]

USCIRF commissioner Gary Bauer has been particularly forthright in his assessment of Nigeria's predicament, insisting that Nigeria is quickly becoming a "killing field" for the nation's Christians. "In large swaths of the country, Christian parents fear for their children every day when they go to school," Bauer said in early 2021. "Those children are targeted by savage Islamists who kidnap and force them to renounce Christ or face death. Every time a Nigerian Christian family worships at a church, they are painfully aware it may be the last thing they do on this earth. The churches are ripe targets for Boko Haram and other jihadists. Christians have been blown up or 'mowed' down in their places of worship."[53]

Those who attribute this violence to mere "bandits" or regard it simply as hostility between farmers and herdsmen "ignore the main truth," Bauer said—namely, that "radical Islamists are committing violence inspired by what they believe is a religious imperative to 'cleanse' Nigeria of its Christians. They must be stopped."

[52] USCIRF, *Annual Report 2021*, 30.
[53] Ibid., 32.

"More Christians have been killed for their faith in Nigeria in the last year than in the entire Middle East," Bauer said, in reference to the year 2020. "Unless we find our voice, what is happening in Nigeria will move relentlessly toward a Christian genocide."[54] Sam Brownback, the former U.S. ambassador-at-large for International Religious Freedom, shares this grim outlook, noting repeated reports from religious-community representatives that "religious freedom in Nigeria deteriorating, including what they assess as an increasing threat of 'mass atrocities,'" adding that "local and international NGOs and religious organizations criticize the government's seeming inability to prevent or mitigate violence between Christian and Muslim communities."[55]

India

Indian Christians trace their history back to AD 52, when the apostle Thomas is believed to have reached their shores to evangelize those living there. Presently there are some 28 million Christians in India, making up just 2.3 percent of the overall population of 1.4 billion, which is overwhelmingly Hindu. India also bears the dubious distinction of being one of the countries of the world where religious freedom has suffered the greatest decline in recent years. As USCIRF noted in its 2021 report, "In 2020, religious freedom conditions in India continued their negative trajectory. The government, led by the Bharatiya Janata Party (BJP), promoted

---

[54] Ibid.

[55] Office of International Freedom, *2020 Report on International Religious Freedom: Nigeria*, U.S. Department of State, May 12, 2021, https://www.state.gov/reports/2020-report-on-international -religious-freedom/nigeria/.

Hindu nationalist policies resulting in systematic, ongoing, and egregious violations of religious freedom."[56]

In India, religious identity is increasingly tied to national identity, meaning that to be considered a "real" Indian, you must be a Hindu, a notion often implicitly—if not explicitly—encouraged by the ruling government. Open Doors' World Watch List of nations where it is most difficult to be a Christian placed India at number 10 in 2021. Less than a decade ago, India was ranked 31, but it has climbed the ranks every year since Narendra Modi, a hardliner of the ruling BJP, came to power as prime minister in 2014.

In India, Christians are persecuted in all areas of public and private life, and regional anti-conversion laws are abused to harass and intimidate Christians. One of the concrete ways the BJP facilitates social restrictions of religious freedom is through such legislation—state-level statutes designed "to regulate religious conversions allegedly accomplished through 'forcible' and 'fraudulent' means, including 'inducement' and 'allurement.' "[57]

In March 2021, the former spokesman of the Catholic Bishops' Conference of India warned that anti-conversion laws in India are a "ready-made tool" for those who wish to persecute Christians. On March 8, the state of Madhya Pradesh passed a so-called Freedom of Religion bill, increasing punishments for "forced conversions," a term critics say is interpreted loosely by authorities to harass Christians and other religious minorities in the mostly Hindu nation. The legislation stipulates up to ten years in jail and a fine of up to $1,375 as punishment for religious conversion through "coercion, force, allurement and fraudulent means and misrepresentation," including marriages solemnized through fraudulent means.

---

[56]   USCIRF, *Annual Report 2021*, 22.
[57]   ACN, *Religious Freedom in the World Report 2021*, 307.

"This Act has the potential to create social disruption since it discriminates against and criminalizes interreligious marriages," said Fr. Babu Joseph, the bishops' former spokesman. "In a multi-religious country like India interreligious marriages have been taking place for millennia and they had produced some outstanding examples religious harmony but all that now comes under the veil of suspicion."[58]

In January 2021, for example, nine Christians were arrested in Madhya Pradesh after a Hindu nationalist group complained of "forced conversions" under the previous government ordinance.[59] Police arrested the parents of a girl along with seven other Christians, charging that the parents had taken the girl to the Christian community center for a prayer meeting under the pretext of taking her to visit her grandmother. The nine Christians were held without bail after presiding judge Yatindra Kumar Guru declared that "it does not seem appropriate to grant bail to the accused, looking into the facts and circumstances."[60]

The arrest drew criticism from human-rights advocates, who said that the move was an act of hostility against Christians. "The new draconian anti-conversion legislation is a tool for majority

[58] Thomas D. Williams, "Christian Leaders Protest 'Anti-Conversion' Laws in India," Breitbart, October 1, 2021, https://www.breitbart.com/faith/2021/10/01/christian-leaders-protest-anti-conversion-laws-in-india/.

[59] Nirmala Carvalho, "Anti-Conversion Law in India a 'Ready Made Tool' to Target Christians, Priest Says," Crux, March 12, 2021, https://cruxnow.com/church-in-asia/2021/03/anti-conversion-law-in-india-a-ready-made-tool-to-target-christians-priest-says.

[60] Thomas D. Williams, "Nine Christians Arrested in India for Alleged "Forced Conversions," Breitbart, February 6, 2021, https://www.breitbart.com/faith/2021/02/06/nine-christians-arrested-india-alleged-forced-conversions/.

vigilante groups to make false complaints and harass the small Christian community," said Sajan K. George, president of the Global Council of Indian Christians. The Freedom of Religion Ordinance "is deliberately misused by right-wing groups and vested interests to exploit existing communal tensions in which Christians are a minority," he said.[61]

Many Hindu nationalists insist that India should be rid of followers of other religions, such as Christianity and Islam. They often resort to the use of violence, particularly targeting Christian converts from a Hindu background. In their villages, Christians are accused of following a "foreign faith" and suffer frequent physical attacks. If they do not "re-convert," their community may completely ostracize them, with a devastating effect on their ability to get jobs, earn an income, and buy food.

In its 2017 report on religious freedom in India, USCIRF noted an ongoing deterioration of conditions for Christians and other religious minorities due to a multifaceted campaign by Hindu-nationalist groups such as Rashtriya Swayamsevak Sangh (RSS), Sangh Parivar, and Vishva Hindu Parishad. "These [religious-minority] groups face challenges ranging from acts of violence or intimidation to the loss of political power," the report stated.[62]

As bad as the situation was in 2017, hate crimes and targeted violence against Christians in India during just the first two months of 2019 showed a startling jump of 57 percent over the same period in 2018, according to a report of the Religious Liberty Commission of the Evangelical Fellowship of India (EFI).[63] During January

---

61 Ibid.
62 USCIRF, "India," *Annual Report 2018*, https://www.uscirf.gov/ sites/default/files/Tier2_INDIA.pdf.
63 "Report Shows 57 Percent Jump in Aggression against Christians in India," *Morning Star News*, March 4, 2019, https://

and February of that year, seventy-seven incidents of "hate and targeted violence against Christians" were documented in India as compared with the forty-nine cases recorded during the same period in 2018. The EFI report said that official figures are invariably low because most cases of persecution go unreported—either because the victim and witnesses are too frightened to speak out or because the police ignore the harassment and fail to file mandatory First Information Reports.

The sharp rise in Christian persecution for 2019 had already been forecast by Release International (RI)—a UK-based charity that helps persecuted Christians around the world—which warned that persecution against Christians would rise in India. "These are countries that have long been on the list but we're seeing an upwards curve, an alarming rise in persecution," said RI spokesman Andrew Boyd, underscoring India's "militant Hinduism."[64]

While many cases of violence are instigated by citizens, other cases involve abuse by law-enforcement officials. On January 13, 2019, female police officers interrupted a Christian worship service in Uttar Pradesh, India's most populous state, where Christians make up a tiny minority, and arrested four women and two men, including Sindhu Bharti, the female pastor who was conducting the worship service. At the police station, one of the female police officers forcefully struck Bharti, rendering her unconscious.

"Boiling tea was forcibly thrust in her mouth because the police thought that she was feigning her unconsciousness," said Madhu

---

morningstarnews.org/2019/03/report-shows-57-percent-jump-in-aggression-against-christians-in-india/.

[64] Thomas D. Williams, "Report: Christian Persecution in India Jumps by 57% in 2019," Breitbart, March 20, 2019, https://www.breitbart.com/asia/2019/03/20/report-christian-persecution-in-india-jumps-by-57-in-2019/.

Bharati, an eyewitness to the event. "When that did not work, they poured two jugs of cold water on her face, not caring that it was already severely cold due to winter."[65] Pastor Bharti had to receive medical treatment for her injuries.

The cases of Christian persecution recorded in the first two months of 2017 were very close in number to those in 2018—fifty cases as opposed to forty-nine—which made the leap to seventy-seven cases in 2019 all the more disturbing.

A 2020 report by Persecution Relief, an ecumenical forum in India, also showed a significant increase in attacks against Christians in India over the last five years. The report, released on October 15, chronicled 157 cases of persecution of Christians, including four murders, between July 1 and September 30, 2020. "Our findings are based on those who make direct calls to our toll-free numbers and others who inform us," said Persecution Relief founder Shibu Thomas, adding that these recorded incidents are "only the tip of an iceberg."[66]

Christians do not report many incidents "for fear of retribution from the attackers and also of police and other government officials, who are hand in glove with the attackers, mostly right-wing Hindu activists," Thomas said.[67]

According to International Christian Concern (ICC), attacks on Christians and their churches in India continue to be reported in greater number and severity. "Much of the violence is perpetrated by radical Hindu nationalists who believe they have the tacit

---

[65]   "Report Shows 57 Percent Jump in Aggression."

[66]   "Christian Shot Dead inside Indian Church as Persecution Intensifies," UCA News, October 26, 2020, https://www.ucanews.com/news/christian-shot-dead-inside-indian-church-as-persecution-intensifies/90032#.

[67]   Ibid.

approval of the BJP-led government to perpetrate acts of violence against India's religious minorities," ICC noted.

In April 2020, USCIRF designated India as a CPC for the first time since 2004, declaring that the government engages in or tolerates "particularly severe" violations of religious freedom. "In 2019, religious freedom conditions in India experienced a drastic turn downward, with religious minorities under increasing assault," USCIRF stated in its 2020 report.[68]

"Following the Bharatiya Janata Party's (BJP) re-election in May, the national government used its strengthened parliamentary majority to institute national level policies violating religious freedom across India, especially for Muslims," it declared. "Violence against Christians also increased, with at least 328 violent incidents, often under accusations of forced conversions," the report found. "These attacks frequently targeted prayer services and led to the widespread shuttering or destruction of churches."

The national and various state governments "allowed nationwide campaigns of harassment and violence against religious minorities to continue with impunity, and engaged in and tolerated hate speech and incitement to violence against them," the report states. "Based on these developments, in this report USCIRF recommends CPC designation for India," it said.[69]

China

The People's Republic of China, under the unopposed, authoritarian control of the Chinese Communist Party (CCP), is one

---

[68] USCIRF, *Annual Report 2020*, April 2020, 20. https://www.uscirf.gov/sites/default/files/USCIRF%202020%20Annual%20Report_42720_new_0.pdf.

[69] Ibid.

of many states whose constitutions formally guarantee religious freedom while in practice such freedom is virtually nonexistent. Article 36 of China's 1982 constitution declares: "Citizens of the People's Republic of China enjoy freedom of religious belief. No state organ, public organization or individual may compel citizens to believe in, or not to believe in, any religion; nor may they discriminate against citizens who believe in, or do not believe in, any religion." While asserting that the state protects "normal religious activities," the constitution goes on to prohibit the use of religion for activities that "disrupt public order, impair the health of citizens or interfere with the educational system of the state." It adds that religious organizations and activities must not be "subject to any foreign domination." Only the five faith traditions — Buddhism, Taoism, Islam, Protestantism, and Catholicism — are officially recognized, and only those governed by state-sanctioned "patriotic" associations. This means that the underground Catholic Church, independent Christian "house churches," and other religious entities not controlled by the state enjoy no rights at all.

Although exact data are unavailable, some 5 percent of China's 1.4 billion people are Christian, with 60 to 80 million Protestants and roughly 12 million Catholics, the latter evenly divided between the state-run Chinese Catholic Patriotic Association and the underground Church, which is faithful to Rome.[70] Despite severe repression, Christianity is flourishing in China, and the Council on Foreign Relations estimates that the number of Chinese

---

[70] Sarah Cook, *The Battle for China's Spirit: Religious Revival, Repression, and Resistance under Xi Jinping* (Washington, DC: Freedom House, 2017), 42, https://freedomhouse.org/sites/default/files/FH_ChinasSprit2016_FULL_FINAL_140pages_compressed.pdf.

Protestants has grown by an average of 10 percent annually since 1979.[71] There are now more Christians in China than members of the CCP, and China is on track to have the world's largest Christian population by 2030.

Especially since the rise to power of Xi Jinping, general secretary of the CCP since 2012, the party has assumed ever stricter control over religious activities in the country, resorting to prison, torture, and pervasive surveillance to maintain its absolute power over churches and people of faith. Since early 2014, local authorities have intensified efforts to stem the spread of Christianity amid official rhetoric about the threat of "Western" values and the need to "Sinicize" religions or integrate them into the Chinese social-ist mentality. Despite formal recognition of freedom of religion, in point of fact the CCP has arrogated to itself total control over religious practice and bans any unlicensed religious worship, edu-cation, or assembly. To register as a state-sanctioned Christian organization, religious leaders must receive training to "adapt" doctrine to government and CCP thinking. The Communist Party is officially atheist, and CCP members and members of the armed forces are required to be atheists and are forbidden from engaging in religious practice of any sort.

Beginning in 2014, the CCP has engaged in a fierce campaign to remove crosses from even party-controlled Christian churches, with authorities insisting that the crosses must go because "Christianity does not belong in China."[72] In the eastern coastal province of Zhejiang's city of Wenzhou, known for its large Christian

---

[71] Eleanor Albert, "Christianity in China," Council on Foreign Relations, last updated, October 11, 2018. https://www.cfr.org/backgrounder/christianity-china.

[72] Frances Martel, "Communists Warn Citizens: 'Christianity Does Not Belong in China,'" Breitbart, October 7, 2020, https://

population, party officials ordered the removal of hundreds of crosses and the demolition of dozens of churches that allegedly violated construction regulations, even though several had received prior approval from local officials.[73]

As part of its "Sinicization" process, the CCP has also sought to replace images of Jesus Christ with photos of President Xi. In 2017, Chinese officials threatened to deny Christians poverty-relief packages unless they substituted images of Jesus in their homes with photos of Xi. The measure, carried out in the Jiangxi Province, was part of a government plan to "melt the hard ice" in the hearts of Christians toward communism, authorities said. One official declared that the move was necessary because Christians are "ignorant" and need to be taught to worship the state, not God.

Officials across Henan Province have similarly forced Christian churches to replace the Ten Commandments with quotes from President Xi.[74] "Support religious community in interpreting religious thought, doctrines, and teachings in a way that conforms with the needs of the progress of the times," reads one of the Xi quotes. "Resolutely guard against the infiltration of Western ideology, and consciously resist the influence of extremist thought."

One pastor from a state-run Protestant church said that the CCP's latest move is part of a systematic plan to erode Christian

www.breitbart.com/faith/2020/10/07/communists-warn-citizens-christianity-does-not-belong-china/.

[73] Albert, "Christianity in China."

[74] Leah MarieAnn Klett, "China Makes Churches Replace Ten Commandments with Xi Jinping Quotes: 'This Is What the Devil Has Always Done,'" *Christian Post*, September 17, 2019, https://www.christianpost.com/news/china-makes-churches-replace-ten-commandments-with-xi-jinping-quotes-this-is-what-the-devil-has-always-done-233002/.

doctrine in the country, adding that the ultimate goal of the party is to "become God."

The pastor, who spoke under the condition of anonymity, said the government first bans unauthorized religious assemblies. "Then it dismantles crosses and starts to implement the 'four requirements' by ordering the national flag and 'core socialist values' to be placed in churches. Surveillance cameras to monitor believers and religious activities are then installed. The last step is to replace the Ten Commandments with Xi Jinping's speeches."

The activities of state-sanctioned religious organizations are regulated by the State Administration for Religious Affairs, which manages all aspects of religious life, including religious leadership appointments, selection of clergy, and interpretation of doctrine. In a controversial 2018 secret deal between the Vatican and the CCP, Pope Francis yielded to the Communist Party part of the Church's authority to name Catholic bishops in the country.

According to regulations imposed in February 2018, children under the age of eighteen are barred from participating in religious activities and religious education, and religious-affairs bureaus in localities including Henan, Shandong, Anhui, and Xinjiang have released letters telling parents not to take their children under eighteen to such activities. The law mandates the teaching of atheism in schools. Authorities require teachers working in high schools in Zhejiang, Jiangxi, and Henan Provinces to sign a letter pledging to hold no religious beliefs. For their part, students are required to submit to an interview with school authorities if they declare religious beliefs on mandatory forms.

Pressure to denounce religion is also brought to bear on adults, and many Chinese companies now require workers to sign a "no-faith commitment" attesting to their atheism. According to Feng-gang Yang of Purdue University's Center on Religion, "faith-based organizations are perceived as one of the most serious threats to the Communist party."[75]

Particularly disturbing is the installation of surveillance and tracking devices in churches across China as part of the authorities' desire for greater control over the movements of Christians in the country. Regular scanning reveals who are consistently attending services, and fingerprints and scans are being used to monitor and track not only those attending worship services but also their families.[76] The increased surveillance is part of China's Sharp Eyes Project, which intends to achieve "blind-spot-free monitoring" of citizens, including in rural regions of the country.

The Chinese government has created "an Orwellian surveillance state with an unprecedented ability to gather private information about its citizens," which it is now using to monitor Christians, USCIRF reported in July 2020. The Chinese government has "installed hundreds of millions of surveillance cameras across the country" and has "systematically installed cameras in churches to identify and target anyone who attends services," USCIRF noted. Moreover, "China's exportation of its surveillance technology and repressive model holds dire implications for religious freedom around the world."[77]

[75] Council on Foreign Relations, "Christianity in China," October 11, 2018, https://www.cfr.org/backgrounder/christianity-china.

[76] See International Christian Concern, "China Increases Church Surveillance and Monitoring," Persecution.org, November 16, 2019, https://www.persecution.org/2019/11/16/china-increases -church-surveillance-monitoring/.

[77] USCIRF, virtual hearing on "Technological Surveillance of Religion in China," July 22, 2020. https://www.uscirf.gov/events/ hearings/uscirf-virtual-hearing-technological-surveillance -religion-china.

The Coming Christian Persecution

Religious freedom in China has gotten worse under the leadership of Xi Jinping, said USCIRF chairperson Gayle Manchin, who underscored the "tremendous suffering the people of China have experienced under the Chinese Communist government. USCIRF has been warning about religious freedom violations in China since the Commission was created in 1998, and the situation has only deteriorated since then."[78]

"Throughout the country, Chinese authorities have raided underground house churches, arrested Christians who refuse to join the state-run churches, and banned children younger than 18 years old from attending services," Manchin noted, adding that the Communist Party "is deliberately using technology to undermine religious freedom and other fundamental rights."[79]

Vice Chair Tony Perkins said that the CCP uses artificial intelligence systems combining information from video surveillance, facial and voice recognition, GPS tracking, and other data "in order to track certain religious communities."

"Authorities even installed cameras on the pulpits of churches and other houses of worship, allowing the Party to identify and monitor anyone who attends services," Perkins said.[80]

Chris Meserole, deputy director for the Artificial Intelligence and Emerging Technology Initiative at the Brookings Institution, testified that the CCP has harnessed digital technologies to make its repression of religion more effective. "As with authoritarians elsewhere, the CCP has long been able to repress public forms of religious organizations, practices, identities, and beliefs, particularly

---

[78] Gayle Manchin, opening remarks, virtual hearing on "Technological Surveillance of Religion in China."

[79] Ibid.

[80] Tony Perkins, opening remarks, virtual hearing on "Technological Surveillance of Religion in China."

in urban areas," Meserole said. "But private forms of religiosity, including those practiced within one's home, have proven more diffi-cult to monitor and repress. Digital technologies have changed that. As processors, sensors, and cameras have proliferated, the extent of religious life that the CCP can surveil has expanded dramatically."[81]

Pakistan

Open Doors considers the Islamic Republic of Pakistan to be the fifth worst country for Christians, where followers of Jesus face extreme persecution in every area of their lives and live under the constant threat of mob attacks. As a tiny minority of the heav-ily Muslim population, all Christians "suffer from institutional-ized discrimination, illustrated by the fact that occupations seen as low, dirty and derogatory are reserved for religious minorities like Christians by the authorities," the organization stated, and Christians can even be victims of bonded labor.[82] As less than 2 percent of the population, Christians have often been victims of the country's harsh blasphemy laws, which are arbitrarily enforced, almost exclusively against religious minorities. In its 2020 report, USCIRF revealed that nearly eighty individuals remain imprisoned in Pakistan for blasphemy, with at least half facing a life sentence or death.

The report said that religious-freedom conditions across Pakistan continue "to trend negatively" and the systematic enforcement of

[81] Chris Meserole, "Technological Surveillance of Religion in China," Brookings, July 22, 2020, https://www.brookings.edu/ testimonies/technological-surveillance-of-religion-in-china/.

[82] Lindy Lowry, "The 10 Most Dangerous Places for Christians," January 15, 2020, Open Doors, https://www.opendoorsusa. org/christian-persecution/stories/the-10-most-dangerous -places-for-christians/.

blasphemy laws and authorities' failure to address forced conversions to Islam has "severely restricted freedom of religion or belief."[83] In its subsequent report (2021), USCIRF said that "religious freedom conditions in Pakistan continued to worsen" during 2020, and the government "systematically enforced" blasphemy laws and failed to protect religious minorities from abuses.[84] There was "a sharp rise in targeted killings, blasphemy cases, forced conversions, and hate speech targeting religious minorities," including Christians, the report declared. In 2020, there were thirty Christians, including seven on death row, jailed in Pakistan on charges of blasphemy, the report noted, including Asif Pervaiz, a thirty-seven-year-old Christian garment-factory worker sentenced to death in September 2020.

Pakistan's penal code criminalizes acts and speech insulting religion or defiling the Quran, the prophet Muhammad, places of worship, or religious symbols. These vague provisions are "frequently abused" to levy false accusations against Christians and other religious minorities, USCIRF observes. The law prescribes severe punishments—including the death penalty—for blasphemy. While the state has never actually implemented the death penalty for this crime, people accused of blasphemy often face threats to their life from extrajudicial forces, such as Muslim lynch mobs, and many alleged blasphemers are killed by street vigilantes with no trial. In July 2020, a U.S. citizen accused of blasphemy was shot dead in a courtroom in Peshawar during a hearing of his case. His murderer received massive support from the Pakistani public, who hailed him as a "holy warrior" of Islam for the assassination.[85]

---

[83] USCIRF, "Pakistan," *Annual Report 2020*, 32, https://www.uscirf.gov/sites/default/files/Pakistan.pdf.

[84] USCIRF, *Annual Report 2021*, 36.

[85] Gabrielle Reyes, "Pakistan Sentences Christian Man to Death for 'Blasphemous Text,'" Breitbart, September 9, 2020, https://

Even the few Christians belonging to the middle class are not exempt "from being marginalized or persecuted in an Islamic culture," Open Doors has noted, and "believers are always at risk because of the country's notorious blasphemy laws."[86] Despite international pressure, Pakistan has refused to relax these laws.

Emblematic in this regard is the now well-known case of Asia Bibi, a Christian woman and mother of five who was jailed for nearly a decade on trumped-up blasphemy charges.[87] In June 2009, Pakistani police arrested Bibi for blasphemy following complaints by Muslim women, backed up by an imam, who claimed that Bibi had insulted the prophet Muhammad, and the following year she was sentenced to death by hanging. The accusations stemmed from a dispute between Bibi and a group of Muslim coworkers. She had been harvesting berries with a group of Muslim women who grew angry with her for drinking out of the same metal water bowl as they, insisting that she was not permitted to do so because, as a Christian, she was unclean.

The woman also accused Bibi of insulting the Prophet, a charge that she vehemently denied. She claims that when her coworkers made derogatory statements about her faith, she merely answered: "I believe in my religion and in Jesus Christ, who died on the cross for the sins of mankind. What did your Prophet Muhammad ever do to save mankind?"

Wilson Chowdhry, chairman of British Pakistani Christian Association, said that Bibi was the victim of intense persecution

---

www.breitbart.com/asia/2020/09/09/pakistan-sentences
-christian-man-death-blasphemous-texts/.

[86] Lowry, "10 Most Dangerous Places."

[87] "Sentenced to Death for a Sip of Water," *New York Post*, August 25, 2013, https://nypost.com/2013/08/25/sentenced-to-death -for-a-sip-of-water/.

for comparing Christ with the Prophet. "She spoke about the wonderful sacrifice Christ made of his life for us and asked the simple question, 'What has Muhammad done for you?' For that, this torture, this beating, this isolation, attempts to assassinate her," he said. "We've never heard of such animosity that would result in, in essence, the whole country being against her. It has been really awful; she's been separated from her five children for the whole period of that time," he added. The "pernicious blasphemy laws of Pakistan have to be terminated; they serve no purpose in modern-day society and are not even sanctioned by the Quran," he said.[88]

Former governor of Punjab Salman Taseer and former minister for minorities Shabbaz Bhatti, Pakistan's only Christian minister, were both assassinated for raising concerns over Bibi's incarceration and calling for a review of the country's blasphemy laws. Bibi's death sentence was finally overturned in October 2018, provoking violent protests led by the anti-blasphemy Islamist Tehreek-e-Labbaik Pakistan (TLP) party. In the wake of Bibi's acquittal, Islamists began attacking random travelers who identified themselves as Christians.[89]

As Shazia Khokhar, a Pakistani Christian woman, testified before the UN Human Rights Council in Geneva in 2018, in Pakistan, "once an individual is accused of blasphemy, he is presumed guilty and the law fails to safeguard against people willing to use violence." The blasphemy law "creates an atmosphere of

---

[88] Tola Mbakwe, "Nine Years in Prison for Asia Bibi," *Premier Christian News*, June 15, 2018, https://premierchristian.news/en/news/article/nine-years-in-prison-for-asia-bibi.

[89] Edwin Mora, "Report: Pakistan's Christians Living in Terror over Asia Bibi Case," Breitbart, November 20, 2018, https://www.breitbart.com/national-security/2018/11/20/report-pakistans-christians-living-in-terror-over-asia-bibi-case/.

religious intolerance and has contributed to the institutionalization of discrimination against religious minorities," she added. "As a poor Christian, from a low caste, Asia Bibi was among the most vulnerable to get accused," Khokhar noted, adding that the legal system, which is theoretically designed to protect the innocent, "failed to protect her in any way."[90]

It is, in fact, Christian women who often suffer most, being "targeted for both their faith and their gender," Open Doors has asserted.[91] It is credibly estimated that some one thousand girls and women are converted to Islam against their will each year, and many of these are kidnapped, forcibly married, and subjected to rape. Local police are often accused of complicity in these cases by failing to investigate them properly. When the cases are investigated, authorities often question the women in front of the men they were forced to marry, pressuring them to deny coercion.[92]

In 2019, the Associated Press reported that hundreds of Pakistani Christians girls had been sold as brides to China, which experiences a massive gender deficit because of the country's long-standing one-child policy.[93] The report stated that 629 girls and women from across Pakistan had been sold as brides to

---

90 "Women Activists Highlight Persecution of Christians in Pak at UN," *Business Standard*, last updated March 13, 2018, https:// www.business-standard.com/article/news-ani/women-activists-highlight-persecution-of-christians-in-pak-at-un-118031300082_1. html.

91 Lowry, "10 Most Dangerous Places."

92 USCIRF, "Pakistan," *Annual Report 2020*, https://www.uscirf. gov/sites/default/files/Pakistan.pdf.

93 Breitbart London, "Hundreds of Pakistani Christians Sold as Brides to China," Breitbart, December 7, 2019, https:// www.breitbart.com/europe/2019/12/07/hundreds-pakistani -christians-sold-brides-china/.

Chinese men and taken to China in just one year but that little was done to prosecute the traffickers because government officials were "fearful of hurting Pakistan's lucrative ties to Beijing." According to Saleem Iqbal, a Christian activist who has helped parents rescue several young girls from China, the government put "immense pressure" on officials from the Federal Investigation Agency (FIA) pursuing trafficking networks to get them to desist in their inquiry. "Some (FIA officials) were even transferred," Iqbal said. "When we talk to Pakistani rulers, they don't pay any attention."[94]

Pakistan's blasphemy laws, forced conversions, and the sale of Christian women do not exhaust the expressions of Christian persecution in the country, which at times become deadly. One of the most horrific attacks in recent years was the Easter Day massacre of Christians in March 2016, when a suicide bomber blew himself up in the Gulshan-e-Iqbal Park in Lahore, killing at least 72 persons, mostly women and children, and injuring 320.[95] Hundreds of Christian families had gathered in the park to celebrate Easter when twenty-eight-year-old Yusuf Farid, a member of the radical Islamist group Jamaat-ul-Ahrar, a branch of the Taliban, detonated his explosive vest just outside the exit – only feet away from the children's play area. Survivors said they saw bodies dismembered by the blast sprawled in pools of blood, and police confirmed the use of metal balls that sprayed in every direction to increase the lethal effect of the bomb. Among the victims were more than thirty

---

[94] Ibid.
[95] "Pakistan: kamikaze fa strage di cristiani a Lahore, 72 morti, maggior parte donne e bambini," ANSA, March 29, 2016, https://www.ansa.it/sito/notizie/mondo/2016/03/27/pakistan-kamikaze-in-parco-53-morti_aec2ba12-9efb-4cb0-ad0c-3a543b6e27ab.html.

small children, who at the time of the blast were playing sports and games in the park.

Unfortunately, Christian persecution in Pakistan is getting worse, not better. Cecil Chaudhry, executive director of the National Commission of Justice and Peace, noted in early 2021 that incidents of forced conversions and marriages, hate speech against religious and sectarian minorities, and killings in the name of religion had all increased in Pakistan during 2020.[96]

Conclusion

Shocking as it is, the preceding exposition of the state of Christian persecution in eight countries—North Korea, Afghanistan, Iraq, Syria, Nigeria, India, China, and Pakistan—provides but a window into a problem that extends far beyond the boundaries of these nations. Anti-Christian hostility is now so widespread as to constitute a pandemic in its own right. As readers will have observed, nearly every one of these hot spots—like other modern states—pays lip service to religious freedom in its official documents, a stark reminder that mere "parchment barriers" (to use James Madison's phrase) do not avail without institutions and the will to back them up.

As noted earlier, it is a constant finding of reports by human-rights and religious-liberty watchdogs that Christian persecution is growing *worse*, not better, a trend we will examine further in chapter 8.

But first we will situate the contemporary phenomenon of Christian persecution in its historical and spiritual contexts. As

---

[96] Kamran Chaudhry, "A Grim Year for Pakistan's Persecuted Religious Minorities," UCA News, January 18, 2021, https://www.ucanews.com/news/a-grim-year-for-pakistans-persecuted-religious-minorities/91029.

extensive and overwhelming as that phenomenon is in the twenty-first century, it is not new. To grasp the significance of today's anti-Christian aggression, we must go back to the time when Jesus Christ walked the earth. Hunted as a baby, hounded during His public life, and ultimately executed in the most brutal fashion at the age of thirty-three, Jesus never knew "success" in the worldly sense. Moreover, He repeatedly promised His disciples that they, too, would be "hated" for following Him. Let us now turn to Jesus' personal experience of hostility and the roadmap He laid out for future generations of believers.

2

A Theology of Antipathy
Jesus' Promise of Ongoing Persecution

One simple fact that has strengthened oppressed Christians down through the ages has been the entirely *expected* nature of the abuse. From the Apostolic Age to the present, no follower of Christ can reasonably say that he never knew persecution was coming. Even before His disciples knew what the "cross" was, Jesus made it quite apparent that it would accompany all those who chose to associate themselves with Him. People sometimes speak of the "prosperity gospel" or the "gospel of success," but except in the most metaphorical of senses, such terminology stands diametrically opposed to the message of Jesus. While no Christian can be certain of reaping material benefits from his faith, all Christians can be sure that the more closely they follow Christ, the more they will experience the persecution that was the hallmark of His own life on earth.

In this chapter, we will recall Jesus' experience of persecution and how it accompanied Him throughout His life, culminating in His Passion and Crucifixion. Along the way, we will ponder His promises of persecution for His disciples, what that meant for them, and what it means for us.

While the Gospel passages quoted will be familiar to most Christians, what some readers may find striking is just how often and how insistently Christ spoke about persecution, both in relation to Himself and to His followers. Compiling the material in one place reveals just how central the message of persecution was to Jesus' public ministry and, by extension, to the Church He founded.

Hostility toward Jesus

Persecution started early for Jesus and accompanied Him until the end of His earthly sojourn. A hint of the rejection He was to experience showed itself while He was still in His mother's womb—manifested in the lack of a place for him in the inn at His ancestral home of Bethlehem, an unfriendliness expressed poetically by St. John in the opening chapter of his Gospel: "He was in the world, and the world was made through him, yet the world knew him not. He came to his own home, and his own people received him not" (John 1:10–11).

When, as an infant, Jesus is presented in the temple, the prophet Simeon takes Him in his arms and tells His mother, Mary, that He is destined to be "a sign that is spoken against" and that "a sword will pierce through your own soul also" (Luke 2:34–35).

This hostility grows much more acute in the violent reaction of King Herod to news of the birth of the Infant Jesus, brought to him by the Magi. Deeply troubled, Herod disingenuously requests more detailed information about this newborn King of the Jews "that I too may come and worship him" (Matt. 2:8). When the Magi fail to bring him news, returning to their country by another route, Herod flies into a rage.

"Then Herod, when he saw that he had been tricked by the wise men, was in a furious rage," Matthew recounts, "and he sent and killed all the male children in Bethlehem and in all that region who were two years old or under, according to the time which he had ascertained from the wise men" (Matt 2:16). Warned by an angel in a dream, Joseph flees to Egypt with Mary and Jesus, and there they stay. It is only after the death of Herod that Joseph, visited in another dream by an angel of the Lord, decides to return to Israel. Learning, however, that Herod's son Archelaus is now ruling in Judea in place of his father, Joseph—again instructed in a dream—takes Mary and Jesus to settle in Galilee, in the town of Nazareth.

In His own description of the rejection He experiences, Jesus casts the reaction to His mission in terms of light and darkness, truth and falsehood. It is no mere human dislike or conflict of personalities, He insists, but is rooted in people's state of soul. "This is the judgment, that the light has come into the world, and men loved darkness rather than light, because their deeds were evil. For every one who does evil hates the light, and does not come to the light, lest his deeds should be exposed. But he who does what is true comes to the light, that it may be clearly seen that his deeds have been wrought in God" (John 3:19–21).

In other words, some will love Jesus because they love truth and love the light. They will be drawn to Him who is the way, the truth, and the life (John 14:6). Others, however, whose hearts are dark and who fear the truth will find in Jesus a stumbling block. He will appear to them as an enemy set out to thwart their plans, an adversary who must be removed. John the Baptist offers similar testimony about Jesus and the reaction He is destined to receive. "He who comes from above is above all. . . . He bears witness to what he has seen and heard, yet no one receives his testimony; he who receives his testimony sets his seal to this, that God is true" (John 3:31–33). In this case, John emphasizes that it is the divine character of Jesus' message that provokes either the welcome or the repudiation.

To be sure, Jesus also says and does plenty of things that stoke the ire of those who are already ill-disposed toward Him. Early in John's Gospel we find Jesus chasing the money changers and merchants out of the temple with a whip, overturning their tables and driving out their livestock. "You shall not make my Father's house a house of trade!" he exclaims (see John 2:16). Asked for some sign to prove His authority for His actions, Jesus answers with the enigmatic, "Destroy this temple, and in three days I will raise it up" (John 2:19). By acting with such authority in the temple, however, Jesus sets Himself up as a rival to those who believe it is their domain—namely, the scribes and the Pharisees.

These Jewish leaders begin watching Jesus more closely, scrutinizing His words and actions. When, on the sabbath, Jesus heals an invalid, a man who had been afflicted for thirty-eight years, at the pool of Bethesda in Jerusalem the scribes and the Pharisees rebuke the cured man when they see him carrying his sleeping mat, as Jesus had instructed him to do. What follows in John's Gospel is a passage that sums up the growing hostility toward Jesus and where it would necessarily lead.

> This was why the Jews persecuted Jesus, because he did this on the sabbath. But Jesus answered them, "My Father is working still, and I am working." This was why the Jews sought all the more to kill him, because he not only broke the sabbath but also called God his Father, making himself equal with God. (John 5:16–18)

This situation is mirrored in the synoptic Gospels as well. In Matthew's narrative, Jesus defends His disciples when they are accused of breaking the sabbath by picking heads of grain and eating them; He tells the Pharisees that "the Son of man is lord of the sabbath" (Matt. 12:8).[97] He then proceeds into the synagogue,

---

[97] See also Mark 2:23-24; Luke 6:1-5.

where there is a man with a withered hand. He heals the man, provoking the wrath of the Jewish leaders. The passage ends on an ominous note: "But the Pharisees went out and took counsel against him, how to destroy him" (Matt. 12:14), or, as Luke puts it, "they were filled with fury and discussed with one another what they might do to Jesus" (Luke 6:11).[98]

Herein we find the immediate motives for the Jews' persecution of Jesus: He seems to spurn the law by working on the sabbath and He does so with impunity, justifying His actions by saying He is imitating His Father, Lord of the sabbath. And thus Jesus adds: "Very truly I tell you, the Son can do nothing by himself, he can only do what he sees the Father doing, because whatever the Father does the Son also does" (John 5:19).

Rather than back down, Jesus gets right in the face of the Jewish leaders, accusing them of infidelity to their own Scriptures by their failure to recognize and accept Him. "You search the scriptures, because you think that in them you have eternal life; and it is they that bear witness to me; yet you refuse to come to me that you may have life" (John 5:39–40).

He then reproves them further: "Do not think that I shall accuse you to the Father; it is Moses who accuses you, on whom you set your hope. If you believed Moses, you would believe me, for he wrote of me. But if you do not believe his writings, how will you believe my words?" (John 5:45–47). In other words, Jesus hits the Pharisees harder still, insisting that by rejecting Him, they are, in fact, failing to believe the words of Moses, in whom they have put their trust.

Yet another factor in the ballooning hatred for Jesus among the Jewish leaders is His growing popularity among the people,

---

[98] See also Mark 3:6.

who began to wonder aloud whether He is the Messiah, a notion the leaders find repugnant, in part because of Jesus' lowly origins as a Galilean. "When the Christ appears, will he do more signs than this man has done?" some asked. "The Pharisees heard the crowd thus muttering about him, and the chief priests and Pharisees sent officers to arrest him" (John 7:31–32). Not a little envy surely enters the picture as well. As we read elsewhere, "when Jesus finished these sayings, the crowds were astonished at his teaching, for he taught them as one who had authority, and not as their scribes" (Matt. 7:28–29).[99] In other words, the crowds are drawing unfavorable comparisons between the scribes and Jesus, and this would not have endeared to them the one they considered a Galilean upstart.

Disregarding the anger He has stirred up thus far, Jesus goes further still, to the point of calling the Jews sons of the devil rather than children of Abraham. "If you were Abraham's children, you would do what Abraham did, but now you seek to kill me, a man who has told you the truth which I heard from God; this is not what Abraham did. You do what your father did," Jesus tells them (John 8:39–41). The Jews then insist that they are God's children, which Jesus again denies, insisting that if God were their Father, they would accept Him, since He came from God. "You are of your father the devil, and your will is to do your father's desires. He was a murderer from the beginning, and has nothing to do with the truth, because there is no truth in him" (John 8:44).

Jesus then returns to an argument He has used before: that if the Jews reject Him, it is because they do not love the truth. "When he [the devil] lies, he speaks according to his own nature, for he is a liar and the father of lies. But, because I tell the truth, you do not believe me," Jesus tells them. "Which of you convicts me of sin? If I tell the truth, why do you not believe me? He who is of God hears the words of God; the reason why you do not hear them is that you are not of God" (John 8:44–47).

The eighth chapter of John's Gospel ends with the culmination of this discourse, in which Jesus commits His greatest "offense" yet by equating Himself with God. "Your father Abraham rejoiced that he was to see my day; he saw it and was glad," He says. The Jews respond, "You are not yet fifty years old, and have you seen Abraham?" To which Jesus replies, "Truly, truly, I say to you, before Abraham was, I am." This is not merely the assertion that He has seen Abraham but the far graver adoption of the words of God to describe Himself: "I am." At this, the Jews "took up stones to throw at him; but Jesus hid himself, and went out of the temple" (John 8:56–59).

The tension grows more intense still in John 9 when Jesus heals a man born blind, again on the sabbath. This evident miracle even causes a division in the ranks of the Pharisees themselves. "Some of the Pharisees said, 'This man is not from God, for he does not keep the sabbath.' But others said, 'How can a man who is a sinner do such signs?' There was a division among them" (John 9:16). When the formerly blind man himself attempts to stand up for Jesus, insisting that only a holy man could work the signs He has, the Pharisees rebuke him and drive him away. Later, the man again meets Jesus and acknowledges him as the Messiah, "worshipping" him. At this Jesus says, "For judgment I came into this world, that those who do not see may see, and that those who see may become blind." Some of the Pharisees nearby hear Him say this and say to Him, "Are we also blind?" Jesus answers: "If you were blind, you would have no guilt; but now that you say, 'We see,' your guilt remains" (John 9:39–41).

The Coming Christian Persecution

In the following chapter, we find Jesus once again asserting His divinity, which draws from the Jews a charge of blasphemy. "My Father, who has given them to me, is greater than all, and no one is able to snatch them out of the Father's hand. I and the Father are one," Jesus asserts. At this the Jews again take up stones to stone Him. Jesus says to them, "I have shown you many good works from the Father; for which of these do you stone me?" The Jews answer, "We stone you for no good work but for blasphemy; because you, being a man, make yourself God" (John 10:29-33).

A further motivation for the Jews' aggression toward Jesus emerges in John 11, following the death of Lazarus and Jesus' raising him from the dead. This act generates even more belief among the people, and the Jewish leaders begin to fear repercussion from their Roman rulers. "So the chief priests and the Pharisees gathered the council, and said, 'What are we to do? For this man performs many signs. If we let him go on thus, every one will believe in him, and the Romans will come and destroy both our holy place and our nation,'" the Gospel states. Then one of them, the high priest Caiaphas, says to them, "You know nothing at all; you do not understand that it is expedient for you that one man should die for the people, and that the whole nation should not perish." St. John relates that Caiaphas did not say this on his own, but "being high priest that year he prophesied that Jesus should die for the nation, and not for the nation only, but to gather into one the children of God who are scattered abroad." And the passage ends, "So from that day on they took counsel how to put him to death" (John 11:47-53).

In the following chapter, Jesus explains that as happens in nature, fruitfulness and indeed "glory" emerge from a willingness to let go of one's own life. This description of His coming Passion also provides a lesson for His followers: not to cling to their lives on earth but to be willing to relinquish them. "The hour has come for the Son of man to be glorified," he declares. "Truly, truly, I say to you, unless a grain of wheat falls into the earth and dies, it remains alone; but if it dies, it bears much fruit. He who loves his life loses it, and he who hates his life in this world will keep it for eternal life" (John 12:23-25).

So far, we have looked only at John's Gospel, but similar events are recorded in the synoptic Gospels as well, including the Pharisees' anger over the disciples' failure to wash their hands before eating—which Jesus defends—and parables aimed directly at the scribes and Pharisees and their mismanagement of their mission, such as the parable of the wicked tenants. This latter parable elicits the following response: "When the chief priests and the Pharisees heard his parables, they perceived that he was speaking about them. But when they tried to arrest him, they feared the multitudes, because they held him to be a prophet" (Matt. 21:45-46).[100]

After this, Jesus launches into an extended diatribe against the Jewish leaders and their hypocrisy, which most certainly did not ingratiate Him with them. "But woe to you, scribes and Pharisees, hypocrites! because you shut the kingdom of heaven against men; for you neither enter yourselves, nor allow those who would enter to go in," Jesus begins. "Woe to you, scribes and Pharisees, hypocrites! for you traverse sea and land to make a single proselyte, and when he becomes a proselyte, you make him twice as much a child of hell as yourselves" (Matt. 23:13-15). Constantly poking the bear, He goes on to call them "blind guides," "blind fools," "whitewashed tombs," "snakes," and a "brood of vipers," repeatedly labeling them hypocrites. "So you also outwardly appear righteous to men, but within you are full of hypocrisy and iniquity," he states (Matt. 23:28).

---

[100] See also Mark 12:1-12.

In the end, the Pharisees hate Jesus for His devastating reproaches of their hypocrisy, for His apparent flouting of the externalities of the law that they love, for His alleged blasphemy, for His increasing popularity, for His willingness to fraternize with tax collectors and sinners, for creating the risk of a violent Roman reaction, and for His overfamiliarity with God, whom He calls "Father." He is in every way a threat to their status and authority and a thorn in their side.

It is during His Last Supper, however, that Jesus offers His apostles His clearest teaching on the ultimate resistance and hostility He will soon face. In this instance, He reveals the most explicit motivation for the hatred directed at Him: it is, in fact, hatred of God Himself. By torturing and killing Him, they give vent to their wrath against God.

> He who hates me hates my Father also. If I had not done among them the works which no one else did, they would not have sin; but now they have seen and hated both me and my Father. It is to fulfil the word that is written in their law, "They hated me without a cause." (John 15:23-25)

When, in the end, Jesus is apprehended by the temple guard in the Garden of Gethsemane, He makes it very clear that the choice is ultimately His, not theirs, and that He is fulfilling the will of His Heavenly Father. Just as Jesus had eluded being stoned or thrown off a cliff because His hour "had not yet come," now that His hour has arrived, He hands Himself over willingly.

Peter, in fact, reaches for his sword and strikes the high priest's servant, cutting off his ear, but Jesus declares: "Put your sword back into its place; for all who take the sword will perish by the sword. Do you think that I cannot appeal to my Father, and he will at once send me more than twelve legions of angels? But how then should the scriptures be fulfilled, that it must be so?" (Matt 26:52–54).

At the same time, Jesus rebukes His captors, shining a light on their injustice and baseness. "Have you come out as against a robber, with swords and clubs to capture me? Day after day I sat in the temple teaching, and you did not seize me. But all this has taken place, that the scriptures of the prophets might be fulfilled" (Matt 26:55–56).

Hostility toward the Disciples of Jesus

Jesus not only foretold His own Passion and death, preparing His disciples for the agony of seeing Him brutally tortured and killed; He also foretold their own sharing in His fate, insisting that whoever follows Him will partake of His Passion as well. It is because of their union with Jesus that this will happen, He asserts, and thus persecution is a mark of the true disciple's intimate sharing in the life and mission of Jesus, just as the world's love and acceptance is a sure sign that a would-be disciple has not attained to this union.

In St. Matthew's Gospel, Jesus offers a series of counsels to His disciples, warning them of coming persecutions and urging them not to fear those who can kill the body but cannot kill the soul (Matt. 10:28). "Behold, I send you out as sheep in the midst of wolves; so be wise as serpents and innocent as doves," He tells them. "Beware of men; for they will deliver you up to councils, and flog you in their synagogues, and you will be dragged before governors and kings for my sake, to bear testimony before them and the Gentiles" (Matt. 10:16–18). Jesus never sugarcoats the mission of His disciples: persecution is part and parcel of the task He puts before them and a vital component of their witness before the peoples.

Jesus also urges His followers to trust in the Holy Spirit for wisdom to know what to say in moments of trial. Jesus proposes that rather than relying on earthly wisdom or carefully crafted argumentation, they should offer themselves as mouthpieces of God's wisdom: "When they deliver you up, do not be anxious how you are to speak or what you are to say; for what you are to say will be given to you in that hour; for it is not you who speak, but the Spirit of your Father speaking through you" (Matt. 10:19–20).

The scope of the persecution they will face extends even into their homes and most intimate relationships, Jesus cautions them. "Brother will deliver up brother to death, and the father his child, and children will rise against parents and have them put to death; and you will be hated by all for my name's sake. But he who endures to the end will be saved" (Matt. 10:21–22). Over and over Jesus tells His followers not to expect to be loved and welcomed in this world but, quite the contrary, to be "hated by all." He is setting them up not for a worldly victory but for an eternal one.

He also reminds them that this persecution has a cause, and that cause is Jesus Himself. A good apprentice should always aspire to be like his master, and if he learns well, he should expect the same treatment. "A disciple is not above his teacher, nor a servant above his master; it is enough for the disciple to be like his teacher, and the servant like his master," He says. "If they have called the master of the house Beelzebul, how much more will they malign those of his household." If one's Leader has been maligned as a devil—the opposite of what He is—then a true disciple should also expect to be unjustly accused as a hater, a bigot, a simpleton, and an enemy of progress.

Jesus is not only Lord and Master, however. He also identifies personally with His disciples—so totally that He experiences their suffering as His own. Whatever is done—good or bad—to His followers is done personally to Him, and as Head of the Church, He suffers in the suffering Church as well. When Jesus meets Saul on the road to Damascus, He declares: "Saul, Saul, why do you persecute me?" He does not ask why Saul persecutes *His disciples*, but *Him*. Thus, when Saul asks Him who He is, Jesus replies: "I am Jesus, whom you are persecuting" (Acts 9:4-5). The persecution lived by the Church is persecution of Jesus Himself.

At the same time, despite the certainty of violent opposition, Jesus assures His followers that this suffering is not to be feared. A Christian knows that he is not a sprinter but a marathoner and that the finish line is not worldly success, fame, and fortune but eternal life. "So have no fear of them; for nothing is covered that will not be revealed, or hidden that will not be known. What I tell you in the dark, utter in the light; and what you hear whispered, proclaim upon the housetops," He declares, while reassuring them of their preciousness in God's eyes. "And do not fear those who kill the body but cannot kill the soul; rather fear him who can destroy both soul and body in hell. Are not two sparrows sold for a penny? And not one of them will fall to the ground without your Father's will. But even the hairs of your head are all numbered. Fear not, therefore; you are of more value than many sparrows" (Matt. 10:26-31).

In the end, a Christian's brave and loyal witness—to stand with Jesus no matter the cost—will be rewarded in kind. It is Jesus Himself who will advocate for the faithful Christian on the last day, and thus he need not fear judgment. "So every one who acknowledges me before men, I also will acknowledge before my Father who is in heaven; but whoever denies me before men, I also will deny before my Father who is in heaven" (Matt. 10:32-33).

The Coming Christian Persecution

There is something about the Savior's task that is divisive, Jesus warns. He is not only the Prince of Peace but also the one who demands that a stand be taken—for Him or against Him. People will be forced to take sides, and those who are not with Him will be against Him, and those who do not gather with Him will ultimately scatter (Matt. 12:30). He calls His disciples to radical discipleship, not polite afternoon tea and crumpets. "Do not think that I have come to bring peace on earth; I have not come to bring peace, but a sword," He insists. "For I have come to set a man against his father, and a daughter against her mother, and a daughter-in-law against her mother-in-law; and a man's foes will be those of his own household" (Matt. 10:34–36).

In the end, Jesus concludes, a Christian is summoned to be willing to give up his life, to let go of earthly aspirations and to seek heavenly ones, both for himself and those he loves. By losing his life in this way, he will save it. "He who loves father or mother more than me is not worthy of me; and he who loves son or daughter more than me is not worthy of me; and he who does not take his cross and follow me is not worthy of me," Jesus says. "He who finds his life will lose it, and he who loses his life for my sake will find it" (Matt. 10:37–39). These were the words that energized the martyrs of the early Church and continue to energize martyrs two thousand years later.

Jesus also seems to suggest that persecution will intensify as the world approaches its final days. "Then they will deliver you up to tribulation, and put you to death; and you will be hated by all nations for my name's sake," He declares. "And then many will fall away, and betray one another, and hate one another. And many false prophets will arise and lead many astray. And because wickedness is multiplied, most men's love will grow cold. But he who endures to the end will be saved. And this gospel of the kingdom will be preached throughout the whole world, as a testimony to all nations; and then the end will come" (Matt 24:9–14).[101]

Persecution is not only guaranteed to Christ's followers. It is also a *choice* that they are called to make, since many times they will be able to avoid it through compromise. An ongoing temptation for believers is to accommodate the world, to cling to life, and to allow ourselves to be "assimilated." This, Jesus warns, is a temptation we must resist. "If any man would come after me, let him deny himself and take up his cross and follow me," He states. "For whoever would save his life will lose it; and whoever loses his life for my sake and the gospel's will save it" (Mark 8:34–35).

One of the more consoling teachings Jesus offers regarding the violence and malevolence His disciples will confront is its source in intimacy with Him. It is because a disciple identifies with Jesus, shares His life and mission, and lives in union with Him that he will suffer resentment and rancor.

Nowhere is this brought out more clearly than in Jesus' discourse at the Last Supper, as recorded by St. John. "If the world hates you, know that it has hated me before it hated you. If you were of the world, the world would love its own; but because you are not of the world, but I chose you out of the world, therefore the world hates you" (John 15:18–19). First, Jesus urges His followers to remember that He Himself was rejected by the world, so when it happens to them, they will be prepared. Next, He asserts that the *reason* for the world's hatred is that His disciples belong to Him and not to the world. His choice of them has removed them from the world. They are *in the world* but no longer *of the world*, and thus the world does not love them as its own.

---

[101] See also Mark 13:9–13.

"Remember the word that I said to you, 'A servant is not greater than his master,'" Jesus continues. "If they persecuted me, they will persecute you; if they kept my word, they will keep yours also. But all this they will do to you on my account, because they do not know him who sent me" (John 15:20-21). Once again, Jesus ties His own persecution to his persecutors' ignorance of the Father. Since they do not know God the Father, they cannot recognize God the Son. But just as Jesus is hated because of the Father, so will His disciples be hated on account of His name. Jesus adopts this same parallelism when speaking of mission: "As the Father has sent me, even so I send you" (John 20:21) as well as of the communion of believers: "As thou, Father, art in me, and I in thee, that they also may be in us, so that the world may believe that thou hast sent me" (John 17:21).

To this discourse, Jesus adds two key points. First, He explains to them *why* He is warning them about coming aggression—namely, to keep them from stumbling when it arrives. Next, He explains the *motivation* of those who persecute Christians, to help His followers to forgive as He forgave, "for they know not what they do" (Luke 23:34).

"I have said all this to you to keep you from falling away," Jesus tells them at the Last Supper. "They will put you out of the synagogues; indeed, the hour is coming when whoever kills you will think he is offering service to God. And they will do this because they have not known the Father, nor me. But I have said these things to you, that when their hour comes you may remember that I told you of them" (John 16:1-4). Jesus explains to His apostles that He warns them of the coming persecution so that they may not falter in their mission. It would be easy for the apostles to wonder whether they were indeed on the right path if their religious leaders said they were not. It would be easy for today's believers to question their path when, instead of success, they meet with apparent failure. They could *stumble*, rethink their choice, but Jesus tells them: "They will put you out of the synagogues." He urges them to be ready for the same treatment He received and not to stumble when it happens. He also warns them that their persecutors will often believe that in persecuting them, they are offering service to God. We will see in the following chapter, for instance, how radical Islamists insist that their persecution of Christians is an act of worship of Allah, who demands from them jihad.

A portion of Christ's teaching on the coming hostilities to His followers is revealed in the form of an intimate prayer to His Father, uttered during the Last Supper and recorded by St. John the Evangelist. In it, Jesus reiterates His understanding that Christians no longer belong to the world and therefore will be rejected by the world. He also adds an endearing plea to His Father to defend them from Satan and to strengthen them for the mission that lies ahead.

> I have given them thy word; and the world has hated them because they are not of the world, even as I am not of the world. I do not pray that thou shouldst take them out of the world, but that thou shouldst keep them from the evil one. They are not of the world, even as I am not of the world. Sanctify them in the truth; thy word is truth. As thou didst send me into the world, so I have sent them into the world. (John 17:14-18)

At the very end of John's Gospel, we are presented with the moving scene of Christ's encounter with Simon Peter, in which the prince of the apostles is granted the occasion to repudiate his former denials of his Lord by reasserting his love three times. When he has done so, Jesus gently prepares him for the martyrdom that awaits him in the future. Although these words were directed specifically to Peter, they contain a precious lesson for all followers of Jesus.

> Truly, truly, I say to you, when you were young, you girded yourself and walked where you would; but when you are old, you will stretch out your hands, and another will gird you and carry you where you do not wish to go." (This he said to show by what death he was to glorify God.) And after this he said to him, "Follow me." (John 21:18-19)

Christ's apostles understood this only too well. It's true: with the exception of John the Beloved, they abandoned their Lord on Calvary. But in the years to come, every last one of them took up his own cross. All of the apostles were put to death for the faith except John, who nevertheless suffered persecution and who miraculously survived an attempt to put him to death. The first Christians were also the first martyrs—the first of countless martyrs, all of whom gave their lives for the risen Lord.

3

Sanguis Christianorum
The Church in the Patristic Age

The nascent Christian Church suffered bloody persecution on and off for three centuries, facing hostility both from the Jewish community and from the Roman Empire. Of the first thirty-one popes, a remarkable twenty-eight are believed to have died as martyrs, and forty-eight of the first fifty popes have been recognized as saints. Numerous other Christians died as martyrs during the three centuries leading up the legalization of Christianity in AD 313. "In the first three centuries, living a Christian life in Rome offered the surest possible way of being exposed to the risk of martyrdom," wrote Cardinal Ratzinger. "This gave the pope a 'martyrological' character."[102]

This vital period in the history of the Church, known as the "Age of the Martyrs," offers a key point of reference for Christian persecution more generally, since, in it, the very existence of Christianity hung in the balance and the Christian response to persecution was forged and consolidated. It has continued as a touchstone

---

[102] Joseph Ratzinger, *God and the World: Believing and Living in Our Time, a Conversation with Peter Seewald* (San Francisco: Ignatius Press, 2002), 381–382.

for suffering Christians of every subsequent generation and thus deserves an in-depth treatment that we will not replicate for the sporadic persecutions of later centuries. Although the violence and aggression suffered by Christians under the Roman Empire does not nearly account for all systematic persecution of Christians, it merits particular attention befitting its unique place in the history of the Church.

Generations of Catholics have become familiar with notable early Christian martyrs of Rome and North Africa through the Roman Canon of the Mass. That venerable list includes the eleven apostles and continues with Popes Linus, Cletus, Clement, Sixtus, and Cornelius, followed by Sts. Cyprian, Lawrence, Chrysogonus (who was beheaded and his body thrown into the sea during the Diocletian persecution), John and Paul (beheaded by Julian the Apostate around AD 362), and the brothers Cosmas and Damian (stoned and then beheaded in Syria in AD 287, during the Diocletian persecution). It later enumerates the New Testament figures of John the Baptist, Stephen, Matthias, and Barnabas; then more from the Apostolic Age: Ignatius, Alexander, Marcellinus, Peter, Felicity, Perpetua, Agatha, Lucy, Agnes, Cecilia, and Anastasia.

The martyrdom of Christians under the Roman Empire took many gruesome forms. Christians who were Roman citizens, such as the apostle Paul, had the "privilege" of being executed by beheading, which at least brought a quick end. Noncitizens were subject to more prolonged ordeals, including crucifixion, being burned to death, and confrontations with wild beasts. This last form of punishment was particularly gruesome and meant exposure in the arena to a variety of ferocious animals, such as leopards, boars, and lions.

Official persecution waxed and waned, depending on the disposition of the reigning emperor and the whims of local leaders.

In his *De mortibus persecutorum* (*On the Deaths of the Persecutors*), Lactantius, an early Christian author who acted as adviser to the emperor Constantine, chronicled the persecution of Christians before his time under the emperors Nero, Domitian, Decius, Valerian, and Aurelian as well as under his contemporaries, Diocletian, Maximian, Galerius, and Maximinus. According to Lactantius—as well as the Roman historians Tacitus and Suetonius—Nero was the first emperor to enact a statewide persecution of Christians.[103] In Lactantius's account, Nero's ire was aroused when the apostle Peter came to Rome and built up the Church there, making many converts.

When Nero heard of those things, and observed that not only in Rome, but in every other place, a great multitude revolted daily from the worship of idols, and, condemning their old ways, went over to the new religion, he, an execrable and pernicious tyrant, sprung forward to raze the heavenly temple and destroy the true faith. He it was who first persecuted the servants of God; he crucified Peter, and slew Paul.[104]

The historian Tacitus, a Roman senator with no sympathy for the members of the new religion, wrote that Nero had "an immense

---

[103] Cornelius Tacitus, *The Annals*, ed. Alfred John Church, William Jackson Brodribb (New York: Perseus, 1942), 15.44, http://www.perseus.tufts.edu/hopper/text?doc=Perseus%3Atext%3A1999.02.0078%3Abook%3D15%3Achapter%3D44; Suetonius, *Nero* 16.2. All of the passages from Tacitus are taken from this section of *The Annals*.

[104] Lactantius, *The Manner in Which Persecutors Died*, in *Ante-Nicene Christian Library*, vol. 22, *The Works of Lactantius*, vol. 2 (Edinburgh: T. and T. Clark, 1871), chap. 2, 166.

multitude" of Christians arrested, having some covered with the skins of wild beasts to be torn to death by dogs. In Tacitus's view, what prompted Nero to hunt and destroy Christians was that he needed to convince the Roman people that the great fire of Rome was not the result of an imperial order. "Consequently, to get rid of the report, Nero fastened the guilt and inflicted the most exquisite tortures on a class hated for their abominations, called Christians by the populace," Tacitus wrote.

> Christus, from whom the name had its origin, suffered the extreme penalty during the reign of Tiberius at the hands of one of our procurators, Pontius Pilatus, and a most mischievous superstition, thus checked for the moment, again broke out not only in Judaea, the first source of the evil, but even in Rome, where all things hideous and shameful from every part of the world find their center and become popular.

Writing dispassionately of the torments of Nero's victims, Tacitus says:

> Accordingly, an arrest was first made of all who pleaded guilty; then, upon their information, an immense multitude was convicted, not so much of the crime of firing the city, as of hatred against mankind. Mockery of every sort was added to their deaths. Covered with the skins of beasts, they were torn by dogs and perished, or were nailed to crosses, or were doomed to the flames and burnt, to serve as a nightly illumination, when daylight had expired.

No more admiring of the emperor than of the Christians, Tacitus notes that Nero offered his own gardens for the spectacle of the massacre of the faithful. He put on a show in the circus, "while he mingled with the people in the dress of a charioteer or stood aloft on a car." His exaggeratedly severe treatment of the Christians backfired, however, as people were moved with pity on seeing them. "Hence, even for criminals who deserved extreme and exemplary punishment, there arose a feeling of compassion; for it was not, as it seemed, for the public good, but to glut one man's cruelty, that they were being destroyed."

Between AD 30 and 311, a total of fifty-four emperors ruled the empire, but only about a dozen actively harassed Christians, and none until Decius (249-251) deliberately enacted an empire-wide persecution. Until then, persecution came mainly at the instigation of local rulers, albeit with Rome's approval and according to the law, since Christianity was illegal. Together with Decius, Diocletian (284-305) became legendary for his ruthless persecution of Christians.

Besides the more enthusiastic pursuers of Christians, there were some who took a more passive approach toward the officially illegal band of believers. The emperor Trajan, for example, who ruled from AD 98 to 117, famously adopted a sort of "Don't ask, don't tell" approach to the Christian community, instructing his provincial governors not to hunt down Christians but simply to prosecute them whenever they were reported.

Trajan's exchange with Pliny the Younger, the Roman governor of Bithynia and Pontus, is so instructive that it is worth examining in greater depth. Pliny wrote to Trajan around AD 112 requesting direction on how to deal with the rapidly growing Christian population in the empire.

"Having never been present at any trials concerning those who profess Christianity, I am unacquainted not only with the nature of their crimes, or the measure of their punishment, but how far it is proper to enter into an examination concerning them," Pliny wrote. He went on to ask "whether repentance entitles them to a pardon" and moreover "whether the very profession of Christianity, unattended with any criminal act, or only the crimes themselves inherent in the profession are punishable."[105]

"Do not go out of your way to look for them," he wrote. "If indeed they should be brought before you, and the crime is proved, they must be punished."[106]

Pliny's treatment of Christians, along with Trajan's reply, reveals much about how the Roman Empire viewed the burgeoning body of believers. Pliny continued:

> In the meanwhile, the method I have observed towards those who have been brought before me as Christians is this: I asked them whether they were Christians; if they admitted it, I repeated the question twice, and threatened them with punishment; if they persisted, I ordered them to be at once punished: for I was persuaded, whatever the nature of their opinions might be, a contumacious and inflexible obstinacy certainly deserved correction.

In other words, Pliny believed that according to the law, the simple fact of professing Christianity was a punishable offense, independent of any other crimes, and that the only way for Christians to escape punishment was to deny their faith. Pliny goes on to recount how he distinguishes false Christians from the real thing: by

---

[105] Pliny the Younger, Letter XCVII to the emperor Trajan, in *Letters of Pliny*. All quotations from Pliny in this section are taken from this letter.

[106] Trajan, Letter XCVIII to Pliny, in *Letters of Pliny*, ed. F. C. T. Bosanquet, trans. William Melmoth (2001) Project Gutenberg, https://gutenberg.org/files/2811/2811-h/2811-h.htm.

obliging those charged with being Christians to offer an invocation to the Roman gods and burn incense before a statue of the emperor.

> An anonymous information was laid before me containing a charge against several persons, who upon examination denied they were Christians, or had ever been so. They repeated after me an invocation to the gods, and offered religious rites with wine and incense before your statue (which for that purpose I had ordered to be brought, together with those of the gods), and even reviled the name of Christ: whereas there is no forcing, it is said, those who are really Christians into any of these compliances: I thought it proper, therefore, to discharge them.

Pliny also recounts the case of others charged with being Christians who admit they had associated with Christians but were willing to denounce their error to escape punishment. The only crime he could discover, he said, "was evidence of an absurd and extravagant superstition." Pliny wrote that he was consulting Trajan as "a matter highly deserving your consideration," because of the growing popularity of the Christian sect among "persons of all ranks and ages, and even of both sexes."

"In fact, this contagious superstition is not confined to the cities only, but has spread its infection among the neighboring villages and country," he wrote. "Nevertheless, it still seems possible to restrain its progress."

In his brief reply, Trajan praises Pliny for his prudence in dealing with Christians, approving his practices.

> You have adopted the right course, my dearest Secundus, in investigating the charges against the Christians who were brought before you. If indeed they should be brought before

you, and the crime is proved, they must be punished; with the restriction, however, that where the party denies he is a Christian, and shall make it evident that he is not, by invoking our gods, let him (notwithstanding any former suspicion) be pardoned upon his repentance.[107]

While Trajan's letter effectively expressed the Roman state policy of not aggressively pursuing Christians, he also made it clear that being a Christian was a crime in and of itself and that when provoked, the state required no further justification to punish Christians than their identity as such. It also meant that when members of the local population harbored animus toward the Christian community or individual Christians, they could denounce them and have them brought to trial. In these cases, the burden of proof would fall upon the Christians to demonstrate that they were not, in fact, what they were accused of being.

Pope Clement of Rome (†99)

Despite Trajan's relatively relaxed approach to punishing Christians, there were noteworthy martyrs even during his reign, beginning with St. Clement, Peter's third successor as bishop of Rome, who served as pope from AD 88 to 99. According to Tertullian, writing around 199, the Roman Church believed that Clement was ordained personally by St. Peter.[108]

Pope Clement was the author of an important epistle to the Christians in Corinth, one of the oldest extant Christian documents outside the New Testament. In this epistle, Clement distinguishes the three orders of bishop, priest, and deacon. The

---

[107] Letter XCVIII to Pliny.
[108] Tertullian, De praescriptione haereticorum 32.

epistle was also the first work to establish the primacy of Rome, as Clement gives authoritative instructions to a local church other than his own. Little is known with certainty of his martyrdom, but according to one ancient text, Trajan banished Clement to the Crimea. In prison, Clement is said to have led a ministry among his fellow prisoners for which he was executed by being tied to an iron anchor and thrown from a boat into the Black Sea.[109]

In the first years of the twelfth century, Pope Paschal II built a church to honor St. Clement. The church still stands in Rome in the valley between the Esquiline and Coelian Hills, on the road connecting the Colosseum to the Church of St. John Lateran. It is considered the most perfect model of an early basilica in Rome. It is said to have been erected on the site of a fourth-century church possibly constructed under the emperor Constantine. This earlier church was itself erected upon a pagan temple of Mithras, whose ruins under St. Clement's can still be visited today.

Ignatius of Antioch (†107)

Another to fall prey to Trajan was Ignatius, bishop of Antioch and a disciple of the apostle John. Born in Syria around the year 50, Ignatius—also called Theophorus (God bearer)—was a friend of fellow martyr St. Polycarp and was named and anointed the third bishop of Antioch by St. Peter himself.

The very ancient *Martyrdom of Ignatius* (*Martyrium Ignatii*) is an eyewitness account of the saint's execution and the events leading up to it, primarily the journey from Syria to Rome.[110] The text

---

[109] See the apocryphal Greek Acts of his martyrdom: Franz Xaver von Funk, *Opera patrum apostolicorum* (1878), 28

[110] *The Martyrdom of Ignatius*, trans. Alexander Roberts and James Donaldson, in *The Ante-Nicene Fathers*, vol. 1, ed. Alexander Roberts, James Donaldson, and A. Cleveland Coxe (Buffalo,

is believed to have been written by Philo, deacon of Tarsus, and the Syrian Rheus Agathopus, who accompanied Ignatius on the voyage to Rome.

The *Martyrdom* relates that Ignatius managed to navigate through the storms of persecution unleashed by the emperor Domitian upon the Christians of Syria and to inspire hope and strengthen the weak against the terrors of the persecution. When Trajan ascended to the throne in the year 98, however, Ignatius met his match. In the ninth year of his reign, Trajan decreed that the Christians should unite with their pagan neighbors in the worship of the gods, stipulating the penalty of death for anyone who refused to offer the prescribed sacrifice. Ignatius was soon arrested and led before Trajan, who was staying in Antioch at the time.

Trajan interrogated Ignatius personally and accused him of violating the imperial edict, declaring him guilty of being a Christian. Trajan condemned him to death with the following sentence: "We command that Ignatius, who affirms that he carries about within him Him that was crucified, be bound by soldiers, and carried to the great [city] Rome, there to be devoured by the beasts, for the gratification of the people."[111]

During his voyage to Rome, chained to a company of ten Roman soldiers, Ignatius composed seven letters that are still considered among the most precious treasures of the early Christian

---

NY: Christian Literature Publishing, 1885), revised and edited for New Advent by Kevin Knight https://www.newadvent.org/fathers/0123.htm.

[111] *The Martyrdom of Ignatius 2*, in *The Ante-Nicene Fathers*, vol. 1, ed. Alexander Roberts, James Donaldson, and A. Cleveland Coxe (Buffalo, NY: Christian Literature Publishing, 1885), revised and edited for New Advent by Kevin Knight, http://www.newadvent.org/fathers/0123.htm.

Church. His *Letter to the Romans*, in particular, describes his deep desire for martyrdom as the means of becoming a "true disciple" of Jesus Christ. Once he had arrived in Rome, Ignatius prayed publicly to Jesus for an end to the persecution of Christians, while affirming that he considered himself blessed to be able to hasten to the Lord as a martyr. In a public spectacle on December 20, 107, probably in the newly completed Flavian Amphitheater (the Colosseum), he was thrown to the lions, and afterward the Christians present gathered his bones, wrapped them in linen, and conveyed them to Antioch as relics.

Polycarp (ca. †155)

Ignatius's friend Polycarp, the bishop of Smyrna (the site of the modern city of Izmir, Turkey), was martyred considerably later, most likely on February 23 in AD 155 or 156, during the proconsulship of Lucius Statius Quadratus, when Antoninus Pius was emperor. Ignatius spoke with Polycarp during his trip from Antioch to Rome, since the soldiers accompanying him had to pass through Smyrna, and it was Polycarp who later collected the seven letters Ignatius wrote during that voyage.

Polycarp's martyrdom is particularly edifying, and the story was handed down through a second-century manuscript known as *The Martyrdom of Polycarp*, the earliest account of Christian martyrdom outside the New Testament, written in the form of a letter sent from the church in Smyrna to another church in Asia Minor at Philomelium.[112] The letter, written partly from the point of view of an eyewitness, narrates the arrest of the elderly Polycarp as well as the Romans' attempt to execute him by fire.

---

[112] Paul Foster and Sara Parvis, *Writings of the Apostolic Fathers* (London: Continuum International Publishing, 2007).

Polycarp was an old man—at least eighty-six—and probably the last surviving person to have known an apostle, having been a disciple of St. John the Evangelist. This was one reason he was greatly revered as a teacher and Church leader.

According to *The Martyrdom of Polycarp*, it was the throng—whipped up in bloodlust after witnessing the execution of the young Christian Germanicus, torn apart by wild beasts—that demanded the arrest and execution of Polycarp. Informed that his arrest was imminent, Polycarp intended to stay in the city but was eventually persuaded to leave and took up residence with friends in the nearby countryside. As an aside, the text states that the Christian Church does not approve of pursuing martyrdom, calling it "something the Gospel does not teach us to do."[113] At prayer three days before he was arrested, Polycarp had a vision of the pillow under his head in flames and announced to those who were with him, "I will be burned alive."

When his second hiding place was discovered, Polycarp decided that his execution must be God's will. The governor told Polycarp that he could go free if only he would curse Christ, but Polycarp memorably answered: "For eighty-six years I have been his servant and he has done me no wrong. How can I blaspheme against my king and savior?"[114]

During the reign of the Stoic philosopher Marcus Aurelius (161–180), Christian blood flowed more profusely than ever before, despite the fact that Marcus himself did not actively persecute the nascent community of believers. Marcus adopted the official position of his predecessor Trajan, which had also been followed by Hadrian and Antoninus Pius. But instructed by his

[113] *The Martyrdom of Polycarp* 4.
[114] Ibid., 9.

philosophical mentors, Marcus became convinced that Christianity was a dangerous revolutionary force, preaching and engaging in gross immoralities such as cannibalism, atheism, infanticide, and incest.[115]

During his reign, fiercely anti-Christian literature proliferated for the first time, most notably Celsus's *The True Doctrine*. Marcus also permitted anti-Christian informers to move freely, with the result that bloody persecutions broke out in various regions. In Lyons in 177, the local bishop was martyred, bringing Irenaeus to the office. In addition, Justin, the first Christian philosopher, was martyred during Marcus's reign.

The emperor Septimius Severus (193–211) issued a rescript prohibiting imperial subjects under severe penalties from becoming Christians. As a probable consequence of this decree, five catechumens at Carthage were seized and cast into prison.

Perpetua and Felicity (†203)

We are blessed to possess a genuine, contemporary description of the deaths of the Christians Perpetua, Felicity, and companions, chronicled in an account titled *The Passion of the Holy Martyrs Perpetua and Felicity*, one of the oldest extant Christian texts. The martyrdom took place at Carthage, in the Roman province of Africa, in modern-day Tunisia.

Vibia Perpetua was a young married noblewoman, believed to have been twenty-two years old at the time of her death, and the mother of an infant, whom she was nursing. Perpetua's father was a pagan, but her mother and two brothers were Christians,

---

[115] See Bart Wagemakers, "Incest, Infanticide, and Cannibalism: Anti-Christian Imputations in the Roman Empire," *Greece & Rome* 57, no. 2 (October 2010): 337–354.

one still a catechumen. Perpetua was arrested and imprisoned as a catechumen and was baptized in jail while awaiting her execution. Her father came to visit her twice in prison, pleading with her to save herself by abjuring her faith, which she refused to do.

Felicity was a Christian slave in her eighth month of pregnancy, imprisoned with Perpetua. Perpetua and Felicity were martyred along with three companions, Revocatus, Saturninus, and Saturus. Another companion of theirs, the Christian Secundulus, died in prison before he could be executed. As it happened, Felicity gave birth to her child in prison. While she was in labor she cried out, and one of the servants said to her, "You who are in such suffering now, what will you do when you are thrown to the beasts, which you disdained when you refused to sacrifice?" Felicity memorably replied, "Now it is I who suffer what I suffer; but then there will be another in me, who will suffer for me, because I also am about to suffer for Him." She gave birth to a baby girl, who was adopted by a Christian woman after Felicity's death.

At Perpetua's trial, the procurator Hilarianus attempted to dissuade her from her course, urging: "Spare the grey hairs of your father, spare the infancy of your boy, offer sacrifice for the well-being of the emperors," to which Perpetua replied, "I will not do so." "Are you a Christian?" Hilarianus asked, and she replied resolutely, "I am a Christian."

On the day of their martyrdom, during the birthday celebrations for the emperor Septimius Severus in AD 203, the five were led out into the amphitheater, and when they came within sight of Hilarianus, they said to him, "You judge us, they say, but God will judge you." All were scourged, and then Saturninus and Revocatus were made to face a leopard and a bear, which mauled them to death. Saturus first was made to face a wild boar, but the boar ended up goring to death the hunter who had supplied him. Next, guards bound Saturus and laid him on the dirt floor near a bear, but the bear would not come forth from its den. Finally, a leopard was loosed on him, which killed him with one bite, unleashing vast amounts of blood.

The young women, stripped and then clothed with nets, were led out before a fierce heifer. The first to face the cow, Perpetua was tossed into the air and fell to the ground. When she looked up, she saw that Felicity had also been knocked to the ground by the cow. She approached her to help her up, and both of them stood together. They were then led to the executioner in front of the people and were dispatched with a thrust of the sword between their ribs.

Cecilia (†230)

Cecilia is one of several virgin martyrs commemorated by name in the ancient Roman Canon of the Mass, and devotion to her goes back to the earliest centuries of the Church. In the Canon, Cecilia's name appears in the midst of other female martyrs of Rome—namely, Agatha, Lucy, Agnes, and Anastasia. In the third century, Pope Urban I built a church in Cecilia's honor in the Trastevere quarter of Rome, on what is believed to be the site of the house where she lived and was martyred.[116]

In iconography, Cecilia is often depicted with an organ. She is the patron saint of music and musicians because it was written that as the musicians played at her wedding, she "sang to the Lord in her heart." She is also the patroness of Rome's Academy of Music, founded in 1584, which bears her name.

---

[116] Jacobus de Voragine, *The Golden Legend*, trans. William Granger Ryan (Princeton: Princeton University Press, 1993), vol. 2, 323.

The Coming Christian Persecution

Though many fanciful stories about St. Cecilia appeared during the fifth and sixth centuries, her existence and martyrdom are undisputed facts. Because she is one of the most venerated martyrs of Christian antiquity, her feast has been celebrated in the Roman Church at least since the fourth century, and the oldest historical account of her death is found in the *Martyrologium Hieronymianum*, which was compiled at that time.

The Acts of St. Cecilia place her martyrdom during the reign of Emperor Alexander Severus, although other accounts offer alternative chronologies, and she could have died as early as the late second century.

Cecilia was buried on the Appian Way, quite possibly in the Catacomb of Callistus in a crypt adjoining the chapel of the popes. Her body was later transferred to the ancient church of Rome bearing her name, which is still preserved in the Trastevere neighborhood. Pope Urban's original church was rebuilt by Pope Paschal I, who reigned in the early ninth century. Paschal wanted Cecilia's relics to repose in the church, and eventually he located them in the Catacomb of Praetextatus. Some have theorized that they may have been transported there from the Catacomb of Callistus to save them from sacking by the Lombard invaders, but this is not known with certainty.

The Coming of the Great Persecution

The year 250 marked a dramatic upturn in systematic persecution of Christians in the Roman Empire. In January of that year, the emperor Decius (249-251) issued an edict ordering all to sacrifice to the gods and present a certificate proving they had done so. Bishops were to be put to death; other Christians were to be punished and tortured until they recanted. Soon afterward, Pope Fabian was martyred. Prompted by civil unrest and a series of barbarian invasions and believing that the favor of the gods was needed to protect the empire, Decius was making every effort to unite Romans in showing support for Rome's deities. While not specifically directed at Christians, his edict posed a particular problem for all monotheists. Decius died in AD 251 while fighting the barbarian Goths in a swamp, just a year after issuing the edict. But his successors stuck to the plan.

The emperor Valerian (253-260) sent two letters to the Senate mandating firm steps against the Christians. The first letter, sent in 257, ordered Christian clergy to sacrifice to the Roman gods or face banishment. The second letter, issued in 258, was harsher still, ordering the immediate execution of Christian leaders and requiring Christian senators to sacrifice to the Roman deities or lose their titles and property. Moreover, if they should continue to refuse, they were to be executed. The letter also decreed that Roman matrons must deny the Christian faith or lose their property and face banishment, and that civil servants and members of the imperial household who would not worship the Roman gods should be reduced to slavery and sent to work on the imperial estates.[117] Since Christians were well established at that time—some in very high positions—Valerian's intent was to portray everyone who would not sacrifice to the Roman gods as unpatriotic and un-Roman.

Lawrence (†258)

One of the more notable casualties of Valerian's persecution of Christians was the thirty-three-year-old Lawrence, one of the seven deacons of the city of Rome under Pope Sixtus II. Lawrence,

---

[117] W. H. C. Frend, *The Rise of Christianity* (Philadelphia: Fortress Press, 1984), 326.

believed to have been a Spaniard, had encountered the future Pope Sixtus II in Caesaraugusta (modern Zaragoza), where Sixtus was one of the most famous and esteemed teachers. Lawrence became a disciple of the venerable master, and both eventually traveled to Rome together. When Sixtus became pope in 257 — a pontificate that would last less than a year — he ordained Lawrence a deacon and appointed him, despite his young age, "first" among the seven deacons who served in the cathedral church (proto-deacon). Both Sixtus and Lawrence would bear witness to Christ to the shedding of blood in the very same week.

The fourth-century *Depositio martyrum* tells us that Lawrence was executed on August 10, 258, just four days after the decapitation of Pope Sixtus II. St. Cyprian, the holy bishop of Carthage, offered an account of the death of Sixtus in one of his letters, noting the environment of great uncertainty and unease in the Church because of increasing hostility toward Christians in the Roman Empire.

"Valerian has issued an edict to the Senate to the effect that bishops, presbyters and deacons shall suffer the death penalty without delay," Cyprian wrote. "Senators, distinguished men and members of the equestrian class, are to be deprived of their rank and property, and if, after forfeiting their wealth and privileges, they still persist in professing Christianity, they too are to be sentenced to death."

"I must also inform you that Sixtus was put to death in a catacomb on August 6, and four deacons with him," Cyprian wrote. "Moreover, the prefects in Rome are pressing this persecution zealously and without intermission, to such a point that anyone brought before them is punished and his property is claimed for the imperial treasury."[118] The catacomb to which Cyprian alludes

---

[118] St. Cyprian, Epistle 80; CSEL, 3, 839–840.

is that of St. Callixtus in Rome, where Sixtus was captured while celebrating Mass. His remains were buried in the cemetery of St. Callixtus after his execution. Along with four deacons martyred with Sixtus, two other deacons, Felicissimus and Agapitus, were put to death the same day, leaving Lawrence as the only deacon left alive in Rome.

"I ask you to make these facts known to the rest of our fellow bishops, in order that by the exhortation of their pastors the brethren everywhere may be strengthened and prepared for the spiritual combat," Cyprian continued in his letter. "Let all our people fix their minds not on death but rather on immortality; let them commit themselves to the Lord in complete faith and unflinching courage and make their confession with joy rather than in fear, knowing that in this contest the soldiers of God and Christ are not slain but rather win their crowns."[119]

Not long afterward, Lawrence was also arrested, and according to St. Ambrose, bishop of Milan from 374 to 397, the Roman prefect Decius demanded that he hand over the treasures of the Church. But instead of gold, Lawrence brought out Rome's poor, among whom he had divided the treasure, in place of alms. Ambrose also wrote that when Pope Sixtus II was being led away to his death, he comforted Lawrence, who wished to share his martyrdom, by saying that he would follow him in three days.[120]

According to a tradition widely diffused by the fourth century and repeated by Ambrose, Lawrence patiently sustained a terrible martyrdom, being roasted alive on a gridiron, described with poetic detail by Prudentius in his hymn on St. Lawrence.[121] The legend

[119] Ibid.
[120] St. Ambrose, *De officiis ministrorum* 1.41.205–207.
[121] Prudentius, *Peristephanon*, Hymnus II.

states that at one point during the excruciating ordeal, the deacon looked at his tormentors and quipped: "You may turn me over now; this side is done." While certain details of the martyrdom cannot be verified with any certainty, there is no doubt that St. Lawrence was a real historical personage who was martyred on August 10, 258, at the agro Verano, where a basilica in his honor still stands today.

Lawrence's sentence to death by fire was also inflicted on other Christians during Valerian's reign, such as the Spanish deacons Eulogius and Augurius, burned alive in the amphitheater of Tarraco (Tarragona) in AD 259.

Cyprian of Carthage (†258)

In August 257, a year before the arrest and execution of Sixtus and Lawrence, Roman soldiers arrested Cyprian in North Africa on charges of atheism for his refusal to sacrifice to the Roman gods according to the directives handed down by Valerian. Cyprian was brought before the Roman proconsul Paternus, who interrogated him as to his identity and office. Cyprian responded directly: "I am a Christian and a bishop. I know no other gods besides the one, true God who made heaven and earth, the sea and all that is in them. This is the God we Christians serve, to this God we pray day and night for you and for all mankind."[122] Paternus sentenced Cyprian to be led off into exile to the city of Curubis, some sixty miles from Carthage. Cyprian arrived in Curubis on September 14, 257, one year to the day before his martyrdom.[123]

---

[122] Msgr. Charles Pope, "The Life of Saint Cyprian of Carthage," pt. 3, https://hcscchurch.org/the-life-of-saint-cyprian/.
[123] Ibid., pt. 4.

As we have seen, in August 258, Cyprian learned that Pope Sixtus II had been put to death in the catacombs on the sixth of that month, together with four of his deacons. Around this time, Galerius Maximus, who had replaced Paternus as proconsul in North Africa, had Cyprian brought back to Carthage from his exile, since Valerian had ordered the swift execution of all Christian leaders, and thus the bishop awaited his final sentence in his own gardens. On September 13, 258, Cyprian was imprisoned on the orders of Galerius Maximus, to be tried the following day.

The public examination of Cyprian by Galerius Maximus on September 14, which took place before a sizable crowd, has been preserved.[124] Cyprian first reiterated his refusal to offer sacrifice to the pagan deities, after which Galerius pronounced the following verdict:

> You have long lived an irreligious life, and have drawn together a number of men bound by an unlawful association, and professed yourself an open enemy to the gods and the religion of Rome; and the pious, most sacred and august Emperors ... have endeavoured in vain to bring you back to conformity with their religious observances; whereas therefore you have been apprehended as principal and ringleader in these infamous crimes, you shall be made an example to those whom you have wickedly associated with you; the authority of law shall be ratified in your blood.

[124] W. H. C. Frend, *The Rise of Christianity* (Philadelphia: Fortress Press, 1984), 319.

Reading then from a written tablet, Galerius said, "It is the sentence of this court that Thascius Cyprianus be executed with the sword," to which Cyprian replied, "Thanks be to God."[125]

Cyprian was led to a hollow surrounded by trees, into which many of the people climbed. Cyprian took off his cloak and knelt down and prayed. Then he stood up, removed his outer garment and gave it to his deacons, and stood in his linen tunic in silence, awaiting the executioner. The Christian brethren laid down cloths and handkerchiefs to catch his blood. He tied a blindfold around his own eyes with the help of a priest and a deacon and was subsequently beheaded. For the rest of the day, his body was exposed to satisfy the curiosity of the pagans. But at night, the Christian brethren bore him with candles and torches to the cemetery of Macrobius Candidianus in the suburb of Mapalia, where they laid him to rest.[126]

The Christian persecution under Emperor Valerian was relatively short-lived, as he was captured by the Persians in battle in AD 260. His son Gallienus, perhaps linking his father's swift demise to his crackdown on Christians, repealed his father's edict and proclaimed freedom of worship for all. Following Gallienus's declaration, Christians enjoyed some forty years of relative peace with little in the way of official persecution. All of that changed in AD 303, however, when the emperor Diocletian and his junior co-emperor, Galerius (both former soldiers who saw Christianity as a threat to traditional

---

[125] *Acta proconsularia S. Cypriani* 4–5, quoted in David M. Gwynn, *Christianity in the Later Roman Empire: A Sourcebook* (London: Bloomsbury, 2015), 10.

[126] See Deacon Pontius, *The Life and Passion of Saint Cyprian*, trans. Robert Ernest Wallis, in *The Ante-Nicene Fathers*, vol. 5, ed. Alexander Roberts, James Donaldson, and A. Cleveland Coxe (Buffalo, NY: Christian Literature Publishing, 1886).

Roman beliefs), unleashed an active campaign against the Christians that has come down to us under the title of the "Great Persecution."

Diocletian began his reign in 284, and during the first fifteen years of his rule, he purged the Roman army of Christians and surrounded himself with vocal adversaries of Christianity.

Cosmas and Damian (ca. †287)

Cosmas and Damian were twins born in Arabia who suffered martyrdom in Syria during Diocletian's reign. According to tradition, the brothers were skilled doctors, and they are invoked as patron saints of pharmacists and physicians. Already in the fifth century, the names of Cosmas and Damian were remembered in the Canon of the Mass.

The brothers were arrested by order of Lysias, the prefect of Cilicia, who ordered them under torture to renounce their Christian faith. According to one account, the brothers remained true to their faith, even while enduring being hung on a cross, stoned, and shot with arrows, before finally being executed by beheading. They were martyred together with their younger brothers Anthimus, Leontius, and Euprepius.

Churches dedicated to Cosmas and Damian were erected in Jerusalem, Egypt, and Mesopotamia as early as the fourth century, and devotion to the two saints spread rapidly in both East and West. The Eastern emperor Justinian I (527–565) restored the city of Cyrus and dedicated it to the twins but brought their relics back with him to Constantinople. After experiencing a cure that he credited to the intercession of Cosmas and Damian, Justinian built and adorned in Constantinople a church dedicated to them, which became a famous place of pilgrimage.

In Rome, Pope Felix IV (526–530) rededicated the Library of Peace (Bibliotheca Pacis) as a basilica of St. Cosmas and Damian in the Forum of Vespasian, which is famed for its sixth-century mosaics depicting the saints' entry into Heaven, accompanied by the Roman martyrs Peter and Paul.

The Great Persecution

In the winter of 302, Diocletian's son-in-law and co-emperor, Galerius, urged Diocletian to commence a general persecution of the Christians. Somewhat less passionate than Galerius, Diocletian hesitated and sought guidance first from the oracle of Apollo at Didyma. When the oracle's answer was interpreted as favorable to Galerius's position, the emperors called a general persecution on February 24, 303. Through a series of proclamations, they ordered the destruction of churches, the confiscation of ecclesiastical property, and the burning of Christian texts and records.

The Christian historian Eusebius, a contemporary of Diocletian, wrote that "an imperial decree was published everywhere" in the nineteenth year of Diocletian's reign (AD 303) "ordering the churches to be razed to the ground and the Scriptures destroyed by fire, and giving notice that those in places of honor would lose their places, and domestic staff, if they continued to profess Christianity, would be deprived of their liberty."[127] When captured, Christians were given the opportunity to recognize the Roman gods by performing a public sacrifice to them or to face punishment.

And so began the ten years of the Great Persecution. "Soon afterwards," Eusebius tells us, "other decrees arrived in rapid succession, ordering that the presidents of the churches in every place

---

[127] Eusebius, *History of the Church*, trans. G.A. Williamson (New York: Penguin Classics, 1989), VIII.2.

should all be first committed to prison and then coerced by every possible means into offering sacrifice."

When the persecution began, Lactantius was in Nicomedia, where he wrote that a "fit and auspicious day was sought out for the accomplishment of this undertaking; and the festival of the god Terminus, celebrated on the sevens of the kalends of March, was chosen, in preference to all others, to terminate, as it were, the Christian religion."[128]

According to Eusebius, there were thousands of martyrs during this period and "each one endured different forms of torture."

"The body of one was scourged with rods. Another was punished with insupportable rackings and scrapings, in which some suffered a miserable death," he wrote. Eusebius describes in some detail the martyrdom of one Peter, a servant of the palace in the city of Nicomedia, saying he would "leave our readers to infer from his case the sufferings of the others."[129] This Peter was brought forward before the rulers and commanded to sacrifice, "but as he refused, he was ordered to be stripped and raised on high and beaten with rods over his entire body, until, being conquered, he should, even against his will, do what was commanded."

But as he was unmoved by these sufferings, and his bones were already appearing, they mixed vinegar with salt and poured it upon the mangled parts of his body.

---

[128] Lactantius, *De Mortibus Persecutorum* 12, quoted in Gwynn, *Christianity in the Later Roman Empire*, 19.

[129] Eusebius, *The History of the Church* VIII.6.2–4, trans. Arthur Cushman McGiffert, in *Nicene and Post-Nicene Fathers*, Second Series, vol. 1, ed. Philip Schaff and Henry Wace (Buffalo, NY: Christian Literature Publishing, 1890).

As he scorned these agonies, a gridiron and fire were brought forward. And the remnants of his body, like flesh intended for eating, were placed on the fire, not at once, lest he should expire instantly, but a little at a time. And those who placed him on the pyre were not permitted to desist until, after such sufferings, he should assent to the things commanded. But he held his purpose firmly, and victoriously gave up his life while the tortures were still going on.

Similarly in Egypt, Eusebius recounts, "thousands of men, women, and children, despising the present life for the sake of the teaching of our Saviour, endured various deaths."[130]

Some of them, after scrapings and rackings and severest scourgings, and numberless other kinds of tortures, terrible even to hear of, were committed to the flames; some were drowned in the sea; some offered their heads bravely to those who cut them off; some died under their tortures, and others perished with hunger. And yet others were crucified; some according to the method commonly employed for malefactors; others yet more cruelly, being nailed to the cross with their heads downward, and being kept alive until they perished on the cross with hunger.

Eusebius remarks that these tortures and killings did not take place just over a few days but over years, often with dozens martyred on a given day. He says he was eyewitness to the martyrdom of a "large crowd" in Thebes, with "some suffering decapitation, others tortured by fire; so that the murderous sword was blunted,

---

[130] Eusebius, *The History of the Church* VIII.8.1–2.

and becoming weak, was broken, and the very executioners grew weary and relieved each other."[131]

Agnes (†304)

Agnes, a twelve-year-old girl, was perhaps the last Christian to be martyred under the emperor Diocletian and, of all the virgin martyrs of Rome, was held in the highest honor by the primitive church. Agnes is believed to have been a member of the Roman nobility, born in AD 291 and raised in a Christian family. The ancient Roman calendar of the feasts of the martyrs (*Depositio martyrum*), dating from AD 354, assigns Agnes's feast to January 21, and her name—which means "lamb"—is the first of the virgin martyrs mentioned in the Roman Canon of the Mass.

Although the Fathers of the Church and Christian poets extolled Agnes's virginity and heroism under torture, the only certain detail of her martyrdom is her young age. St. Ambrose gives her age as twelve[132] and St. Augustine as thirteen,[133] while Pope St. Damasus I depicts her as "hastening to martyrdom from the lap of her nurse."[134] In his narrative, Damasus states that immediately after the promulgation of Diocletian's imperial edict against the Christians, Agnes voluntarily declared herself a Christian and suffered martyrdom by fire, concerned only with veiling her body from the gaze of the heathen multitude, which she accomplished with her flowing hair. Ambrose, on the other hand, declared that

[131] Eusebius, *The History of the Church* VIII.9.4.

[132] St. Ambrose, *De virginibus* I.2; *PL*, XVI, 200–202.

[133] St. Augustine, Sermo 273, 6; *PL*, XXXVIII, 1251.

[134] St. Damasus, In St. Agneten, 3, quoted in Johann Peter Kirsch, "St. Agnes of Rome," *Catholic Encyclopedia*, vol. 1 (New York: Robert Appleton, 1907), New Advent, http://www.newadvent.org/cathen/01214a.htm.

the judge originally ordered Agnes to be burned alive but, when the flames failed to consume her, instructed that she be decapitated. All of these accounts date back to the fourth century, the period in which Agnes died.

After her execution, Agnes was buried beside the Via Nomentana in Rome. Constantina, the daughter of the emperor Constantine I, was said to have been cured of leprosy after praying at Agnes's tomb, and she appears in the scenes from the life of Agnes on the fourteenth-century Royal Gold Cup in the British Museum.

In the Wake of the Great Persecution

The torture and deaths of thousands of Christians and the demolition of Christian churches and administrative buildings were not the only casualties of the Great Persecution. Diocletian dealt ruthlessly with what he considered subversive literature and made it a point to destroy not only Christian buildings but even more so, precious Christian texts and records, as a form of *damnatio memoriae*. Our present lack of precise records of Christian martyrs and their treatment by the empire is due not only to the natural attrition common to ancient historical events. The chief reason we possess so few original accounts of histories and martyrdoms—which were zealously chronicled and preserved by the Christian community—is that Diocletian made a concerted effort to wipe out the corpus of Christian literature.[135] He destroyed copies of Sacred Scripture wherever he found them and burned any other Christian texts he could get his hands on, determined not to allow "corrupt doctrines" to spread in the empire by means of written communication. As Lorne D. Bruce has written: "The

---

[135] See James Westfall Thompson, *The Medieval Library* (Chicago: University of Chicago Press, 1939), 18.

extent of our knowledge of the persecution in the west is, of course, based upon the fortuitous character of the sources that remain."[136] Scholars believe that Christian libraries suffered irremediable damage in 303–304, and volumes of priceless historical records were obliterated.[137]

Galerius eventually ended the Great Persecution in AD 311 with his Edict of Toleration—together with his co-emperors, Constantine and Licinius—reportedly as an effort to appease the Christian God after Galerius had contracted a particularly abhorrent disease.[138] In his edict, Galerius said that despite the harsh penalties inflicted upon them, the Christians "indeed persisted in the same folly, and we saw that they were neither paying to the gods in heaven the worship that is their due nor giving any honor to the god of the Christians."[139]

"So in view of our benevolence and the established custom by which we invariably grant pardon to all men, we have thought proper in this matter also to extend our clemency most gladly, so that Christians may again exist and rebuild the houses in which they used to meet, on condition that they do nothing contrary to public order," he continued, while adding that in return the Christians must pray for his recovery. "Therefore, in view of this our clemency, they are in duty bound to beseech their own god for our security, and that of the state and of themselves, in order that

---

[136] Lorne D. Bruce. "A Note on Christian Libraries during the 'Great Persecution,' 303–305 A.D.," *Journal of Library History (1974–1987)* 15, no. 2 (Spring 1980): 132.

[137] See Henri Leclercq. "Bibliothèques" in Fernand Cabrol, ed. *Dictionnaire d'archéologie chrétienne et de liturgie*, 15 vols. in 30 (Paris: Librairie Letouzey et Ané, 1907–1953), vol. 2, pt. 1, cols. 859–862.

[138] Eusebius, *The History of the Church* VIII.16.3–5, 17.1.

[139] Ibid., VIII.17.6–10.

in every way the state may be preserved in health and they may be able to live free from anxiety in their own homes."

Freedom of worship was not universally and permanently granted until AD 313, when Constantine issued what has become known as the Edict of Milan, a letter from Constantine and his co-emperor, Licinius, to eastern governors, legalizing Christianity in the empire.

By all accounts, the Christian Church began as an utter failure, at least from a worldly perspective. To be a Christian in those days was to sign up for harassment, abuse, imprisonment, and often death. But as Hilaire Belloc wrote: "The Church is a perpetually defeated thing that always outlives her conquerors."

While the drama of the first centuries of Christianity provides countless examples of heroic witness to Jesus, this was hardly the end of the story of Christian persecution. Down through the ages, Christians have faced ongoing persecution in various forms, sometimes institutionally, often in more random fashion: the Protestant Reformation; the French Revolution; the missionaries in Canada, Japan, Korea, and elsewhere; the Spanish Civil War; the great totalitarian repressions of the twentieth century—all reveal an anti-Christian animus smoldering under the surface, always ready to be reignited into active persecution.

In the following pages, we will turn to another central aspect of the persecution of Christ's followers: its causes. Why is it that more than 75 percent of religious persecution in the world is directed toward Christians, who preach love of God and neighbor, mercy, peace, and forgiveness? What is it about Christians—or their faith—that seems to provoke such animosity? To that topic, we now turn.

4

The Cross as Target
Why the Special Hostility toward Christians?

Various theories have been advanced as to why Christians have been a particular magnet for persecution ever since the foundation of the Church. While Christians themselves have generally accepted the fact of persecution as a mark of authenticity and faithfulness to Jesus, others have proposed that there is something essentially intolerable about Christianity that provoked even the famously tolerant Roman Empire to treat Christians with cruelty.

Monotheism alone, for instance, cannot explain the unique hostility toward the followers of Jesus. The Jews, in obedience to the first commandment, declined to take part in many of the religious rituals prescribed by the Roman emperors and yet were generally given a pass when it came time to enforce their civic duty. Being Jewish was not illegal in the Roman Empire, whereas being a Christian was.

So many explanations have been offered for hatred of Christians and Christianity in the modern era that it is impossible to single out one or two as decisive. It is, however, worth trying to identify some distinctive characteristics of Christianity that together arouse recurring aggression.

The Coming Christian Persecution

Let us begin with the views of Christianity promoted by two prominent eighteenth-century intellectuals who both downplayed Christian persecution under the Roman Empire and blamed the Christians themselves for whatever punishments were meted out to them. Since these two figures—who bore no love for Christianity or the Church—are often cited in our own day as authoritative voices in understanding hostility toward Christians, their interpretations of Christian persecution are highly relevant to our investigation.

Voltaire's Attack on the Martyrs

The French Enlightenment writer François-Marie Arouet (1694–1778), better known by his pen name, Voltaire, was famous for his wit as well as for his attacks on the Catholic Church. In his *Treatise on Tolerance*—his first major philosophical work—Voltaire called for tolerance among religions and targeted religious fanaticism for his harshest rebukes, especially that of the Jesuits (under whom Voltaire had received his early education).[140]

On examining Christian persecution under the Roman Empire and the history of the martyrs, Voltaire came to the remarkable conclusion that the fault for martyrdom lay entirely with the Christians themselves. It was not the Romans who were intolerant, he contended; rather, it was the Christians who were themselves intolerant by insisting on the uniqueness of their religion and their right to be different. Voltaire produces only the slightest historical documentation to back up his claims; instead, he relies primarily on his rhetorical prowess to present the Romans as highly

---

[140] Voltaire, *Treatise on Tolerance* (1763), trans. Jonathan Bennett (2017), Early Modern Texts, https://www.earlymoderntexts.com/assets/pdfs/voltaire1763.pdf.

reasonable characters who simply could not have done what has been imputed to them.

"The ancient Romans, from Romulus until the days when the Christians disputed with the priests of the Empire, you don't see a single man persecuted for his views," thus exemplifying supreme tolerance of atheists as well as of adherents of other faiths, Voltaire insisted. "Caesar, who gave us roads, laws, and games, never sought to compel us to abandon our Druids for him, though he was the chief priest of the nation that had conquered us."

"All religions were tolerated. How could the Romans have sought out and persecuted obscure members of one cult at a time when they permitted all other religions?" he asks. If the Christians had only been able to behave like followers of other religions, he argues, they would have been fine. It was the "unthinking zeal" of a few intemperate Christians such as St. Polyeuctes, he suggests, that "was probably the source of all the persecutions."[141]

Yet a number of texts seem to contradict Voltaire's claims. In his 311 Edict of Toleration, the emperor Galerius, one of the most aggressive persecutors of the Christians, declared quite candidly that it was the Christians' insistence on following the dictates of their own religion rather than worshipping the emperor that most vexed him. "For through some perverse reasoning such arrogance and folly had seized and possessed them that they refused to follow the path trodden by earlier generations and perhaps blazed long ago by their own ancestors, and made their own laws to suit their own ideas and individual tastes and observed these; and held various meetings in various places," he wrote.[142]

---

[141] Ibid., 14, 15, 17, 18.
[142] Eusebius, *The History of the Church* VIII.17.7.

Voltaire takes issue with popular accounts of Christian martyrs, insisting that they seem entirely unlikely, given the Romans' record of tolerance toward others. "We are told that as soon as the Christians appeared they were persecuted by these same Romans—who didn't persecute anyone. It seems to me that this statement is entirely false," Voltaire declares. "It is said that Nero persecuted them. Tacitus tells us that they were accused of setting fire to Rome, and were abandoned to the fury of the people."[143]

Voltaire then attempts to undermine the authority of the Roman historian through insinuation, without, however, producing any opposing facts of his own:

> It is up to the wise reader to see the point at which one should distrust the truthfulness of historians; what credit one should give to what solemn authors, born in an enlightened nation, affirm about public events; and what limits to one's credulity should be set regarding anecdotes that these same authors pass on without any evidence.[144]

In explaining away St. Lawrence's martyrdom, Voltaire proposes that it was really just a big misunderstanding. "For instance, when St. Lawrence refused to give to the Roman prefect Cornelius Secularis Christian money that he held in safe keeping, the prefect and Emperor would naturally be angry," he asserts. "They did not know that St. Lawrence had distributed the money to the poor, and done a charitable and holy act. They regarded him as a rebel, and had him put to death."[145] Voltaire would have known this was untrue, since just prior to Lawrence's death the Emperor Valerian has issued

---

[143] Voltaire, *Treatise on Tolerance*, 15, 16.
[144] Ibid., 17.
[145] Ibid., 18.

an edict declaring that all bishops, priests, and deacons were to be put to death immediately. Just four days before Lawrence's death, soldiers had executed Pope Sixtus II, who was celebrating Mass in the Catacomb of Saint Callixtus, along with four deacons—a fact unrelated to pecuniary concerns. The five of them were martyred for no other crime than that of being followers of Christ, which was hardly the result of a simple misunderstanding.

Voltaire also attempts to make the case that Christians were offensive to their rulers and provoked them by violently censuring their practices.

"So the martyrs were men who made an outcry against 'false gods.' It was a very wise and very pious thing to refuse to believe in them; but if, not content with worshipping God in spirit and in truth, they broke out violently against the established cult, however absurd it was, we have to admit that they were themselves intolerant," Voltaire states.[146]

It is worth pointing out that Voltaire was hardly indifferent to organized religion and Christianity in particular, as readers may well have noticed. "Atheism is the vice of a few intelligent persons, and superstition is the vice of fools," he wrote in his *Philosophical Dictionary*, adding that superstition "born in Paganism, adopted by Judaism, infested the Christian Church from the earliest times."[147] Or, as he put it in a letter to Frederick the Great, "Christianity is the most ridiculous, the most absurd, and bloody religion that has ever infected the world." Like many Enlightenment figures, Voltaire found religious faith and reason to be inimical to each other, and in the face of what he took as inherent incompatibility, he opted for reason.

---

[146] Ibid.

[147] Voltaire, *Philosophical Dictionary*, s.v. "Superstition."

The Coming Christian Persecution

Edward Gibbon

The English historian Edward Gibbon (1737–1794) took up Voltaire's polemic against the Christian martyrs across the Channel and published *The History of the Decline and Fall of the Roman Empire* in six volumes between 1776 and 1788. Influenced by Voltaire and by his own deep dislike of organized religion, Gibbon challenged the commonly accepted account of early Church history by reckoning far smaller numbers of Christian martyrs than had been traditionally accepted. Gibbon was hostile to Islam and Judaism but harbored special antipathy toward Christianity, blaming the otherworldly concerns of Christians rather than the loss of Roman virtue and identity for the decline of the Roman Empire. Like Voltaire, Gibbon depicted Roman paganism as *tolerant* and Christianity as *intolerant*, indulging himself in extended ridicule of the early Church and her primitive beliefs.

"The primitive Christians perpetually trod on mystic ground, and their minds were exercised by the habits of believing the most extraordinary events," Gibbon wrote with pragmatic scorn.[148] "They felt, or they fancied, that on every side they were incessantly assaulted by daemons, comforted by visions, instructed by prophecy, and surprisingly delivered from danger, sickness, and from death itself, by the supplications of the church."

> The real or imaginary prodigies, of which they so frequently conceived themselves to be the objects, the instruments, or the spectators, very happily disposed them to adopt with the same ease, but with far greater justice, the authentic wonders of the evangelic history; and thus miracles that

---

[148] Edward Gibbon, *History of the Decline and Fall of the Roman Empire*, I.XV.4.

exceeded not the measure of their own experience, inspired them with the most lively assurance of mysteries which were acknowledged to surpass the limits of their understanding. It is this deep impression of supernatural truths which has been so much celebrated under the name of faith; a state of mind described as the surest pledge of the divine favor and of future felicity, and recommended as the first, or perhaps the only merit of a Christian. According to the more rigid doctors, the moral virtues, which may be equally practised by infidels, are destitute of any value or efficacy in the work of our justification.[149]

In other words, for Christians, gullibility was prized higher than moral goodness, he proposed.

Gibbon also took issue with the refusal of many primitive Christians to enlist in the army or to occupy public office. "This indolent, or even criminal disregard to the public welfare, exposed them to the contempt and reproaches of the Pagans, who very frequently asked, what must be the fate of the empire, attacked on every side by the barbarians, if all mankind should adopt the pusillanimous sentiments of the new sect," Gibbon wrote.[150]

Gibbon was particularly offended by what he saw as a Christian "condemnation of the wisest and most virtuous of the Pagans, on account of their ignorance or disbelief of the divine truth," a spiritual intolerance that excluded virtuous pagans from participating in salvation simply because they failed to acknowledge Christ. The primitive church "delivered over, without hesitation, to eternal torture, the far greater part of the human species," he wrote.

[149] Ibid.
[150] Gibbon, *Decline and Fall* I.XV.5.

A charitable hope might perhaps be indulged in favor of Socrates, or some other sages of antiquity, who had consulted the light of reason before that of the gospel had arisen. But it was unanimously affirmed, that those who, since the birth or the death of Christ, had obstinately persisted in the worship of the daemons, neither deserved nor could expect a pardon from the irritated justice of the Deity.

These rigid sentiments, which had been unknown to the ancient world, appear to have infused a spirit of bitterness into a system of love and harmony. The ties of blood and friendship were frequently torn asunder by the difference of religious faith; and the Christians, who, in this world, found themselves oppressed by the power of the Pagans, were sometimes seduced by resentment and spiritual pride to delight in the prospect of their future triumph.[151]

Gibbon did, in fact, write in a supercilious tone redolent of Voltaire's, with the same evident contempt for Christianity. "About fourscore years after the death of Christ, his innocent disciples were punished with death by the sentence of a proconsul of the most amiable and philosophic character, and according to the laws of an emperor distinguished by the wisdom and justice of his general administration," Gibbon wrote of Trajan.[152]

Like Voltaire, Gibbon attributed the persecution of the Christians to their own intolerance and inability to get along under a benevolent and otherwise tolerant government. It is unsurprising that the nations of antiquity, built upon tolerance, should "unite

---

[151] Ibid., I.XV.4.
[152] Ibid., II.XVI.1.

with indignation against any sect or people which should separate itself from the communion of mankind, and claiming the exclusive possession of divine knowledge, should disdain every form of worship, except its own, as impious and idolatrous."[153]

In short, the Christians were guilty of "inflexible obstinacy" and thus deserving of the persecutions that inevitably befell them.[154] Moreover, it was the intransigence of the Christians—he asserted—that ensured the severe punishments they received, since they had the easy option of simply sacrificing to the emperor to escape or at least mitigate such punishment. By stubbornly refusing, they rightly provoked the wrath of the magistrates into whose power they had fallen:

> Punishment was not the inevitable consequence of conviction, and the Christians, whose guilt was the most clearly proved by the testimony of witnesses, or even by their voluntary confession, still retained in their own power the alternative of life or death. It was not so much the past offence, as the actual resistance, which excited the indignation of the magistrate. He was persuaded that he offered them an easy pardon, since, if they consented to cast a few grains of incense upon the altar, they were dismissed from the tribunal in safety and with applause.[155]

Those "humane" judges endeavored to reclaim, rather than to punish, those deluded enthusiasts, Gibbons continued:

> Varying his tone according to the age, the sex, or the situation of the prisoners, he frequently condescended to set

153 Ibid.
154 Ibid., II.XVI.2.
155 Ibid., II.XVI.3.

before their eyes every circumstance which could render life more pleasing, or death more terrible; and to solicit, nay, to entreat, them, that they would show some compassion to themselves, to their families, and to their friends.

If threats and persuasions proved ineffectual, he had often recourse to violence; the scourge and the rack were called in to supply the deficiency of argument, and every art of cruelty was employed to subdue such inflexible, and, as it appeared to the Pagans, such criminal, obstinacy.[156]

Gibbon's efforts to exonerate the Roman Empire's treatment of the early Christians earned him the disdain of certain historians who found his account overblown. His unbalanced treatment of the topic and the failure of his contemporaries to reject it is "a proof of the unphilosophical and indeed fanatical animosity against Christianity, which was so prevalent during the latter part of the eighteenth century," wrote the Scottish historian Sir James Mackintosh in 1836.[157]

"The sixteenth chapter I cannot help considering as a very ingenious and specious, but very disgraceful extenuation of the cruelties perpetrated by the Roman magistrates against the Christians," Mackintosh wrote. "It is written in the most contemptibly factious spirit of prejudice against the sufferers; it is unworthy of a philosopher and of humanity."[158]

A half century later, the Franco-English historian Hilaire Belloc—who was a great fan of Gibbon as a writer and waxes eloquent

---

[156] Ibid.

[157] James Mackintosh, *Memoirs of the Life of the Right Honourable Sir James Mackintosh*, ed. Robert James Mackintosh (London: E. Moxon, 1836), vol. 1, 246.

[158] Ibid., 245.

on Gibbon's mastery of the English language—also found him wanting as a historian, primarily for his visceral dislike of Christianity. "Gibbon had little historical sense, and, on the top of that, did not wish to tell the truth, but rather to attack. On which account he is a bad historian. But as a writer—what a writer!" Belloc wrote.[159] "He so hated the Christian religion that he did, not once, but a hundred times, suppress essential facts, wilfully distorting and wilfully over-emphasizing," Belloc added later in the same work.[160]

Both Voltaire and Gibbon raise some questions of fact regarding the Romans' treatment of Christians that deserve closer examination. Was it true that the empire was tolerant of a broad diversity of beliefs? Was its hostility to Christians the result of misunderstanding or the stubborn arrogance of the believers themselves?

Roman Persecution

The fact is that the Roman persecution of Christians had very precise motives. It is true that the Roman state was remarkably tolerant toward a diversity of religions, but there were two notable exceptions to this general indifference. The Romans did not tolerate any cult that was hostile to the state or any cult that was exclusive of all others. The foundation for these exceptions was political expediency rather than any dogmatic zeal, and it was on the latter issue where Christians ran afoul of the Roman state.

There was one notable exception to Roman intolerance of one-god believers, and that was the Jewish nation, whose faith was clearly exclusive. Like Christianity, Judaism did not allow for

---

[159] Hilaire Belloc, "On Gibbon" in *A Conversation with an Angel and Other Essays* (London: Harper and Brothers, 1928), 130.
[160] Ibid., 136.

mingling in the activities of other faiths, and no Jew could participate in the rites of any other religion or the official worship of the state. And yet the Jewish religion was not persecuted in the Roman Empire but was rather the subject of the state's special protection. Why? There were three reasons for Roman indulgence of the Jews: the venerable age of the faith, the identity between faith and nation, and Judaism's general disinterest in proselytism. As historian Philip Hughes has noted: "The religion of the Jew was part of his nationality and, as such the traditional Roman policy, which tolerated all differences in the one loyalty, tolerated the Jew's religion and protected it."[161] Moreover, the Jews notoriously kept to themselves, and non-Jewish converts to the faith were rare, and therefore, their numbers did not notably increase.

If the Christian Church had never sought the conversion of the Gentiles to the faith but had remained an innocent offshoot of Judaism, it would probably have gotten a pass as well. The Roman authorities initially regarded the Christians as members of a Jewish sect and treated them as such. The differences between the Christians and the Jews seemed to be mere internal religious quarrels, with which the Roman state did not wish to be involved.[162] But the Jewish leaders themselves soon made it clear to the Roman officials that in Christianity they had to deal with a new, nonnational religion. The differences became ever more manifest, and Christianity emerged in the Roman mind as a religion unto itself. What the Romans saw were members of their own nation—rich and poor, slaves and free, soldiers and civilians, men and women, young and old—converting in droves to the new, upstart faith. This

---

[161] Philip Hughes, *A History of the Church*, vol. 1, *The World in Which the Church Was Founded* (London: Sheed and Ward, 1948), 158.

[162] See Acts 25:18-21.

caused consternation. The new religion, exclusive in its beliefs and precluding worship of the emperor, was not only unlawful in the technical sense but was a looming threat. The seeds of active persecution were sown.

Popular sentiment, too, became increasingly hostile as rumors spread depicting followers of the young sect as monsters of depravity, meeting in secret for the performance of bloody and obscene rites. Thus, by Nero's time (54–68), the Christians, who were known by that name in Rome, had become numerous and were the objects of popular suspicion and hatred. Nero took advantage of this hatred to make Christians scapegoats for his own misdeeds and proceeded to set a horrifying precedent in how to deal with the new, illegal religion.

As we saw in chapter 4, the policies of emperors such as Trajan, Valerian, and Diocletian had dire consequences for the lives of believers. But those specifically Roman responses to Christianity do not provide a complete answer to the question of why Christians have been persistently singled out for persecution over the centuries. Had Christian persecution existed solely as a phenomenon of the first centuries in a specific political context, we could chalk the whole affair up to an unfortunate confluence of destinies, a sort of perfect storm erupting in aggression and violence. But this is not the case. Hostility toward Christianity was not limited to the Roman Empire or the first centuries of the Christian era. It continued down through the centuries and has become increasingly virulent in our time.

So once again, the question must be asked: Why such abiding contempt and abhorrence for Christians and their religion? What elements intrinsic to the faith itself have made it—and continue to make it—the object of such loathing?

The Coming Christian Persecution

The *Letter to Diognetus*

A fairly detailed hypothesis about the deeper motives behind the growing antipathy toward Christians can be found in the ancient Christian text the *Letter to Diognetus*. Written by an unknown author sometime between AD 130 and 200, the letter attempts to describe the relationship between Christians and the world, thereby elucidating what it is about them that the "world" finds so irritating and intolerable.

The author first explains that Christians are outwardly not all that different from others. The Christians "are distinguished from other men neither by country, nor language, nor the customs which they observe." They do not live apart in self-made ghettos or communes, nor do they have the marks of some secret society, with peculiar language, handshakes, or other signals to distinguish them from others. Inhabiting Greek as well as barbarian cities, the author continues, they follow "the customs of the natives in respect to clothing, food, and the rest of their ordinary conduct."[163]

So far, so good. Christians eat, dress, talk, and work like other ordinary citizens. And yet there is something different about them, the author suggests, that may explain at least in part the hostility they experience. "They dwell in their own countries, but simply as sojourners. As citizens, they share in all things with others, and yet endure all things as if foreigners. Every foreign land is to them as their native country, and every land of their birth as a land of strangers."

In the eyes of the author of the letter, there is a discernible detachment among Christians that keeps them from rooting so completely in the world, and indeed in the present life, that all their

---

[163] Quotations in this section from the *Letter to Diognetus* are taken from chapters 5 and 6.

hope becomes lodged in that detachment. There were, of course, pagan philosophers who advocated this sort of detachment. The awareness of mortality and the inevitable brevity of life led some to practice even more detachment than the Christians, eschewing any sort of active participation in the affairs of the earthly city. While Christian monks and hermits may have practiced this sort of disengagement, the majority of Christians did not, as our author explains, and yet even the engaged, "secular" Christians bore a mark of otherworldliness that set them apart from their contemporaries. Moreover, what may have been mere resignation to mortality in the case of a Seneca or a Marcus Aurelius was somehow more hopeful and forward-looking in the lives of Christians. And so our author notes that Christians "are in the flesh, but they do not live after the flesh. They pass their days on earth, but they are citizens of heaven."

But spiritual detachment from the affairs of this world is not the only distinguishing mark of Christians, our author observes. He also offers Diognetus specific examples showing how the moral life of Christians, though similar in many ways to that of the pagans, differs in some essential points. "They marry, as do all others; they beget children; but they do not destroy their offspring. They have a common table, but not a common bed," he explains. And thus, while they "obey the prescribed laws," at the same time they "surpass the laws by their lives."

As a result, the author declares, this difference—as subtle and seemingly harmless as it may be—is sufficient to incite the wrath of their compatriots. In a sort of panegyric to the Christian life, the author suggests that the very goodness of the Christians may well be a source of the hatred they often received in return. Christians "love all men, and are persecuted by all. They are unknown and condemned; they are put to death and restored to life," he states.

The Coming Christian Persecution

They are evil spoken of, and yet are justified; they are reviled, and bless; they are insulted, and repay the insult with honour; they do good, yet are punished as evil-doers. When punished, they rejoice as if quickened into life; they are assailed by the Jews as foreigners, and are persecuted by the Greeks; yet those who hate them are unable to assign any reason for their hatred.

In his following chapter, the author of the letter reaches his own conclusion as to what it is about the Christians that sparks such antipathy. For him, it is primarily a moral issue. He bases this conclusion on a parallel he draws between the place of the Christian in the world and the relationship between the soul and the body after the Fall, with a natural antagonism underlying both relationships:

To sum up all in one word—what the soul is in the body, [such] are Christians in the world. The soul is dispersed through all the members of the body, and Christians are scattered through all the cities of the world. The soul dwells in the body, yet is not of the body; and Christians dwell in the world, yet are not of the world.

This, then, is the true source of the animosity the world feels toward Christians, the author argues. The moral goodness of the Christian life—or at least its moral ideal—serves as a constant reproach to an immoral world that wants to be affirmed rather than challenged. "The flesh hates the soul, and wars against it, though itself suffering no injury, because it is prevented from enjoying pleasures; the world also hates the Christians, though in nowise injured, because they abjure pleasures," the letter states.

In this we find echoed the words of the biblical book of Wisdom, which, though traditionally applied to the life and death of

Jesus, are also applicable to His followers. In the following passage, the unrighteous feel challenged and threatened by the life of the just one, who irritates them because his very presence seems a reproach.

> Let us lie in wait for the righteous man, because he is inconvenient to us and opposes our actions; he reproaches us for sins against the law, and accuses us of sins against our training. He professes to have knowledge of God, and calls himself a child of the Lord.
>
> He became to us a reproof of our thoughts; the very sight of him is a burden to us, because his manner of life is unlike that of others, and his ways are strange. We are considered by him as something base, and he avoids our ways as unclean; he calls the last end of the righteous happy, and boasts that God is his father.

As a result, the unjust decide to put the righteous one to the test, to subject him to torments to see whether his words still hold true.

> Let us see if his words are true, and let us test what will happen at the end of his life; for if the righteous man is God's son, he will help him, and will deliver him from the hand of his adversaries. Let us test him with insult and torture, that we may find out how gentle he is, and make trial of his forbearance. Let us condemn him to a shameful death, for, according to what he says, he will be protected. (2:12-20)

Atheists' Particular Animosity toward Christianity

An interesting phenomenon that has emerged in our day is the particular animosity of atheists toward Christians and Christian beliefs. Why do atheists find Christianity intolerable while not experiencing the same antipathy to Buddhism, Hinduism, Judaism, or Islam? The answer to that question may provide a clue as to why Christians have long borne the brunt of religious persecution in the world. The spate of neo-atheist popular literature exemplified by such works as Sam Harris's *The End of Faith: Religion, Terror, and the Future of Reason* (2005) and his *Letter to a Christian Nation* (2007), Daniel C. Dennett's *Breaking the Spell: Religion as a Natural Phenomenon* (2006), Richard Dawkins's *The God Delusion* (2006), Christopher Hitchens's *God Is Not Great: How Religion Poisons Everything* (2007), and Jerry Coyne's *Fact vs. Faith: Why Science and Religion Are Incompatible* (2015) focuses overwhelmingly on Christianity in its attacks on religion in general.

A curious thing about many atheists is their anger and apparent hatred of God. It is curious because one would think that "not believing" in something would render that nonexistent "something" uninteresting and unworthy of attention. While some atheists are indifferent to God and religious belief, a surprising number are actively hostile toward them. The recent publication of numerous books denying the existence of God suggests a proselytizing spirit animating much modern atheism. They not only disbelieve; they also want to convert as many as possible to their disbelief. While much of this hostility to faith manifests itself merely in ridicule, at times it grows darker and more aggressive.

As a target for both their proselytizing and their aggression, atheists overwhelmingly prefer Christians. Rarely will atheists attack Buddhists, Hindus, Jews, or Muslims for their faith. This goes for atheists in Hollywood, in higher education, and in government. In his incisive article titled "Why Atheism Specifically Targets Christianity More Than Other Religions," Joel Furches set out to explain why atheists and agnostics harbor a degree of animosity toward Christianity and Christians that is not in evidence in their dealings with other faith traditions.[164]

As an example, Furches cited Jason Pratt, a former atheist and Christian baiter who used to delight in taunting his Christian classmates in college. "I even had a few [Christians] as roommates. And I frequently took pleasure in ridiculing them. I generally enjoyed playing their intellectual superior, and I enjoyed challenging what they believed," Pratt said. "As I was going through school I had a number of other roommates from various other countries: I had a Muslim from Oman, a Buddhist from South Korea, and various other faiths—and it was interesting, none of them really bothered me too much. Their faith and what they said they believed was not of much concern to me: it was really only the Christians."[165]

This is typical of atheists everywhere, Furches observed, running through atheist literature from Nietzsche to Russell to Dawkins to Graham Oppy. Writers in this vein rarely attempt to debunk New Age beliefs, Scientology, or pantheism—despite their pervasiveness—and they waste little ink criticizing the other "Abrahamic" religions, Judaism and Islam, even though the latter will likely surpass Christianity as a world religion in the next several decades.[166]

---

[164] Joel Furches, "Why Atheism Specifically Targets Christianity More Than Other Religions," *Soapboxie*, October 17, 2022, https://soapboxie.com/social-issues/Atheism-Specifically-Targets -Christianity-Above-Any-Other-Religion-Why.

[165] Ibid.; "True Confessions of a Rocket Scientist: Jason Pratt," podcast, 36:01, Grace Bible Church, June 7, 2015, https://www. visaliaevfree.org/mediaPlayer/#/sermonaudio/2.

[166] Furches, "Why Atheism Specifically Targets Christianity."

The Coming Christian Persecution

Yale professor David Gelernter, a practicing Jew, has described with great acuity how, for many atheists, politics functions as religion, and thus Christianity, with its refusal to deify political programs, can present itself to their minds as a rival worldview deserving derision and hatred.

"Almost all human beings need religion, as subway-riders need overhead grab bars," Gelernter writes.

> The religious impulse strikes conservatives and liberals alike. But conservatives usually practice the religion of their parents and ancestors; liberals have mostly shed their Judaism or Christianity, and politics fills the obvious spiritual gap. You might make football, rock music, or hard science your chosen faith. Some people do. But politics, with its underlying principles and striking public ceremonies, is the obvious religion substitute.
>
> Hence the gross asymmetry of modern politics. For most conservatives, politics is just politics. For most liberals, politics is their faith, in default of any other; it is the basis of their moral life.[167]

If modern atheists do indeed focus on Christianity as their preferred target, the deification of politics goes a long way in explaining why Christians are so often ridiculed and discriminated against, particularly in the West. The pervasiveness of atheism in politically "woke" Hollywood, universities, theater, media, and many other culture-molding institutions helps us understand why atheists find Christian beliefs and Christians themselves so intolerable.

---

[167] David Gelernter, "What Explains the Vicious Left?" *Weekly Standard*, December 31, 2015, https://www.washingtonexaminer.com/weekly-standard/what-explains-the-vicious-left.

Pope Francis on Christian Persecution

Pope Francis is among those who have sought to understand and explain why Christians are so often the targets of hatred and persecution. In early 2020, he explored the topic in a General Audience on the Beatitudes, in which he proposed that an authentic Christian witness often stirs up indignation, anger, and hatred in the worldly minded, and he tied this reaction to the rampant persecution of Christians in the world today.[168]

Reflecting on the Gospel beatitude "Blessed are those who are persecuted for righteousness' sake, for theirs is the kingdom of heaven," the pope said that the practice of Christian virtue stings the ungodly to the core, unleashing hostility and violence. Expressing a line of thought similar to that of the author of the *Letter to Diognetus*, the pope proposed that the beauty of goodness causes pain to those who do not live it. "Poverty in spirit, mourning, meekness, a thirst for holiness, mercy, purification of the heart, and works of peace can lead to persecution for Christ's sake," the pope said, because "the world, with its idols, its compromises and its priorities, cannot approve of this type of existence."

The worldly "can only reject poverty or meekness or purity and declare life according to the Gospel to be an error and a problem, and therefore as something to be vilified," he said, and so the world judges Christians to be "idealists or fanatics."

"The Christian witness, which does so much good to so many people who follow it, irritates those with a worldly mentality," he said, and "they experience it as a reproach." It is not so much the Christian, but the action of God in one's conscience, that provokes this annoyance, he suggested. "When holiness appears and the life of the children of God emerges, there is something uncomfortable

---

[168] Pope Francis, General Audience, April 29, 2020.

in that beauty that calls for taking a stand," Francis said, "either to allow oneself to be challenged and to open oneself to goodness or to reject that light and harden one's heart, even to the point of opposition and fury."

The pope suggested that the same causes of Christian persecution can be found throughout history. "It is odd and striking to see how hostility grows to the point of fury in the persecutions of the martyrs," he said. "Just look at the persecutions of the last century, of the European dictatorships, which give rise to fury against Christians, against the Christian witness and against the heroism of Christians."[169]

Later that year, he returned to the subject, suggesting that "enduring persecution and hostility is part of the Christian vocation," something essential to the "DNA" of Christianity.[170]

Unfortunately, as many analysts have noted, Pope Francis's actions and official policies have not always corresponded to his strong words on the subject of contemporary Christian persecution, and this lack of consistency has undermined the Church's witness.

For example, his 2018 secret accord with the Chinese Communist Party (CCP) on the naming of bishops in the country was seen by many as a betrayal of the millions of faithful members of China's underground Catholic Church who have stayed true to Rome during decades of hostility. When the pope opened the possibility of faithful Catholics joining the state-controlled Catholic Patriotic Association, reversing the policy of his predecessors, many priests felt pressure to join an organization that had endeavored for years to destabilize Rome's authority over Chinese Catholics. They no longer had the defense that to do so was not

[169] Ibid.
[170] Angelus message, July 19, 2020.

permitted by the Catholic Magisterium and thus began looking willfully obstinate rather than faithful to the Church. Moreover, official hostility to Christians in China did not diminish with the Vatican deal with the CCP but actually increased, leading many to observe that the Vatican had sacrificed much and gained nothing by the agreement.

A second example of the pope's unintentionally undermining his own message on Christian persecution stems from his unwillingness to call out or even acknowledge the unique and worrisome phenomenon of radical Islamic terrorism.

In a meeting with popular movements in 2017, the pope denied the existence of Islamic terrorism, while suggesting that Muslims are no more likely to find motivation for violence in their faith than Christians are in theirs. "Christian terrorism does not exist, Jewish terrorism does not exist, and Muslim terrorism does not exist. They do not exist," Francis said.[171]

While he perhaps meant that not all Christians are terrorists and not all Muslims are terrorists—a self-evident fact—his words suggested that no specifically Islamic form of terrorism exists in the world, which is patently false. On several occasions, Pope Francis has insisted that all religions want peace and that no religion promotes violence. The danger of violent radicalization, therefore, would exist equally in all religions. "There are fundamentalist and violent individuals in all peoples and religions—and with intolerant generalizations they become stronger because they feed on hate and xenophobia," he said.

This is simply untrue, and it has been radical Islamists themselves who have countered the pope's theories by insisting that

---

[171] Pope Francis, address to the World Meeting of Popular Movements, February 10, 2017.

their violence is inspired by their faith, as we will have occasion to see in the following chapter.

For his part, Francis has played down any religious motivation for Muslim aggression and insisted that such acts are generated by economic disparities. The Islamists' Christian victims—most of whom are significantly worse off than their Muslim countrymen—may disagree with the Holy Father.

Spiritual Warfare

Illuminating as each of these hypotheses about the sources of Christian persecution might be, there is perhaps a final element that eludes attempts to explain the sources of anti-Christian animus. There is something superhuman, indeed demonic, about the bitterness often experienced by the persecutors of Christians. The reaction often seems completely disproportionate to the disdain or odium one would expect, given the level of irritation Christians can cause.

St. Paul famously wrote that "we are not contending against flesh and blood, but against the principalities, against the powers, against the world rulers of this present darkness, against the spiritual hosts of wickedness in the heavenly places" (Eph. 6:12). There is a spiritual battle going on beyond the material realities of this world in which other forces are at work. Ultimately, the causes of Christian persecution are spiritual, rather than merely rational, and any serious attempt to come to grips with our topic must engage this uncomfortable truth.

5

Haters Gonna Hate?
The Drivers of Christian Persecution Today

Jesus characterized the nature of Christian persecution as hatred of the light and aversion to the truth. As we have seen, this hatred has taken many forms throughout history. In today's world, it has its own peculiarities. According to the director of Open Doors Italy, Cristian Nani, there are nine primary "drivers" of persecution in today's world: radical Islam, communist and postcommunist oppression, religious nationalism, ethnic antagonism, tribal oppression, denominational protectionism, secular intolerance, dictatorial paranoia, and organized crime.[172] This nine-headed hydra of anti-Christian animus reveals just how diverse are the motivations behind the widespread antagonism toward modern disciples of Jesus.

These drivers vary from country to country, although they may also coexist within one country. Sometimes the state itself is the primary origin of persecution, as in North Korea and China; sometimes a religious body or factions within it impel the aggression, such as the situation with radical Islam. In eight of the top ten nations for Christian persecution, the majority religion is Islam,

---

[172] Open Doors, *World Watch List 2021.*

a telling fact. Four of the top ten countries are in Africa, four are in Asia, and two are in the Middle East.

In this chapter, we will see the many ways in which specific manifestations of anti-Christian hatred in the world today have emerged from and reflect the history and ideas we have been following in previous chapters.

Radical Islam

Islamic extremism is the primary driver of Christian persecution in many countries around the world, including Afghanistan, Libya, Pakistan, Yemen, Iran, Nigeria, Iraq, Syria, Sudan, Somalia, and Saudi Arabia. According to the 2022 World Watch List, of the fifty countries where Christian persecution is highest, "Islamic oppression" is the principal driver of persecution in more than half, and thirty-four of those countries have a Muslim majority. Moreover, the "extreme persecution" suffered by Christians in eight of the ten worst nations comes from "Islamic oppression" or is occurring in Muslim-majority nations—namely, Afghanistan (no. 1), Somalia (no. 3), Libya (no. 4), Yemen (no. 5), Eritrea (no. 6), Nigeria (no. 7), Pakistan (no. 8), and Iran (no. 9).

Islam is the world's fastest-growing religion with 1.8 billion followers—almost a quarter (24.1 percent) of the world's population. Global Islam is split into two major denominations—Sunni (75 to 90 percent) and Shia (10 to 20 percent); the division arose out of a disagreement over the succession to Muhammad and over time acquired broader political significance as well as theological and juridical dimensions.

It is important to emphasize right off the bat that radical Islamists make up a small percentage of Islam, and the vast majority of Muslims do not engage in or support Christian persecution. For instance, in the 2016 Marrakesh Declaration, more than 250

Muslim religious leaders, heads of state, and scholars called for the defense of the rights of religious minorities in predominantly Muslim countries. Moreover, the world's largest Muslim political organization, Nahdlatul Ulama, with a membership of tens of millions, has explicitly condemned the use of religion as a pretext for violence, while embracing religious freedom and religious pluralism.

That being said, radical Islamists give a bad name to all Muslims by claiming a religious justification for the oppression of Christians, often insisting that violent jihad is the will of Allah and a duty for all pious Muslims. In its more extreme forms, Islamism has sought the eradication of Christians from certain geographical areas, such as the formation of a geopolitical "caliphate" by the Islamic State, beginning in Mosul, Iraq, in 2014.

There are more than thirty Islamic terror groups in the world, some of which operate in a single nation and others that operate regionally or worldwide. Some of the better-known and more active groups include al-Qaeda (Middle East), al-Shabaab (Somalia), Boko Haram (Nigeria), Hamas (Gaza Strip and West Bank), Hezbollah (Lebanon), the Islamic State of Iraq and the Levant (ISIL), and the Taliban (Afghanistan). According to the Global Terrorism Index 2016, just four Islamic extremist groups were responsible for 74 percent of all deaths from Islamic terrorism in 2015: the Islamic State, Boko Haram, the Taliban, and al-Qaeda. Islamic terrorism exists in both Sunni and Shiite forms, although the majority is Sunni, which is understandable, given the Sunni's demographic superiority.

A particularly revealing explanation of radical Islam's war on Christianity came from Islamist extremists themselves, who, in 2016, offered a detailed repudiation of assertions that they were motivated by economic or sociological considerations rather than religious ones. Shortly before, Pope Francis had expressed his opinion that all religions seek peace and that religious beliefs cannot possibly be the force behind Islamic terrorism. The pope pointed to economic inequalities and a misguided global economy, rather than religion, as the true dynamo driving jihadism.[173]

Addressing Pope Francis by name, spokesmen for the Islamic State assured the pontiff that their *sole* motivation is religious and is sanctioned by Allah in the Quran. In issue 15 of *Dabiq*, the propaganda magazine of the Islamic State, ISIS criticized Pope Francis for his alleged naïveté in clinging to the conviction that Muslims want peace and that acts of Islamic terror are economically motivated.[174]

"This is a divinely-warranted war between the Muslim nation and the nations of disbelief," the authors stated in an article titled "By the Sword." The Islamic State attacked Francis for claiming that "authentic Islam and the proper reading of the Qur'an are opposed to every form of violence," saying that by doing this, "Francis continues to hide behind a deceptive veil of 'good will,' covering his actual intentions of pacifying the Muslim nation."

Pope Francis "has struggled against reality" in his efforts to portray Islam as a religion of peace, the article insisted, before going on to urge all Muslims to take up the sword of jihad, the "greatest obligation" of a true Muslim. Despite the obviously religious nature of their attacks, the article states, "many people in Crusader

---

[173] "Full Text of Pope Francis' In-Flight Presser from Poland," July 31, 2016, Catholic News Agency, https://www.catholicnewsagency.com/news/34293/full-text-of-pope-francis-in-flight-presser-from-poland.

[174] "New Issue of the Islamic State's magazine: Dabiq #15," Jihadology, July 31, 2016, https://jihadology.net/2016/07/31/new-issue-of-the-islamic-states-magazine-dabiq-15/.

[Christian] countries express shock and even disgust that Islamic State leadership 'uses religion to justify violence.' "

"Indeed, waging jihad—spreading the rule of Allah by the sword —is an obligation found in the Qur'an, the word of our Lord," the Islamic State declared. "The blood of the disbelievers is obligatory to spill by default. The command is clear. Kill the disbelievers, as Allah said, 'Then kill the polytheists wherever you find them.' "

The Islamic State also reacted to Pope Francis's description of recent acts of Islamic terror as "senseless violence," insisting that there is nothing senseless about it. "The gist of the matter is that there is indeed a rhyme to our terrorism, warfare, ruthlessness, and brutality," they asserted, adding that their hatred for the Christian West is absolute and implacable.

"The fact is, even if you were to stop bombing us, imprisoning us, torturing us, vilifying us, and usurping our lands, we would continue to hate you because our primary reason for hating you will not cease to exist until you embrace Islam," they wrote. "Even if you were to pay *jizyah* [the tax for infidels] and live under the authority of Islam in humiliation, we would continue to hate you."

In February 2017, Sam Rohrer, the president of the American Pastors Network, warned that many well-intentioned people are in denial over the true nature of Islam by refusing to acknowledge its inherent ties to violent jihad.

Responding to a CBS poll that found that the majority of Democrats believe that Islam is no more violent than Christianity, Rohrer said that many Americans are confused about the Muslim faith and the teachings of the Quran. He added that this view represented a "purposeful denial of facts."

"The view for a long time has been that jihadists, wherever they are, are not at all reflective of Islam, and these are only a small number, who don't speak for Islam," Rohrer said in an interview with the *Christian Post*. "The unfortunate thing about that is that those involved in jihad are the only ones who are really practicing what the Qur'an says."[175]

Those who do not recognize that Islam is more prone to terrorism and violence than Christianity either haven't "done their homework" or are ignoring the truth, Rohrer said, adding that public opinion on Islam is tied to a religious relativism that assumes that "all people worship the same God, or there is no God, or all gods are equal."

It is a "great mistake" to believe that Islam is first and foremost a religion, like Christianity or Judaism, Rohrer suggested. "That is totally wrong, because Islam is primarily a political, legal system. It has religious tenets, but it is a political system accompanied by Sharia law," he said. "By its very commandments," he said, Sharia prohibits Islam from peacefully coexisting with others.

A particularly noteworthy example—among many—of the deep-seated and religiously motivated hatred of Christians by radical Islamists was the videotaped beheading of twenty-one Coptic Christians on a beach in Libya on February 15, 2015. Islamic State jihadists dressed the Christians in orange jumpsuits and made them kneel in the sand along a Libyan beach near Sirte, where they executed them by the sword.

In the video of the execution, a masked ISIS jihadist dressed in military fatigues made a pronouncement before the beheading begins. "All praise is due to Allah the strong and mighty and may blessings and peace be upon the ones sent by the sword as a mercy

---

[175] Stoyan Zaimov, "Democrats Wrong to Think Islam Not Violent, American Pastors Network Prez Says," *Christian Post*, February 15, 2017, https://www.christianpost.com/news/democrats-wrong-islam-not-violent-american-pastors-network-175055/.

to all the worlds," he said. "All crusaders: safety for you will be only wishes especially if you are fighting us all together. Therefore, we will fight you all together. The sea you have hidden Sheikh Osama bin Laden's body in, we swear to Allah we will mix it with your blood," he added.[176]

On the sixth anniversary of the massacre, Pope Francis issued a special message to recall the heroic witness of the Christians. "Today is the day I have in my heart, that February of 2015," the pope said. "I hold in my heart that baptism of blood, those twenty-one men baptized as Christians with water and the Spirit, and that day also baptized with blood. They are our Saints, Saints of all Christians, Saints of all Christian denominations and traditions. They are those who have blanched their lives in the blood of the Lamb, they are those ... of the people of God, the faithful people of God."[177]

In his message, Pope Francis focused on the heroic witness of the Egyptian saints, noting how they were ordinary men who made an extraordinary sacrifice: giving their lives for their faith in Jesus. "They had gone to work abroad to support their families: ordinary men, fathers of families, men with the dream of having children; men with the dignity of workers, who not only seek to bring home bread, but to bring it home with the dignity of work," he said.

---

[176] Jordan Schachtel, "ISIS Beheads 21 Christians, Promises to 'Conquer Rome, By Allah's Permission,'" Breitbart, February 15, 2015, https://www.breitbart.com/national-security/2015/02/15/isis-beheads-21-christians-promises-to-conquer-rome-by-allahs-permission/.

[177] "Video Message of His Holiness Pope Francis in Memory of the Coptic Martyrs Killed in Libya in 2015," Vatican website, February 15, 2021, https://www.vatican.va/content/francesco/en/messages/pont-messages/2021/documents/papa-francesco_20210215_videomessaggio-martiri-copti.html.

"And these men bore witness to Jesus Christ. Their throats slit by the brutality of ISIS, they died saying: 'Lord Jesus!', confessing the name of Jesus."

"It is true that this was a tragedy, that these people lost their lives on that beach; but it is also true that the beach was blessed by their blood," the pope continued. "And it is even more true that from their simplicity, from their simple but consistent faith, they received the greatest gift a Christian can receive: bearing witness to Jesus Christ to the point of giving their life."

"I thank God our Father because He gave us these courageous brothers. I thank the Holy Spirit because He gave them the strength and consistency to confess Jesus Christ to the point of shedding blood," Francis added.

As I mentioned in the preceding chapter, it is unfortunate that Pope Francis's recognition of the heroic martyrdom of Christian witnesses at the hands of Muslim terrorists is not accompanied by a more serious analysis of the phenomenon of anti-Christian Islamic violence. This seeming contradiction is underscored by Francis's very first canonization, performed on May 12, 2013, just two months after his election. On that day, Francis raised the 813 martyrs of Otranto to the glory of the altars, a process already set in motion by his predecessor Pope Benedict XVI. These were Christian laymen, mostly shopkeepers, who were slain by invading Muslims of the Ottoman Empire in the southern Italian coastal city of Otranto in 1480. On August 14, the invaders presented the more than 800 laymen with an ultimatum: either convert to Islam or be slain. A tailor named Antonio Primaldo stepped forward and declared: "Now it is time for us to fight to save our souls for the Lord. And since He died on the Cross for us, it is fitting that we should die for Him"—a proclamation met with a loud cheer. The men were led out to the Hill of Minerva (later renamed the Hill of

Martyrs), where they were beheaded one by one. At the time of the martyrs' canonization in 2013, the *Guardian* newspaper remarked on Francis's unusual decision to avoid during the ceremony making any mention of Islam or the circumstances of their death.[178]

Hindu Nationalism: The Case of India

As we noted in chapter 1, religious affiliation is increasingly tied to national identity in India, especially since the rise to power of the right-wing Bharatiya Janata Party (BJP) in 2014, with the party's close ties to Hindu nationalism. As USCIRF noted in its 2019 report, in countries such as India, "it is increasingly difficult to separate religion and politics, a tactic that is sometimes intentional by those who seek to discriminate against and restrict the rights of certain religious communities."[179] As a driver of anti-Christian harassment and violence, Hindu nationalism often pushes a vision of Christians as unpatriotic and "un-Indian."

India "has a long history as a secular democracy where religious communities of every faith have thrived," and the nation's independent judiciary "has often provided essential protections to religious minority communities through its jurisprudence," USCIRF noted. This is, unfortunately, no longer the case, and India is a prime example of the global rise in anti-Christian hostility. India's history of religious freedom "has come under attack in recent years with the growth of exclusionary extremist narratives—including, at times, the government's allowance and encouragement of mob

---

[178] Lizzy Davies, "Pope Francis Completes Contentious Canonisation of Otranto Martyrs," *Guardian*, May 12, 2013, https://www.theguardian.com/world/2013/may/12/pope-francis-canonise-otranto-martyrs.

[179] USCIRF, *Annual Report 2019*, 2, https://www.uscirf.gov/sites/default/files/2019USCIRFAnnualReport.pdf.

violence against religious minorities," USCIRF continues, "that have facilitated an egregious and ongoing campaign of violence, intimidation, and harassment against non-Hindu and lower-caste Hindu minorities."

Mob violence was "carried out against Christians under accusations of forced or induced religious conversion," the report declares. "In cases involving mobs killing an individual based on false accusations of cow slaughter or forced conversion, police investigations and prosecutions often were not adequately pursued."[180]

While Christians constitute slightly more than 2 percent of India's population, they are victims in 14 percent of cases of religiously motivated violence, and these assaults have spiked since the BJP took power.[181] The highest share of these attacks comes in reaction to allegations of religious conversions. The assaults span from attacks on churches and prayer spaces—even those in homes—to violence against priests, nuns, and ordinary members of the Christian faithful.

On June 29, 2021, Pew Research Center published the results of a major survey revealing that for most of India's Hindus, religious and national identities are closely linked.[182] The survey of religion across India was based on nearly thirty thousand face-to-face

180 Ibid., 174.

181 Harsh Mander, "New Hate Crime Tracker in India Finds Victims Are Predominantly Muslims, Perpetrators Hindus," Scroll.in, November 13, 2018, https://scroll.in/article/901206/new-hate-crime-tracker-in-india-finds-victims-are-predominantly-muslims-perpetrators-hindus.

182 Neha Sahgal, Jonathan Evans, Ariana Monique Salazar, Kelsey Jo Starr, and Manolo Corichi, "Religion in India: Tolerance and Segregation," Pew Research Center, June 29, 2021, https://www.pewforum.org/2021/06/29/religion-in-india-tolerance-and-segregation/.

interviews of adults conducted in seventeen languages between late 2019 and early 2020. The poll sought to measure "multiple dimensions of Hindu nationalism by asking people how important certain attributes or behaviors are to 'true' Indian identity," and it found that nearly two-thirds of India's Hindus (64 percent) "say it is very important to be Hindu to be truly Indian." The survey also found that "support for the BJP is considerably higher among those who say both being Hindu and speaking Hindi are very important to be truly Indian."

Amid this surge of Hindu nationalism in recent years, Indian Christians are constantly pressured by aggressive propaganda. The message "to be Indian, you must be Hindu" means that mobs continue to attack and harass Christians and other religious minorities. The belief that Christians are not truly Indian means that widespread discrimination and persecution is often conducted with impunity, since authorities easily look the other way rather than investigating charges of abuse against Christians. India also continues to block the flow of foreign funds to many Christian-run hospitals, schools, and church organizations, all under the guise of protecting the Indian national identity.[183]

In 2018, India's Supreme Court underscored the deteriorating conditions for religious freedom in some states, asserting that certain state governments were not doing enough to stop violence against religious minorities and, "in some extreme instances, impunity was being granted to criminals engaged in communal violence."[184]

Violence toward Christians has risen exponentially, and in just seven years, the nation climbed from number 31 on the World

---

[183] See Open Doors, *World Watch List 2021*.

[184] USCIRF, *Annual Report 2019*, 174.

Watch List to number10. "India has been going up the list rather steadily for the past five years" and can now be classified as a country with extreme persecution, said Dr. Matthew Rees in 2019, having authored that year's annual report.[185] Rees noted that a key factor pushing India higher on the list is the "toxic narrative around this idea of the connection of Hinduism and being Indian," a notion not just "from the extreme end" of the Hindu nationalist RSS movement but also "creeping into the language of the elected politicians and officials." In Open Doors' 2022 report, India had maintained its number-10 position among the fifty countries where it is most dangerous to be a Christian.

In 2017, Ram Nath Kovind, president of India and BJP spokesperson, described Christians and Muslims as "foreigners of the nation," whereas Ashok Singhal, the leader of the Vishva Hindu Parishad, forecast a BJP victory in 2014 as the beginning of a revolution that would turn India entirely Hindu by 2020, Open Doors' report stated.

Research shows that the rise in Christian persecution "is connected to the BJP party," Rees told the *Wire*. "When influential people use this language, it filters down to the rest of society and we think that is playing a big part in the mob violence and social ostracism."

"If you are not Hindu, then your Indian identity is questioned, and if your identity as an Indian is questioned then also your right to the constitution is questioned," Rees said, adding that a "big factor is the Freedom of Religion Act or 'anti-conversion' legislation"

---

[185] Ruhi Khan, "India 10th Most Dangerous Country to Live in for Christians: Report," *Wire*, February 14, 2019, https://thewire.in/communalism/india-10th-most-dangerous-country-to-live-in-for-christians-report.

that is in force in eight states—Arunachal Pradesh, Odisha, Madhya Pradesh, Chhattisgarh, Gujarat, Himachal Pradesh, Jharkhand, and Uttarakhand."[186]

In June 2021, the Fides News Agency, the official information service of the Pontifical Mission Societies, reported that in the first five months of 2021, India had witnessed at least 127 reported episodes of violence against Christians. Among the complaints registered were religiously motivated attacks by mobs and threats and intimidation of various kinds.

A. C. Michael, a lay Catholic and leader of the United Christian Forum, which operates a toll-free number to monitor incidents of violence against Christians in the country, said that incidents of anti-Christian violence "have become so common that no one feels the need to condemn them anymore, including political, civil society and religious leaders."[187]

Unfortunately, Hindu nationalism as a driver of Christian persecution shows no sign of abating. Attacks against Christians in India increase every year rather than decreasing, and there are no indications that this trend will change anytime soon.

Totalitarianism

It is a tautology to speak of atheistic totalitarianism, since by its very nature, a totalitarian state conceives of itself as a supreme and all-encompassing authority that admits of no other power outside itself. That is, after all, what *totalitarian* means: the state is

---

[186] Ibid.

[187] "In the Midst of the Pandemic, Violence against Christians Does Not Stop," Agenzia Fides, June 11, 2021, http://www.fides.org/en/news/70301-ASIA_INDIA_In_the_midst_of_the_pandemic_violence_against_Christians_does_not_stop.

everything. As Benito Mussolini famously declared, "Everything within the state, nothing outside the state, nothing against the state."[188] Totalitarian regimes control — or attempt to control — everything, from education to literature to media to the economy to security forces: all under a single-party state with an overarching, all-encompassing ideology and a police force willing to use terror to enforce the will of the state and its ideological vision. "A totalitarian regime thus has one political party, one educational system, one artistic creed, one centrally planned economy, one unified media, and one moral code."[189]

For the ancient Roman Empire, this identification of the state with divinity was expressed in the straightforward practice of Caesar's deification. While the empire tolerated other divinities, it did so only as long as all religion was ultimately subject to the state.

At no time has the destructive evil of totalitarianism been more in evidence than in the twentieth century, when atheistic Communism in its many forms and permutations wrought untold damage on vast portions of humanity, whether in the USSR, China, North Korea, Albania, Burma, Romania, Cuba, Vietnam, or Cambodia. Meanwhile, various versions of fascism, most notably the one adopted by National Socialist Germany, similarly assumed complete control over private and public life and actively sought to eliminate any perceived threats to its power. As the historian Paul Johnson has admirably demonstrated, what unites these regimes — whether "left" or "right" — infinitely outweighs

---

[188] Ta-Nehisi Coates, "The Meaning of 'Totalitarian,'" *Atlantic*, March 26, 2014, https://www.theatlantic.com/international/archive/2014/03/the-meaning-of-totalitarian/359615/.

[189] Ibid.

what distinguishes them, since all totalitarianisms ultimately look and act alike.[190]

All of these oppressive, atheistic regimes saw religion, and Christianity in particular, as a perilous foe to be vanquished. The greatest enemy to a totalitarian state is a religion that proclaims the infinite worth and dignity of every human being as well as a higher sovereignty that demands accountability from each person, whether acting in a private or public capacity.

"This century now drawing to a close has known very many martyrs, especially because of Nazism, Communism, and racial or tribal conflicts," St. John Paul II noted in 1998. "People from every sector of society have suffered for their faith, paying with their blood for their fidelity to Christ and the Church, or courageously facing interminable years of imprisonment and privations of every kind because they refused to yield to an ideology which had become a pitiless dictatorial regime."[191] Not only was John Paul himself shot in an attempted assassination; he was also witness in his earlier years to the very totalitarianisms he denounced, since his native Poland suffered first Nazi occupation and then oppressive Soviet communist rule.

Perhaps no one has expressed totalitarianism's hatred of God and Christianity better than the Russian Christian dissident Aleksandr Solzhenitsyn. "The centralized atheism before whose armed might the whole world trembles still hates and fears this unarmed faith as much today as it did 60 years ago," Solzhenitsyn declared in 1983. "All the savage persecutions loosed upon our people by

---

[190] See Paul Johnson, *Modern Times: The World from the 1920s to the 1980s* (London: Weidenfeld & Nicolson, 1983).

[191] Pope John Paul II, *Incarnationis Mysterium*, bull of indiction of the Great Jubilee of the Year 2000 (November 29, 1998), no. 13.

a murderous state atheism, coupled with the corroding effect of its lies, and an avalanche of stultifying propaganda—all of these together have proven weaker than the thousand-year-old faith of our nation. This faith has not been destroyed; it remains the most sublime, the most cherished gift to which our lives and consciousness can attain."[192]

Yet communism's failure to destroy the faith was not due to any lack of effort to do so, Solzhenitsyn insisted, since communism saw the worship of the Christian God as its mortal enemy. The world "had never before known a godlessness as organized, militarized, and tenaciously malevolent as that practiced by Marxism," Solzhenitsyn said. "Within the philosophical system of Marx and Lenin, and at the heart of their psychology, hatred of God is the principal driving force, more fundamental than all their political and economic pretensions."

"Militant atheism is not merely incidental or marginal to Communist policy; it is not a side effect, but the central pivot," he insisted. "To achieve its diabolical ends, Communism needs to control a population devoid of religious and national feeling, and this entails the destruction of faith and nationhood. Communists proclaim both of these objectives openly, and just as openly go about carrying them out," since "the atheistic world longs to annihilate religion."

Totalitarianism continues to drive Christian persecution today just as surely as it did in Stalin's USSR or in Hitler's Third Reich. The explicitly atheist communist regimes in North Korea and

---

[192] Aleksandr Solzhenitsyn. "Men Have Forgotten God," 1983 Templeton Address, *National Review*, December 11, 2018, https://www.nationalreview.com/2018/12/aleksandr-solzhenitsyn-men-have-forgotten-god-speech/.

China, for example, continue to assert their absolute control over every aspect of the lives of citizens, and with expanding powers of surveillance, this draconian control is destined to continue to grow.

The Academy and Disdain for Christian Belief

For many in our modern society, higher education has become an idol. Not only secularists who disdain religious faith but people of faith themselves often look to learning as a source of liberation, meaning, and even salvation. The supposedly inherent antagonism between faith and science comes not from believers but from self-anointed shamans of science, who can accept no other temple than the classroom and no other prophet than the white-coated priests of the laboratory. Most Christians have no trouble whatsoever accepting the beneficial contributions of science, but they draw a line at *worshipping* science as a deity. Because of this, and because of Christians' insistence on a higher authority not subject to the academy's approval, conflict often ensues.

As I have shown elsewhere, the idea that Christianity and science are inherently hostile to one another is a decidedly modern notion, since the bulk of history's most celebrated scientists have been theists.[193] It is the Christian worldview that provided the ground for the scientific method, which adopts these very premises as axiomatic to its pursuits. As the sociologist Rodney Stark has so persuasively shown, science was "stillborn" in the great civilizations of the ancient world, except in Christian civilization.[194] Why is it, Stark asks, that empirical science and the scientific method did not

[193] See Thomas D. Williams, *Greater Than You Think: A Theologian Answers the Atheists about God* (New York: Hachette, 2008).

[194] See especially Rodney Stark, *For the Glory of God: How Monotheism Led to Reformations, Science, Witch-Hunts, and the End of Slavery* (Princeton, NJ: Princeton University Press, 2003) and *The Victory*

develop in China (with its sophisticated society), in India (with its philosophical schools), in Arabia (with its advanced mathematics), in Japan (with its dedicated craftsmen and technologies), or even in ancient Greece or Rome?

The answer, he asserts, is fairly straightforward. Science flourished in societies where a Christian mindset understood nature to be ordered and intelligible, the work of an intelligent Creator. Far from being an obstacle to science, Christian provided the necessary humus in which science took root.

Despite this fact, or perhaps because of it, the modern atheistic and agnostic academy has sought to exorcise itself of its believing past, relegating Christians to the margins of "meaningful" discourse, which descends progressively into utter banality, having excluded truly meaningful topics as unworthy of debate.

The weapon of choice for petty academic dictators in their war on Christianity is not open hostility but rather ridicule and belittlement of religious belief or sentiment. Christians are treated as simpletons, benighted creatures clinging to an unenlightened creed from an unenlightened age. Belief is equated with superstition, while higher education in particular is presented as liberation from the shackles of an ignorant faith. These descendants of the philosophes of the Age of Enlightenment have their hands on the levers of power in much of Western society, and Christians often survive only by keeping their heads down and revealing as little as possible of what they believe.

Students who attend orthodox Christian colleges often have trouble getting accepted for postgraduate work at established secular universities, not because of a lack of talent or academic

---

of Reason: How Christianity Led to Freedom, Capitalism, and Western Success (New York: Random House, 2005).

qualifications but simply because of an intense anti-Christian prejudice permeating the liberal academy. Writing for Bloomberg in 2016, Megan McArdle commented on one egregious example of such bias at work, noting that it was, unfortunately, typical. "What happened on that committee is bigotry, plain and simple," McArdle wrote. "And it's not just a problem for conservative Christians, and people seen as conservative Christians. It's a problem for academia."[195]

While much of the academy's hatred of Christianity is directed toward students who dare to make their faith known, it also finds a pernicious outlet in excluding believers from teaching posts in higher education. Stories abound of search committees at major universities disqualifying candidates for teaching posts a priori because of their Christian background or beliefs.

The Rise of Satanism

Satan, the father of lies and the declared enemy of God and humanity, is active in all forms of Christian persecution. He is the tempter, always looking to stir up hatred and violence against the followers of Jesus. He is the sworn enemy of Christ, looking, above all, to separate humanity from God through sin but also willing to play his part in putting men and women to the test, trying their patience and subjecting them to affliction with the hope that their resolve will fail. He is therefore active in anti-Christian religious extremism, in totalitarianism and atheistic political regimes, in the academy with its hubris and anti-Christian prejudices, and

---

[195] Megan McArdle, "Academics Are So Lefty They Don't Even See It," *Bloomberg*, January 7, 2016, https://www.bloomberg.com/opinion/articles/2016-01-07/academics-are-so-lefty-they-don-t-even-see-it.

in aggressive secularism and worldly vice that sees Christianity as the enemy of its license and perversions.

"The devil has two strategies: the seduction of worldly promises, and when this fails, that of rage," Pope Francis said in March 2020.[196] The first ploy attempted by Satan to separate us from Christ will always be that of a "worldly spirit," Francis said, where he offers "self-realization, careerism, and worldly success, as ways to cover up the cross of Jesus." When this strategy fails, however, the devil often turns to violence and fury. We see this in Christ's Passion, where there is not merely a death sentence, but "there is more, there is humiliation, there is rage. And when there is fury in the persecution of a Christian, the devil is present," the pope said. And so the two thieves crucified with Jesus are "condemned and crucified, but then left to die in peace. Instead, the insults only fall on Jesus."

"The devil knows no middle ground," the pope said. "His pride is so great that he enjoys destroying with rage. Think of the persecution of so many saints, so many Christians, whom he does not kill, but he makes them suffer, and tries by every means to humiliate them to the end." As an example of this rage in the persecution of Christians, Francis offered the example of the Pakistani Christian Asia Bibi, who spent "nine years in prison, suffering the rage of the devil."

Yet while the devil is active everywhere and stokes anti-Christian passions wherever they may be found, he is also sometimes called upon and worshipped, served not in secret or unknowingly but overtly. Satanism has been on the rise in recent years as confused and rudderless people look for meaning in the service of

---

[196] Pope Francis, "Vanity Distances us from Christ's Cross," homily at Mass on March 11, 2020.

evil. Lucifer—the angel of light—is able to present himself both as fearsome and attractive, seducing those who abandon truth as a venomous snake entices its prey into striking distance before attacking.

In late 2019, Dominican Fr. Francois Dermine, an Italian exorcist, denounced what he saw as a steady rise in demonic activity as more and more young people abandon traditional spirituality and turn to the occult. "Satanism is getting much more aggressive and also diffused," the priest said. "Secularization leaves a void. Young people do not have anything to satisfy their spiritual and profound needs. They are thirsting for something, and the Church is not attractive anymore." Since the Church is no longer perceived as a valid option by many young people looking for answers, "they try to find something elsewhere. This something is, many times, the demonic world."[197]

Satanism takes many forms, Fr. Dermine said, and many become exposed to it through occult practices that seem harmless at first. Through these activities, young people risk acquiring "a Satanist mentality," in which familiarity with the demonic world becomes normalized. "There are many groups of Satanism," the priest said, and Satanism often begins with seemingly innocuous games such as the "Charlie Charlie challenge," in which players attempt to summon a malignant Mexican spirit by balancing two pencils in the form of a cross and posing yes-or-no questions to "Charlie." This sort of game introduces children to the

[197] Elise Harris, "Italian Exorcist Says Society Risks Collapse Due to 'Aggressive Satanism,'" *Crux*, December 22, 2019, https://cruxnow.com/church-in-europe/2019/12/italian-exorcist-says-society-risks-collapse-due-to-aggressive-satanism.

occult early, and such practices are becoming more widespread, Dermine said.

As an example, the priest cited the publication of *A Children's Book of Demons*, a manual that gives kids instructions on how to summon up demons. The International Association of Exorcists has issued a statement warning parents of the dangers of the book, which targets children aged five to ten. Written by Aaron Leighton, an illustrator and "fan" of occult practices, the book invites children to call forth demons as a way of dealing with unpleasant issues, such as chores, homework, and getting rid of bullies. "Satanism is not always so explicit, but it is becoming more and more so, and the publication of this book is a sign of this," Fr. Dermine noted, observing that until a few years ago, the publication of such a text would have been inconceivable.

Although many adults try to dismiss occultism as a harmless fad, Fr. Dermine insists it is very real and very dangerous. "It's not only a vague fear, it's a very concrete risk," he said. "We must not underestimate this, because violence among young people is becoming more and more diffused. A violent mentality is very dangerous for our society, very, very dangerous," he said. "Our society risks collapse if it continues like this."

The rise of Satanism has been tied to increased attacks on Christians and church property as well as sacrilegious practices. In May 2020, vandals broke into the Church of Saint-Jean-des-Cordeliers in southwest France and jimmied open the tabernacle to steal the consecrated Hosts. The theft of consecrated Hosts often occurs in conjunction with Satanism, since the satanic rite called a Black Mass uses consecrated Hosts, which Catholics believe to be the Body of Jesus Christ. As Irish priest, Fr. David Jones, noted in late 2018 that the growth of satanic cults has seen a corresponding rise in demand for consecrated Hosts. We know that "consecrated Hosts go missing from churches every month to be sold on the black market and desecrated in satanic rituals," Fr. Jones said.[198]

"It's very easy to get sacred Hosts in Ireland. We know from CCTV that people go to churches when no one is there, and many priests and sacristans are careless about leaving the key to the tabernacle around or in a place that is easily guessed," the priest said. In 2019, Catholics in the United States raised an alarm when the e-commerce company Etsy.com posted an ad for "Real Catholic Hosts, consecrated by a priest." Posted by a business called "Pentagora," the ad said that the purpose of the nine Hosts was "to abuse for classic black fairs or black magic purposes."

Profanations of churches and other Christian sites, which has been steadily rising in Europe, has been tied to multiple causes, one of which is Satanism. In March 2020, vandals broke into the Church of Saint-Pierre-Saint Paul in the town of Trémorel, in northwest France, and desecrated the Hosts. "The tabernacle was forced and the consecrated hosts contained in the ciborium were thrown to the ground and dispersed," said the local bishop of Saint-Brieuc, Denis Moutel. "This act seriously hurts the faithful since it touches the Eucharist, the most sacred reality of our faith."

In July 2020, vandals profaned a Christian church in Goleszów, in southern Poland, painting satanic symbols on the main doors of the building. The perpetrators spray-painted the words "Ora pro nobis, Lucifer"—Latin for "Pray for us, Lucifer"—around an inverted Christian cross along with the Latin words for "the church of the devil." The criminals also painted a pentagram and the number

---

[198] Daniel Hamiche, "Dordogne: profanation et vol dans une église de Bergerac," L'Observatoire de la Christianophobie, May 20, 2020.

666, which refers to the number of the "beast" in the biblical book of Revelation, interpreted by some to be the antichrist.[199]

The following month, presumed Satanists disfigured and toppled a wooden statue of Jesus Christ in Cremona, Italy, leaving a piece of cardboard with the inscription "Satan." The wooden figure, bearing the title "Christ of the River Po" was created by Italian artist Mario Spadari and placed by the river along the Lungo Po road in Cremona on the feast of the Assumption, August 15, but was brought down with rocks and severely disfigured just days later.[200]

Along with overt satanic worship, certain modern institutions and practices are visibly tied to Satan in their abhorrence of innocence, their odium for the family, and their disdain for children. First among these is the international abortion industry, which claims the lives of an estimated 43 million unborn babies each year. Its eerie similarity to the ancient worship of Moloch (Baal), who demanded the sacrifice of infants to appease his bloodlust, manifests the close bond between abortion and Satanism. As San Francisco achbishop Salvatore Cordileone said in January 2022, the "new secular religion of our own time takes on this practice in an almost sacramental way: indeed, abortion has become, for them, their blessed sacrament, what they hold most sacred, the

---

[199] "Profanacja kościoła w Goleszowie! Na drzwiach świątyni namalowano pentagram, 666 i napis 'Módl się za nami, Lucyferze,'" July 7, 2020, wPolityce.pl, https://wpolityce.pl/kryminal/511051-profanacja-kosciola-w-goleszowie

[200] Lucia Landoni, "Cremona, vandalizzata e abbattuta la statua del Cristo del Po," La Repubblica, August 20, 2020, https://milano.repubblica.it/cronaca/2020/08/29/news/cristo_vandalizzato_statua_cremona-265779318/?ref=RHPPLF-BH-I257369211-C8-P5-S2.4-T1.

doctrine and practice upon which their whole belief system is built."[201]

It is unsurprising, therefore, that groups such as the Satanic Temple advertise a "religious abortion ritual," insisting that Satanist women seeking abortions can avoid being subjected to waiting periods and other restrictions on abortion in the name of religious liberty.[202] One of the Satanic Temple's ongoing campaigns bears the name "Religious Reproductive Rights," and the group asserts that "its Satanic abortion ritual exempts TST members from enduring medically unnecessary and unscientific regulations when seeking to terminate their pregnancy. The ritual involves the recitation of two of our tenets and a personal affirmation that is ceremoniously intertwined with the abortion."

"Because prerequisite procedures such as waiting periods, mandatory viewing of sonograms, and compulsory counseling contravene Satanists' religious convictions, those who take part in the religious abortion ritual are exempt from these requirements and can receive first-trimester abortions on demand in states that have enacted the Religious Freedom Restoration Act," they declare on their website.[203]

It is also unsurprising that the abortion industry views Christianity as its greatest enemy and aggressively works to discredit and

---

[201] Thomas D. Williams, "SF Archbishop Decries New Paganism Whose 'Sacrament' Is Abortion," Breitbart, January 25, 2022, https://www.breitbart.com/faith/2022/01/25/sf-archbishop -decries-new-paganism-whose-sacrament-is-abortion/.

[202] Joshua Ceballos, "Satanists Put Up I-95 Billboard Advertising Abortion Law Loophole," *Miami New Times*, December 28, 2020, https://www.miaminewtimes.com/news/satanic-temple-abortion- ritual-advertised-on-miami-billboard-11779916.

[203] The Satanic Temple, https://thesatanictemple.com/pages/ rrr-campaigns.

demonize Christians. Unwilling merely to kill babies, the abortion industry wants to force taxpayers to pay for abortions and to crush opposition to its abhorrent practices.

Pope Francis has also tied the devil directly into contemporary gender ideology, which would blur distinctions between male and female and pervert the order of creation. Francis has used the strongest language imaginable to criticize modern gender ideology, calling it "demonic" in 2014 and comparing it to the educational policies of Hitler. "I ask myself," said Pope Francis in 2015, "if the so-called gender theory is not, at the same time, an expression of frustration and resignation, which seeks to cancel out sexual difference because it no longer knows how to confront it."[204]

The pope's words were echoed by Guinean Cardinal Robert Sarah, who, in a speech for the 2016 National Catholic Prayer Breakfast in Washington, DC, similarly denounced same-sex marriage, transgender bathroom laws, and attacks on the family as the work of the devil. "All manner of immorality is not only accepted and tolerated today in advanced societies, but even promoted as a social good. The result is hostility to Christians, and, increasingly, religious persecution," Cardinal Sarah said. "Nowhere is this clearer than in the threat that societies are visiting on the family through a demonic 'gender ideology,' a deadly impulse that is being experienced in a world increasingly cut off from God through ideological colonialism."[205]

"This is why the devil is so intent on destroying the family," the cardinal said. "If the family is destroyed, we lose our God-given,

[204] Pope Francis, General Audience, April 15, 2015.
[205] Cardinal Robert Sarah, keynote address, National Catholic Prayer Breakfast, May 17, 2016, https://catholicprayerbreakfast.com/wp-content/uploads/Cardinal-Sarah-Keynote_2016-NCPB.pdf.

anthropological foundations and so find it more difficult to welcome the saving Good News of Jesus Christ: self-giving, fruitful love."

"This is why it is so important to fight to protect the family, the first cell of the life of the Church and every society," the cardinal said. "This is not about abstract ideas. It is not an ideological war between competing ideas. This is about defending ourselves, children and future generations from a demonic ideology that says children do not need mothers and fathers. It denies human nature and wants to cut off entire generations from God."

6

White and Red Martyrdom
Is the Post-Christian West Exempt?

There is no doubt that anti-Christian persecution in its more violent forms occurs predominantly in countries where Christians are a *minority*. According to the 2021 World Watch List, the twelve countries where anti-Christian persecution is "extreme" are in Africa, Asia, and the Middle East. Not a single European country found its way onto the list of the fifty countries where it is most dangerous to be a Christian, and the only countries on the list from the Americas are Mexico and Colombia, where Christians face persecution because of drug cartels, guerillas, organized crime, and corruption.

It is understandable that watchdog groups such as Open Doors focus on violence and deaths in ranking countries where it is most dangerous to be a Christian. Religiously motivated killings in the West are not unheard of, but they are relatively rare compared with those in countries under authoritarian regimes or unstable governments or in non-Christian confessional states, such as certain Islamic republics, or those under Hindu nationalism.

Other forms of persecution, however, are on the rise in the post-Christian West. Discriminatory hiring practices, exclusion or near exclusion of believers from certain fields, pressure to "assimilate" in a hypersecular environment or to check one's faith at the door, and other similar phenomena are increasingly evident in countries that pride themselves on being liberal democracies. Even the violent and aggressive forms of persecution are increasing as the West abandons and even repudiates its own heritage.

Growing Anti-Christian Persecution in the West

One might think that the safest place to be a Christian today would be in former Christendom, the "West," where Christianity was embraced, institutionalized, and grew to maturity. One might well expect Christians to suffer incomprehension and hostility in lands where Christianity is unknown or where Christians are a distinct minority, but surely Christians must be secure in places where Christianity made its home and left an indelible mark on the culture. If this ever was the case, it is unfortunately not so today. In modern Europe, cases of violence and harassment against Christians as well as vandalism of Christian sites—such as churches, monuments, and cemeteries—have been increasing year by year.

In its 2019 report, the Vienna-based Observatory on Intolerance and Discrimination Against Christians in Europe (OIDACE) chronicled the increase in Christian persecution throughout Europe, pointing to "a rise in the number of churches, Christian symbols, and cemeteries across Europe being vandalized, desecrated, and burned, compared to previous years."[206] Moreover, the report stated, across Europe, "Christians have been fired, sued,

---

[206] Observatory on Intolerance and Discrimination against Christians in Europe (OIDACE), *Report 2019*, https://www.intolerance-againstchristians.eu/fileadmin/user_upload/publications/files/Report2019_final.pdf.

and even arrested for exercising their freedom of expression or conscience."[207]

"As we have noted in the past, Christians in Europe are not simply experiencing social discrimination, prejudice, or restrictions on freedom. Christians, including clergy, have been attacked or killed for their faith. As in previous years we have continued to see threats and attacks against Christian converts from Islam," the sixty-four-page report declared,[208] offering summary sketches of more than 325 cases of intolerance and discrimination against Christians in Europe in 2018. Germany suffered attacks against Christian churches at an average rate of two per day. Attacks on Christian churches and symbols regularly occurred in 2019 in Belgium, the UK, Denmark, Ireland, Italy, and Spain as well.

At a May 2020 Organization for Security and Co-operation in Europe (OSCE) conference on intolerance and discrimination, a Vatican representative took the occasion to denounce the rise in anti-Christian crimes throughout Europe. Speaking on behalf of the Holy See, Msgr. Janusz Urbańczyk stressed the gravity of anti-Christian violence and noted that the increasing anti-Christian acts across Europe include "threats, violent attacks, murders and profanation of churches and places of worship, cemeteries and other religious properties." In his address, Msgr. Urbańczyk also expressed concern over the spread of the false idea "that religions could have a negative impact or represent a threat to the well-being of our societies."[209]

---

[207] Ibid., 6.

[208] Ibid.

[209] Devin Watkins, "Covid-19: Vatican Urges OSCE to Promote Religious Freedom amid Rising Intolerance," Vatican News, May 28, 2020, https://www.vaticannews.va/en/vatican-city/news/2020-05/holy-see-osce-discrimination-religious-liberty-coronavirus.html.

The Coming Christian Persecution

Though not unique, a particular case in point is France, where anti-Christian incidents rose by a striking 285 percent between 2008 and 2019, according to Ellen Fantini, the former director of OIDACE.[210] Official annual crime statistics for 2018 provided by the French Interior Ministry included 1,063 "anti-Christian acts" and showed that in the ten-year period from 2008 to 2018, there was an increase of some 250 percent in attacks on Christian sites. The Ministry registered 996 anti-Christian acts in 2019 — an average of nearly 3 per day — while noting that the true figure may be higher, since officials do not count fires of undetermined cause at churches across the country.[211] The attacks finally attracted public interest when, in March 2019, a dozen Catholic churches were desecrated across France over the period of *just one week*, including an arson attack on the historic Church of Saint-Sulpice — one of Paris's largest and most important churches.[212] The string of church profanations puzzled both police and ecclesiastical leaders, who mostly refrained from commenting as the violations spread up and down France.

---

210 "'Will They Stop at Burning an Empty Church?': Anti-Christian Attacks Rise in Europe," Catholic News Agency, July 22, 2020, https://www.catholicnewsagency.com/news/45254/will-they-stop-at-burning-an-empty-church-anti-christian-attacks-rise-in-europe.

211 "Statistiques 2019 des actes antireligieux, antisémites, racistes et xénophobes," Ministère de l'Interieur et des Outre-mer, January 26, 2020, https://www.interieur.gouv.fr/Actualites/Communiques/Statistiques-2019-des-actes-antireligieux-antisemites-racistes-et-xenophobes.

212 "Vu d'Espagne. Une vague de profanations d'églises en France," Courrier International, March 20, 2019, https://www.courrier-international.com/article/vu-despagne-une-vague-de-profanations-deglises-en-france.

Christian sites in Europe suffered a record number of attacks in 2019, with some 3,000 Christian churches, schools, cemeteries, and monuments vandalized, looted, or defaced. Citing data provided to the OSCE, Fantini noted that anti-Christian crimes in the UK doubled in just one year, from 2017 to 2018, and are rising in Spain, Germany, and Sweden as well.

A 2020 report by the Gatestone Institute compiling anti-Christian acts perpetrated during 2019 revealed a range of profanation of Christian sites, including arson, defecation, desecration, looting, mockery, Satanism, theft, urination, and vandalism.[213] The greatest number of acts of violence against Christian sites occurred in France, where churches, schools, cemeteries, and monuments are vandalized, desecrated, and burned.

While some of the attacks are secular in nature, many others "reflect a deep-seated hostility toward Christianity," the Gatestone report stated. "Such attacks include smearing feces on representations of Jesus Christ or statues of Mary, the mother of Jesus. Other attacks involve the defilement or theft of Communion wafers, which Roman Catholics believe are transformed into the real presence of Christ when consecrated. Some of these attacks may be the work of Satanists, who use the consecrated host in a ritual called the Black Mass."

"The desecrations have an evident anti-Christian character," wrote Juan Pedro Quiñonero, Paris correspondent for the Spanish newspaper *ABC*. "Drunk with fierce hatred, the vandals want to give their actions a clear anti-religious dimension." In the case of the desecration of Catholic churches, the vandalism "speaks for

---

[213] Soeren Kern, "Europe: Anti-Christian Attacks Reach All-Time High in 2019," Gatestone Institute, January 1, 2020, https://www.gatestoneinstitute.org/15366/europe-anti-christian-attacks.

itself," Quiñonero wrote, "heinous mockeries of the figure of Christ on the cross and the desecration of high altars."[214]

Observers have noted a dangerous confluence of an ever more aggressive secularism with the rise in radical Islam, which together account for much of the anti-Christian violence in Europe. "There is an evolution of acts of profanation against monuments, but also against the Catholic faith itself," said Dominique Rey, bishop of Fréjus-Toulon.[215] "In the past, even if one was not a Christian, the expression of the sacred was respected. We are facing a serious threat to the expression of religious freedom. Secularism must not be a rejection of the religious, but a principle of neutrality that gives everyone the freedom to express his faith."

"We are witnessing the convergence of laicism—conceived as secularism, which relegates the faithful only to the private sphere and where every religious denomination is banal or stigmatized—with the overwhelming emergence of Islam, which attacks the infidels and those who reject the Koran," Bishop Rey continued. "On one hand, we are mocked by the media . . . and on the other, there is the strengthening of Islamic fundamentalism. These are two joint realities."

On the morning of July 26, 2016, two nineteen-year-old Islamic State radicals, Adel Kermiche and Abdel Malik Petitjean, burst into a parish church in Saint-Étienne-du-Rouvray in Normandy,

---

[214] Juan Pedro Quiñonero, "Profanan una docena de iglesias en Francia en la última semana," *ABC*, April 15, 2019, https://www.abc.es/internacional/abci-profanan-docena-iglesias-francia-ultimos-siete-dias-201903191943_noticia.html?ref=https:%2F%2Fwww.gatestoneinstitute.org%2F.

[215] Dominique Rey, "Under Secularism's Shots," interview with the Italian magazine *Il Timone*, August 5, 2019, https://www.iltimone.org/news-timone/under-secolarisms-shots/.

France, while Mass was in progress, shouting, "Allahu Akbar!" They seized the presiding priest, Fr. Jacques Hamel, along with five other members of the congregation and proceeded to slit the priest's throat. Just before his death, Fr. Hamel told one of his assailants, "Be gone, Satan!"[216]

Pope Francis declared the slain French priest to be a Christian martyr, a qualification that would makes the person a saint in the Church's eyes, while also condemning murder committed "in God's name" to be the work of Satan.[217] Without yet formally canonizing Hamel, Francis said that the French priest is in Heaven, noting that "martyrs are blessed (*beati*)," a term the Catholic Church uses for those who have been beatified, or declared to be in Heaven. "You can put this photo in the church, because he is blessed now, and if someone tells you that you do not have the right, tell them that the Pope gave you permission," Francis told the archbishop of Rouen, Dominique Lebrun, after the morning Mass celebrated in the Vatican in honor of the martyred priest. He was referring to a photo of the deceased priest, which the pope had signed.[218]

In an extended reflection on Christian martyrdom, the pope said in his homily that there are "more Christian martyrs" today than in the early days of Christianity. "Today Christians are

---

[216] " 'Va-t'en, Satan': les derniers mots du père Hamel, cités aux obsèques," *L'Express*, August 2, 2016, https://www.lexpress.fr/actualite/societe/religion/la-foule-se-presse-en-la-cathedrale-de-rouen-pour-les-obseques-du-pere-hamel_1817972.html.

[217] Pope Francis, Holy Mass in suffrage of Father Jacques Hamel, September 14, 2016, https://www.vatican.va/content/francesco/en/cotidie/2016/documents/papa-francesco-cotidie_20160914_p-jacques-hamel.html.

[218] "La Messa del Papa in suffragio. 'Padre Hamel è martire e beato,' " *Avvenire*, September 14, 2016, https://www.avvenire.it/chiesa/pagine/rouen-vescovo-padre-hamel-beato-martire-papa.

murdered, tortured, imprisoned, and slaughtered, because they refuse to deny Jesus Christ," he said, and Father Hamel "is part of this chain of martyrs."

"Christians who suffer today—whether it be in prison or by death or torture—in refusing to deny Jesus Christ, they indeed show the cruelty of this persecution. This cruelty that demands apostasy is—let us say the word—satanic." The pope went on to propose what a marvelous thing it would be if all religions could together proclaim: "Killing in the name of God is satanic." Francis's words seemed aimed particularly at the Islamic terrorists who kill as an act of jihad and claim to be accomplishing the will of Allah.

Fr. Jacques Hamel "had his throat cut on the Cross," Francis said, "precisely while he was celebrating the sacrifice of the Cross of Christ." This good, humble man, "who was always trying to make peace, was assassinated as if he were a criminal. This is the satanic thread of persecution." Even as he was accepting his martyrdom at the altar, Fr. Jacques "did not lose his clarity of thought and clearly said the name of the murderer, he said it very clearly: 'Be gone, Satan!'"

"He gave his life for us, he gave his life so as not to deny Jesus," the pope said, while simultaneously accusing the author of his persecution: "Be gone, Satan!" The pope also urged his hearers to ask for the saint's intercession, that from Heaven he might pray to God for the Church on earth: Give us "the meekness, brotherhood, peace, and also the courage to speak the truth: killing in the name of God is satanic," he said. Francis was accompanied at Mass by some eighty French pilgrims who came specifically for the celebration, among them the archbishop of Rouen and the slain priest's sister, Rosine Hamel.

Fr. Hamel's cause for beatification was officially opened at the diocesan level in April 2017, after Pope Francis waived the mandatory five-year waiting period, and the prefect of the Vatican's Congregation for the Causes of Saints said in 2019 that Hamel's case is a "priority" for Pope Francis and will get special attention among the fifteen hundred causes currently under review.[219]

Why is Europe experiencing such a trend toward anti-Christian violence and vandalism? One explanation is the influx of radical Islam, but this does not tell the whole story. It would seem, rather, that as Europe distances itself further and further from its foundation in a Christian belief system, its indifference to faith has evolved in many places into aggressive hostility.

Pope Benedict XVI often urged Europe to recall its "Christian roots," warning that through a separation from its historical and ideological ties to Christianity, Europe and the entire West risked forgetting why they believe in modern concepts such as human rights, the dignity of the human person, the common family of humanity, and the equality of all people. The fundamental truths upon which all of Western democracy rests stand precariously in the balance. As Cardinal Ratzinger (later Benedict XVI) sagely observed in 2004, "This slender remnant of rational basic moral certainty is not the product of reason alone but is based on surviving remnants of insights from the Jewish-Christian tradition" and while this remnant has long ceased to be an undisputed certainty, "a minimum of morality is somehow still accessible in the decomposing Christian culture."[220]

"The basic moral insights revealed by Christianity were so obvious to all and so incontrovertible that even in the conflict

---

[219] "Padre Hamel beato, le carte ora a Roma," *Avvenire*, March 9, 2019, https://www.avvenire.it/chiesa/pagine/padre-hamel-chiusa -la-fase-diocesana-del-processo-di-beatificazione.

[220] Joseph Ratzinger, *Values in a Time of Upheaval* (San Francisco: Ignatius Press, 2005), 66–67.

between confessions they could be regarded as insights that every rational man took for granted," Ratzinger wrote. "But what seemed a compelling, God-given insight of reason retained its evidential character only for so long as the entire culture, the entire existential context, bore the imprint of Christian tradition," a reality that fades with each passing year.

Ratzinger's reflections on Christianity's pivotal role in forming Western culture were not confessional pieties but were shared by well-known atheists as well. The German philosopher Jürgen Habermas, for example, was insistent that many of the benefits we enjoy in free societies have their source in our Judeo-Christian heritage. "Christianity has functioned for the normative self-understanding of modernity as more than a mere precursor or a catalyst," Habermas wrote. "Egalitarian universalism, from which sprang the ideals of freedom and social solidarity, of an autonomous conduct of life and emancipation, of the individual morality of conscience, human rights and democracy, is the direct legacy of the Judaic ethic of justice and the Christian ethic of love."

"This legacy, substantially unchanged, has been the object of continual critical appropriation and reinterpretation," he continued. "To this day, there is no alternative to it. And in light of the current challenges of a postnational constellation, we continue to draw on the substance of this heritage. Everything else is just idle postmodern talk."[221]

The rise in anti-Christian acts in Europe has been accompanied by a similar phenomenon in the United States. The summer of 2020 witnessed a worrisome spate of attacks on U.S. churches without precedent in recent history. In particular, from July 10 to 16,

---

[221] Jürgen Habermas, *Time of Transitions* (Malden, MA: Polity, 2006), 150–151.

Catholic churches across North America suffered a devastating week of vandalism and arson. The week-long spree included the desecration of statues of Jesus and Mary—some of which were beheaded or spray-painted—along with fire and graffiti on church structures.[222]

On July 10, a vandal spray-painted the word *IDOL* on a statue of the Virgin Mary that stands in front of Cathedral Preparatory School in Queens, New York. The rector of Cathedral Prep, Fr. James Kuroly, called the incident an act of hatred. "Obviously, this tragedy saddens us deeply but it also renews our hope and faith in the Lord as he has shown his goodness in the many people who have already reached out to us," said Fr. Kuroly. "We are sincerely grateful for the help we have received as well as the prayers. Please continue praying for those who committed this act of vandalism and hatred toward Our Lady and the Church."[223]

The following day, twenty-four-year-old Stephen Anthony Shields crashed his minivan into the front of Queen of Peace Church in Ocala, Florida, while services were in progress. Shields got out of the car and poured gasoline around the church lobby and lit it on fire, causing extensive damage. Police eventually arrested Shields and charged him with arson and resisting arrest, as well as attempted second-degree murder, since parishioners were attending Mass at the time of the attack.

That same day, arsonists set fire to Mission San Gabriel Arcángel in Los Angeles—a mission founded by St. Junípero Serra in

---

[222] "Catholic Churches across U.S. Suffer Week of Vandalism and Arson," Aleteia, July 17, 2020, https://aleteia.org/2020/07/17/catholic-churches-across-u-s-suffer-week-of-vandalism-and-arson/.

[223] Catholic News Agency, "Statues of Mary Vandalized in Weekend of Catholic Church Attacks," *National Catholic Register*, July 13, 2020, https://www.ncregister.com/news/statues-of-mary-vandalized-in-weekend-of-catholic-church-attacks.

1771—destroying the building's timber roof and sections of the interior. Los Angeles archbishop José Gomez called the mission the "historic cornerstone and the spiritual heart of Los Angeles and the Catholic community here."[224]

That evening, another arsonist set fire to a statue of the Virgin Mary in the Dorchester neighborhood of Boston, outside St. Peter Church. The perpetrator set fire to plastic flowers in the hands of the statue, causing smoke and flame damage to the statue's face, head, and upper body. The statue had been erected decades ago as a memorial to servicemen killed during World War II.

Still that same day, vandals beheaded a statue of the Virgin Mary and knocked the monument off its pedestal at St. Stephen Church in Chattanooga, Tennessee. "What a strange time we live in. Over the weekend, an outdoor statue of the Blessed Mother was beheaded at St. Stephen Parish in Chattanooga," tweeted Bishop Richard Stika of Knoxville. "This is occurring at various spots throughout the United States."

During the night between July 15 and 16, vandals spray-painted the entrance to St. Joseph Church in New Haven, Connecticut, profaning the building with satanic symbols and other graffiti. "At some point between about 9:00 p.m. last night and 6:00 a.m. today, there was an act of vandalism at St. Joseph church, where words and various symbols including a satanic one—an upside-down pentagram within a circle—were painted on the outside doors of the church," said Dominican Fr. John Paul Walker, the church's pastor. The priest asked parishioners to "pray to Our Lord in reparation for this sacrilege, and to St. Michael for protection against all the powers of hell. Please pray, too, for the perpetrator of this action, who is clearly a very disturbed individual in need of serious help."[225] The Archdiocese of Hartford, Connecticut, said on Facebook that the incident followed "an apparent trend of desecrating Catholic spaces throughout the nation, as evidenced by incidents in Chattanooga, Queens, Boston, Sacramento, and Ocala."

"The underlying motive of these sacrilegious attacks is clear: to intimidate and instill fear in the hearts of those who worship Christ," the archdiocese said. "However, our cherished Catholic faith has survived for 2,000 years in the faces of many different oppressors, and it is not about to yield now."

"Therefore, we remain unafraid and resolute in our faith, and we will pray for a conversion of the hearts of those who wish to terrorize us," it said. "Today, even in the midst of anti-Christian sentiment and actions, however, we do not answer hate with hate," it said. "To the contrary, these attacks make our love and unity stronger, and our prayers ever more steadfast."

The troubling rise of anti-Christian attacks in the United States has been accompanied by a similar spike in vandalism, arson, and profanation in Canada. On July 14, two marauders desecrated a statue of Jesus at Sacred Heart Church in Calgary, using spray paint and a marker or chalk. Police were still investigating a similar case at the Grotto of Our Lady of Lourdes in Ontario, where intruders had cut the heads off several statues with a power saw or grinder. These incidents could be dismissed simply as unfortunate actions of

---

[225] Christine Rousselle, "Parishioners 'in Deep Grief' over Removal of Dominicans from Historic New Haven Church," *National Catholic Register*, October 9, 2021, https://www.ncregister.com/cna/parishioners-in-deep-grief-over-removal-of-dominicans-from-historic-new-haven-church.

a few disturbed individuals if they were not increasingly common, a trend that shows no sign of abating. Between 2020 and 2022, Canada saw thirty-eight such hateful attacks on Christian churches.

Persecution with "White Gloves"

St. Jerome coined the expression *white martyrdom*—distinguished from the "red" martyrdom of those who shed their blood for the Faith—to describe monks' and ascetics' practice of daily living for Christ; the term was later used to denote those who suffer persecution because of their faithfulness to Christ, but not up to the point of bloodshed. Similarly, the term *wet martyr* has been used to denote a person who has shed blood or been executed for the faith, whereas *dry martyr* describes a person who has suffered every indignity and cruelty but not shed blood or suffered execution.

Pope Francis has made the distinction between those who undergo violent persecution and those who suffer a more subtle form of oppression. "Around the world today, in Europe, so many Christians are persecuted and give their lives for their faith," the pope said during a General Audience in 2019, "or they are persecuted with white gloves, that is, ostracized and marginalized."[226]

The pope has stated that a healthy pluralism, one that genuinely respects and values differences, "does not entail privatizing religions in an attempt to reduce them to the quiet obscurity of the individual's conscience or to relegate them to the enclosed precincts of churches, synagogues or mosques."[227] To do so would

---

[226] Pope Francis, General Audience in the Vatican's Paul VI Hall, December 11, 2019.

[227] Pope Francis, Apostolic Exhortation *Evangelii Gaudium* (*The Joy of the Gospel*) (January 1, 2013), no. 255.

represent "a new form of discrimination and authoritarianism," he wrote, by arbitrarily imposing the views of an agnostic or non-believing minority and silencing the convictions of the believing majority. "In the long run, this would feed resentment rather than tolerance and peace," he said.

No one can demand that "religion should be relegated to the inner sanctum of personal life, without influence on societal and national life, without concern for the soundness of civil institutions, without a right to offer an opinion on events affecting society," Francis wrote. "Who would claim to lock up in a church and silence the message of Saint Francis of Assisi or Blessed Teresa of Calcutta? They themselves would have found this unacceptable. An authentic faith—which is never comfortable or completely personal—always involves a deep desire to change the world, to transmit values, to leave this earth somehow better that we found it."

What Francis describes is a growing reality in the post-Christian West, where those who allow their Christian faith to inform their choices are often looked upon with scorn and marginalized. "If Christians in the Middle East need to fear the machete," Catholic League president Bill Donohue wrote, "Christians in the Western world need to fear the media, higher education, activist organizations and government. They are the ones advocating, or imposing, a secular agenda on religious institutions."[228]

As Archbishop Cordileone has observed, there has arisen in our day a radical secularism that goes beyond a healthy separation of church and state or respect for the legitimate autonomy of

---

[228] Bill Donohue, "Changing Face of Religious Persecution," Catholic League for Religious and Civil Rights, April 21, 2021, https://www.catholicleague.org/changing-face-of-religious-persecution/.

distinct spheres of knowledge and action. This has become "a sort of religion of its own, one that takes the form of a hyper-aggressive, anti-Christian kind of a secularism," he said. "This is all around us nowadays, and this kind of secularism has all the marks of a religion: infallible dogmas, rituals, saints, creedal statements and condemnation of heretical teachings along with punishment of the heretics who hold them and dare to speak them in public, index of forbidden books, even sacraments."[229]

Similarly, Los Angeles archbishop José Gomez has denounced a deliberate effort "to erase the Christian roots of society and to suppress any remaining Christian influences." In a forceful video address to the Congress on Catholics and Public Life in Madrid, Archbishop Gomez said in 2021 that an "elite leadership class has risen in our countries that has little interest in religion and no real attachments to the nations they live in or to local traditions or cultures."[230]

"This group, which is in charge in corporations, governments, universities, the media, and in the cultural and professional establishments, wants to establish what we might call a global civilization," the archbishop warned. "In this elite worldview, there is no need for old-fashioned belief systems and religions. In fact, as they see it, religion, especially Christianity, only gets in the way of the society they hope to build."

---

[229] "Archbishop Cordileone: 'The Solution to Building a Culture of Life Is Being True Christians,'" *National Catholic Register*, January 24, 2022.

[230] Archbishop José Gomez. "Reflections on the Church and America's New Religions," *LA Catholics*, November 4, 2021, https://archbishopgomez.org/blog/reflections-on-the-church-and-americas-new-religions.

In his critique of "cancel culture" and "political correctness," Gomez said that "often what is being canceled and corrected are perspectives rooted in Christian beliefs—about human life and the human person, about marriage, the family, and more." In modern society, "the 'space' that the Church and believing Christians are permitted to occupy is shrinking," he said. "Church institutions and Christian-owned businesses are increasingly challenged and harassed."

"The same is true for Christians working in education, health care, government, and other sectors," he added. "Holding certain Christian beliefs is said to be a threat to the freedoms, and even to the safety, of other groups in our societies." Gomez went on to suggest that political belief systems based on social justice or personal identity have come to fill the space that Christian belief and practice once occupied. "Whatever we call these movements—'social justice,' 'wokeness,' 'identity politics,' 'intersectionality,' 'successor ideology'—they claim to offer what religion provides." The architects of this movement seek to replace the Christian story with "what we might call the 'woke' story or the 'social justice' story," he said.

This "soft" yet ever more aggressive persecution takes advantage of a redefinition of religious freedom, which in many quarters has been demoted from freedom of belief and practice to mere "freedom of worship," an effort to silence the voice of believers in the public square. In 2018, Archbishop Paul Gallagher, the Vatican's foreign minister, denounced

> a reductionist approach to—or understanding of—freedom of religion or belief. Such an approach ... seeks to reduce religions to the quiet obscurity of the individual's conscience or to relegate them to the enclosed precincts of churches, synagogues or mosques, revealing not only a failure to

appreciate the true sense of freedom of religion or belief, but also the legitimate role of religion in the public square.[231]

Failing to understand this "feeds into sentiments of intolerance and discrimination against Christians, what might well be termed 'the last acceptable prejudice' in many societies," Gallagher said. "If we truly seek a broad approach to prevent and combat intolerance and discrimination, we need to avoid a selective approach and give attention also to such manifestations of intolerance and discrimination."

Princeton Professor Robert George summed up the situation succinctly in a 2019 Facebook post, in which he enumerated the sort of abuse to which Christians are increasingly subjected:

> Evangelicals and Catholics have watched as Democrats and progressives across the country have worked to shut down Catholic and other religious foster care and adoption agencies because, as a matter of conscience, these agencies place children in homes with a mom and a dad. They have watched as cake bakers, florists, caterers, wedding planners, and others (even the pizza shop–owning O'Connor family and the software designer Brendan Eich) have been harassed in efforts to drive them out of business and deprive them of their livelihoods because of their beliefs about marriage and sexual morality. They have watched as the Democratic and progressive mayor of Atlanta terminated the employment of Kelvin Cochran, the city's Fire Chief,

---

[231] Archbishop Paul Richard Gallagher, Address to the 25th Ministerial Council of OSCE, Milan, December 7, 2018, https://press.vatican.va/content/salastampa/it/bollettino/pubblico/2018/12/07/0911/01985.html.

for the same reason—he had published a book upholding Biblical teaching on marriage and sexual morality. They have watched as Democrats and progressives have tried to "cleanse" entire fields of medicine and healthcare of Evangelicals, Catholics, and other pro-life people by imposing on them requirements to implicate themselves in the taking of innocent life by abortion. They watched as Beto O'Rourke proposed—over no truly meaningful opposition from his fellow Democratic presidential aspirants—to selectively yank the tax exempt status from churches and other religious organizations that refused to fall in line with progressive ideological orthodoxy on sex and marriage.[232]

While much damage is done by those who wish to redefine religious freedom as freedom of worship, a more head-on assault on the status of religious liberty itself is being carried out in parallel. At the March 30, 2021, release of the State Department's annual human-rights reports, U.S. Secretary of State Antony Blinken made a special point of "repudiating" the prior administration's emphasis on religious freedom.[233] His predecessor Mike Pompeo had expanded the State Department's efforts to address religious liberty around the globe and had elevated the Office of International Religious Freedom. "Given our own great freedoms, it's a distinctly American responsibility to stand up for faith in every nation's public square,"

---

[232] Robert P. George, Facebook, December 27, 2019, https://www.facebook.com/robert.p.george.39/posts/10219398644569471. Two typographical errors were corrected in this reproduction of the post.

[233] Associated Press, "Blinken Ends Trump Rights Plan Promoting Conservative Agenda," Breitbart, March 30, 2021, https://www.breitbart.com/news/blinken-ends-trump-rights-plan-promoting-conservative-agenda/.

Pompeo said at the roll-out of the International Religious Freedom Report for 2018.[234] Pompeo also convened the independent, nonpartisan Commission on Unalienable Rights, chaired by Harvard law professor Mary Ann Glendon (my mother-in-law), which in 2020 released a report on America's distinctive human-rights tradition, at the core of which stands religious freedom. "Prominent among the unalienable rights that government is established to secure, from the founders' point of view, are property rights and religious liberty," the commission found.

Blinken reversed the prior administration's emphasis on religious freedom, insisting that there is no hierarchy to human rights and that religious liberty is no more basic or fundamental than reproductive and LGBTQ rights. He also scrapped the highly praised report from the Commission on Unalienable Rights, insisting that it was "unbalanced" and did not reflect the views of the Biden administration. "Human rights are also co-equal; there is no hierarchy that makes some rights more important than others," Blinken said. Since international law makes important distinctions among rights, designating some as "non-derogable" (which means that they cannot be suspended even in times of national emergency), Secretary Blinken's problem seems to be with international law itself. Among the rights declared non-derogable in the International Covenant on Civil and Political Rights is the right to enjoy freedom of thought, conscience, and religion.

Religious-freedom champion Nina Shea was quick to call out Blinken, arguing that his alteration of America's human-rights policy

---

[234] Penny Starr. "Pompeo: 2018 Religious Freedom Report Finds 'Extreme Hostility' to All Faiths in China," Breitbart, June 21, 2019, https://www.breitbart.com/national-security/2019/06/21/pompeo-2018-religious-freedom-report-finds-extreme-hostility-to-all-faiths-in-china/.

"does a grave disservice to millions who are persecuted for their faith." Shea, the director of the Hudson Institute's Center for Religious Freedom, said that by downplaying the importance of religious freedom, Blinken "is bowing to trends in domestic partisan political fashions, not responding to realities in a world where the need to oppose religious persecution has become ever more urgent."[235]

Religious freedom "has a place of primacy in American history, law, political tradition, and culture," Shea stated, and the First Amendment's recognition of the right to religious practice in a pluralistic society "has become one of America's signature contributions to international human-rights law." Unfortunately, Blinken's "demotion of religious freedom will be inevitably interpreted by his department to mean that religious freedom is to receive little attention in its agenda," Shea declared.

The Buttiglione Case

Those who dare to profess their Christian faith in public are often deemed unsuitable for public posts in the post-Christian West, even when they make no effort to impose their beliefs on others. In October 2004, a European Parliament committee made history by rejecting a nominee for a Commission post for the first time ever. The candidate was Rocco Buttiglione, a Catholic intellectual and close friend of Pope John Paul II who made the "mistake" of refusing to disassociate himself from Catholic teaching on marriage and sexuality. Buttiglione, who served in Silvio Berlusconi's government as European affairs minister, angered

---

[235] Nina Shea, "Secretary Blinken, Don't Downplay the Importance of Religious Freedom," *National Review*, April 12, 2021, https://www.nationalreview.com/2021/04/secretary-blinken-dont-downplay-the-importance-of-religious-freedom/.

deputies during his hearing by saying he believed homosexual practice to be a sin.

An op-ed at the time from the editors of the *Wall Street Journal Europe* noted that Buttiglione had run afoul of the European Union's "Secular Inquisition."[236] "Judging from the hysterical reaction of the Socialist members of the European Parliament, you'd be forgiven for thinking that Torquemada himself has arisen from his grave to usurp the European Commission's justice and home affairs portfolio and reinstitute the inquisition," declared the paper's editors. While Buttiglione took pains to distinguish between morality and law, it was "a distinction apparently too subtle for most of his audience," the editors added. "Mr. Buttiglione, an Italian philosophy professor, devout Catholic and friend of the Pope, became the first commission appointee ever to be singled out and called unacceptable by a parliamentary committee," the editorial observed.

Seeing that the nomination could not be approved, Italy eventually withdrew its appointment. As the OIDACE bluntly summarized the affair, "Rocco Buttiglione was dismissed by the European Institutions as EU Commissioner because of his Catholic convictions."[237]

Commenting on the fiasco, Jewish law professor Joseph Weiler delivered a speech titled "Christophobia and Laicism"[238] in Vienna on April 27, 2006, in which he stated the following:

---

[236] "Europe's Secular Inquisition," editorial, *Wall Street Journal Europe*, October 13, 2004, 6, https://www.wsj.com/articles/SB109761719065343396.

[237] "Practicing Catholic Rejected as a Member of the European Commission," Observatory on Intolerance and Discrimination Against Christians in Europe, https://www.intoleranceagainstchristians.eu/index.php?id=12&case=17.

[238] Joseph Weiler, "Christophobia and Laicism," Europe for Christ, http://www.europe4christ.net/index.php?id=122&L=7.

As he is asked about homosexuality, he answers as follows: "If you ask for my personal belief, I believe those relations are sinful. But if you ask what I will do as Commissioner responsible for Home Affairs and Justice, I will uphold the law and the Constitution of Europe." He did not even say "wrong," but he said "sinful," which is a religious category. If you are not religious, the word "sin" has no meaning. Now imagine, Rocco Buttiglione was a Jew: First, nobody would ask the question. And second, if the question were asked and he gave exactly the same reply, everybody would consider it the "model" answer: He upholds his tradition (which, as multicultural, we accept), and he is faithful to the Constitution. But if you are Christian you can be booted out. It's a telling story.

Italian historian Ernesto Galli della Loggia wrote that no faithful Catholic could have responded differently than Buttiglione did, and this does not bode well for Catholics in public life. The reaction of the European Parliament "means, in practice, that, with a few exceptions, anyone who adheres to Catholicism or shows it without reticence is no longer suitable to hold a position at the top of the EU," Galli della Loggia wrote, "and that Catholic Christianity is substantially incompatible with the principles on which Europe as an institution is based."[239]

Obergefell and Its Obergefallout

Something similar occurs in the United States across a number of issues, notably the question of same-sex "marriage," which

[239] "Buttiglione's Defense of Christian Principles Fuel an EU Debate," Catholic News Agency, October 15, 2004, https://www. catholicnewsagency.com/news/buttigliones_defense_of_christian _principles_fuel_an_eu_debate.

collides with the beliefs of orthodox Christians. The 2015 Supreme Court decision in *Obergefell v. Hodges* outlawed state bans on same-sex "marriage," declaring it the new law of the land. Although Christians have resigned themselves to this reality, most have not changed their views on the morality of homosexual practice or of same-sex "marriage," and this has often earned them the labels of bigots, homophobes, and "haters" for simply believing that marriage is the union of one man and one woman, a position considered uncontroversial in most civilizations for most of human history.

U.S. Supreme Court justice Samuel Alito uttered prophetic words in his 2015 dissent in the *Obergefell v. Hodges* case, warning that the ignominious decision would be used as a stick with which to beat those who uphold traditional marriage. In his dissent, Alito predicted that the ruling would be employed "to vilify Americans who are unwilling to assent to the new orthodoxy." Though the majority decision paid lip service to the rights of conscience of those who disagreed with the ruling, Alito seemed to have little doubt of what the real outcome would be. "Perhaps recognizing how its reasoning may be used, the majority attempts, toward the end of its opinion, to reassure those who oppose same-sex marriage that their rights of conscience will be protected," Alito observed. "We will soon see whether this proves to be true. I assume that those who cling to old beliefs will be able to whisper their thoughts in the recesses of their homes, but if they repeat those views in public, they will risk being labeled as bigots and treated as such by governments, employers, and schools."[240]

---

[240] Obergefell et al. v. Hodges, Director, Ohio Department of Health et al. (2015), 6–7, https://www.supremecourt.gov/opinions/14pdf/14-556_3204.pdf.

Numerous cases have already proven the prescience of Alito's remarks, and the negative fallout for Christians from the *Obergefell* decision shows no signs of abating. On October 10, 2019, during a CNN townhall on LGBTQ issues, the former Democratic presidential candidate Beto O'Rourke proclaimed that churches failing to toe the secular line on gay and transgender rights would lose their tax-exempt status in his administration. In other words, a presidential candidate threatened to use the power of his office to strip churches of their status if they refused to renounce basic Christian beliefs regarding the complementarity of men and women, sexual morality, and the nature of marriage.

Not content with the mere legalization of same-sex "marriage," the homosexual lobby has sought to use its newfound powers to bully Christians into celebrating what they know to be immoral. Several high-profile court cases have revolved around trying to coerce Christian bakers into producing cakes and pastries that honor same-sex "marriage." In each case, the bakers were perfectly willing to serve anyone who came to their establishment and never tried to discriminate against any of their clients. They merely drew the line at using their creativity to promote something they believe to be evil. This commonsense distinction was not enough for the radical LGBT lobby, which has attempted in each case to force Christians to violate their consciences.

In 2016, a bakery owned by a Christian family in Longview, Texas, was inundated with threats and hate mail after the owners declined to bake a wedding cake for a gay marriage. Irate LGBT activists posted vulgar and derogatory reviews on Yelp and other social-networking platforms, targeting Edie and David Delorme, who own the Kern's Bake Shop. Others made threats against the business and their family. "See you in Hell, lady," read one message. "Racist criminals. This business is run by a homophobic piece of s***," another message read.

The popular Christian evangelist Franklin Graham was quick to voice support for the Delormes. "Here we go again—gays attacking Christians for what they believe. They want to force everyone to accept and condone their lifestyle which God's Word defines as sin—but they are blatantly intolerant of others," Graham posted on his Facebook page.

The Delormes are members of a local Baptist church and have always striven to run their bakery according to their Christian beliefs, including a long-standing policy to turn away any business that mighty conflict with their religious beliefs. It is not just a question of sexual morality. The bakery won't make any tobacco- or alcohol-related cakes either, and no "risqué" cakes of any kind.

"We feel like if we are going to be putting our name on something, we want it to encourage Godly values," Edie said. This does not mean that they will not serve homosexual customers but merely that they will not make a cake celebrating a ceremony they believe is sinful.

In a similar case, Aaron and Melissa Klein, Christian bakers in Oregon who owned Sweet Cakes by Melissa, were fined $135,000 by the Oregon government in 2015 because they declined to bake a wedding cake for a lesbian couple.[241] The Kleins are Evangelical Christians who believe that marriage is the union of one man and one woman, and they run their business consistent with their faith as part of their Christian testimony and ministry to the community. In their lawsuit, the two women claimed they felt "mentally raped," as part of a list of eighty-eight symptoms of emotional distress they experienced at being refused a cake. The forum "concludes

[241] "Oregon Christian Bakers Wedding Cake Case Going to Court," February 23, 2016, Breitbart, https://www.breitbart.com/politics/2016/02/23/oregon-christian-bakers-wedding-cake-case/.

that $75,000 and $60,000, are appropriate awards to compensate for the emotional suffering they experienced," wrote Alan Mc-Cullough, administrative law judge for Oregon's Bureau of Labor and Industries, in his order.[242]

Another Christian baker, Jack Phillips, was ordered by a Colorado judge to bake cakes for same-sex "marriages" or face a possible jail sentence. As an Evangelical Christian, Phillips refuses to cooperate with something he understands to be offensive to God—same-sex "marriage"—and therefore he does not make cakes for gay weddings. Phillips' case eventually made it all the way to the Supreme Court, and he ended up winning in 2018 on a technicality—namely, that a Colorado commissioner showed open hostility by saying that Phillips' Christian beliefs on marriage were "despicable."[243] The Court opted not to resolve the broader question of whether Christians can be forced to participate in same-sex weddings against their beliefs.

Hate Crimes

As Western society moves further and further from its Christian roots, biblical teachings that seemed to be unexceptional and self-evident a generation ago begin to look more and more like

---

[242] Jim Hoft, "Lesbians Claim 'Mental Rape' After Christian Family Wouldn't Bake Them Cake," *Gateway Pundit*, April 25, 2015, https://www.thegatewaypundit.com/2015/04/lesbians-claim-mental-rape-after-christian-family-wouldnt-bake-them-cake/.

[243] Ken Klukowski, "Supreme Court Sides with Masterpiece Cakeshop in Same-Sex Wedding Ruling," Breitbart, June 4, 2018, https://www.breitbart.com/politics/2018/06/04/supreme-court-sides-with-masterpiece-cakeshop-in-same-sex-wedding-ruling/.

intolerable bigotry. People are increasingly asked to approve of behavior they know to be wrong or risk being labeled as intransigent extremists. One of the ways that radical secularists have responded has been through hate-crimes legislation.

In 2021, for instance, the Scottish Parliament passed the Hate Crime and Public Order bill, which, while eliminating the offense of blasphemy, created a new crime of "threatening, abusive or insulting material" that is "likely" to stir up hatred against a protected group.[244] It also criminalized "possessing inflammatory material" with a view to communicating the material in circumstances where it is likely that hatred would be stirred up.

Prior to the bill's passage, the director of the Catholic Parliamentary Office, Anthony Horan, warned that the legislation could enshrine "cancel culture" in law. "A new offence of possessing inflammatory material could even render material such as the Bible and the *Catechism of the Catholic Church* inflammatory," Horan said. "The Catholic Church's understanding of the human person, including the belief that sex and gender are not fluid and changeable, could potentially fall foul of the new law."[245]

Unsurprisingly, one of the groups pushing for passage of the bill was Scotland's atheists, who rightly saw in the legislation a chance to silence purveyors of biblical morality. The convener of Atheists Scotland, Ian Stewart, praised the bill, asserting that "it

[244] Hate Crime and Public Order (Scotland) Bill (April 23, 2020), Scottish Parliament, https://www.parliament.scot/-/media/files/legislation/bills/current-bills/hate-crime-and-public-order-scotland-bill/stage-3/bill-as-amended-at-stage-3.pdf.

[245] "Freedom to Disagree Must Be Protected, Say Scotland's Bishops," Scottish Catholic Media Office, July 29, 2020, https://scmo.org/news-releases/perma/1596013200/article/freedom-to-disagree-must-be-protected-say-scotland.html.

will enable the prosecution of all Scotland's religions and their Holy Books for spreading hatred."[246]

"It is utterly unacceptable ... in progressive, social democratic Scotland that squalid, Bronze Age village disputes, as described in the Holy Books, about control of women, goats or water should give Scotland's 'Holy Willies' authority to spout out vitriol against atheists, agnostics, apostates, sceptics, non-believers, women, trans people and homosexuals," Stewart declared in the Dundee newspaper the *Courier*. Stewart said that his group intended to "monitor all Holy Books, sermons in places of worship and the social media accounts of the various religions" in order to report any offenders to police to be criminally prosecuted.

On February 14, 2022, a court in Finland similarly heard arguments against Member of Parliament (MP) and medical doctor Päivi Räsänen and Bishop-Elect and Dean Juhana Pohjola, who were charged by Finland's prosecutor general with "hate crimes" for publicly expressing their Christian beliefs regarding marriage.[247]

The International Lutheran Council noted that the charges stem from a 2004 booklet called *Male and Female He Created Them: Homosexual Relationships Challenge the Christian Concept of Humanity*, published by Luther Foundation Finland. The booklet, authored by Dr. Räsänen, articulates traditional biblical teaching

---

[246] Kurt Zindulka, "Scottish Hate Crime Bill: Atheists Plan to Target Christians for 'Spreading Hate,'" Breitbart, August 30, 2020, https://www.breitbart.com/europe/2020/08/30/scotland-atheists-to-target-christians-for-spreading-hate-under-proposed-hate-crime-bill/.

[247] See Christopher Manion, "Religious Freedom on Trial in Finland," Population Research Institute, February 15, 2022, https://www.pop.org/religious-freedom-on-trial-in-finland/?eType=Emai lBlastContent&eId=63201cc6-1ecf-4f28-81b8-bec8b01d331a.

on human sexuality and recounts the Christian understanding of marriage, the path of Räsänen's conversion, and the history of the Finnish Parliament's legalization of homosexual partnerships, which led to the legalization of same-sex "marriage." Dean Pohjola was also charged in the indictment because he is editor-in-chief of Luther Foundation Finland's publications, including the booklet.

"As a Christian, I do not want to and cannot discriminate against or despise anyone created by God," Pohjola said when he was charged. "Every human being, created by God and redeemed by Christ, is equally precious. At the same time," he continued, "this does not remove the fact that, according to the Bible and the Christian conception of man, homosexual relations are against the will of God, and marriage is intended only between a man and a woman. This is what the Christian church has always taught and will always teach."

Human-rights lawyer Paul Coleman of the Alliance Defending Freedom International, who has assisted in the suit, said a case like this is a "canary in the coalmine" for freedom of speech throughout the Western world. He added that he would characterize the first day of the trial "as a modern-day Inquisition or heresy trial. And the heresy was that Päivi and Bishop Juhana were on trial against the new sexual orthodoxy of the day."

The Bible as Bigotry

Hate-crimes legislation is not the only arrow in the quiver of those wishing to silence Christian belief. Christianity's refusal to get with the times has generated growing animosity and even proposals to coerce Christians into updating their moral teachings to conform to the standards of progressivism. A noteworthy example was a 2015 essay in the *New York Times* suggesting that

Christians must either fully embrace the gay lifestyle or be forced into doing so.[248]

Op-ed writer Frank Bruni, one-time *Times* restaurant critic and a gay activist, wrote that Christians who hold on to "ossified," biblically based beliefs regarding sexual morality have no place at America's table and proposed that Christians take homosexual relations "off the sin list." In one fell swoop, Bruni trashed all believing Christians as "bigots," saying that Christians' negative moral assessment of homosexual relations is "a choice" that "prioritizes scattered passages of ancient texts over all that has been learned since—as if time had stood still, as if the advances of science and knowledge meant nothing."

In other words, if you still cling to your benighted views and your "ancient texts," you are living in the past and your views merit no respect, he suggested. Bruni's solution to the impasse was not some sort of goodwill compromise or a treaty of mutual respect, but a take-no-prisoners ultimatum to Christians to abandon their beliefs or else. When Bruni said that Christians' understanding of sexual morality is "a choice," what he meant was that there is a way out without completely losing face: just embrace the new morality preached by mainstream liberal churches that see nothing wrong with any sexual arrangement one is comfortable with; then we will accept you. Bruni took it upon himself to explain how the Bible can be interpreted to read that God is really fine with sodomy and that all the antiquated prohibitions against adultery, fornication, and "men lying with other men" are a quaint vestige of an archaic worldview that went out definitively with Freud.

---

[248] Frank Bruni, "Bigotry, the Bible and the Lessons of Indiana," *New York Times*, April 3, 2015, https://www.nytimes.com/2015/04/05/opinion/sunday/frank-bruni-same-sex-sinners.html.

The Coming Christian Persecution

The scary part about Bruni's essay was not his awkward attempt at playing the biblical scholar but the undertone of evident disdain for Christians and his proposal that those who resist should be forcibly reeducated. Christians' refusal to bend with the times does not stem from faithfulness to God, Bruni proposed, but from willful obstinacy that must be broken. "So our debate about religious freedom should include a conversation about freeing religions and religious people from prejudices that they needn't cling to and can indeed jettison, much as they've jettisoned other aspects of their faith's history, rightly bowing to the enlightenments of modernity," Bruni wrote.

But what if Christians don't want to change? What if they don't want to "bow to the enlightenments of modernity"? What if they are convinced that the modern worldview is not the most enlightened path when it comes to the ultimate meaning of life and death, time, and eternity? "Religion," writes Bruni, "is going to be the final holdout and most stubborn refuge for homophobia. It will give license to discrimination." And thus it must be stamped out. Bruni cited fellow gay activist Mitchell Gold, founder of the advocacy group Faith in America, as saying that church leaders must be made to take homosexuality off the sin list. "His commandment is worthy—and warranted," Bruni agreed.

As recently as 2016, Harvard law professor Mark Tushnet urged liberals to stamp out aggressively the losers of the culture wars, whom he identified as Christians and conservatives. "The culture wars are over; they lost, we won," Tushnet wrote confidently.

> For liberals, the question now is how to deal with the losers in the culture wars. That's mostly a question of tactics. My own judgment is that taking a hard line ("You lost, live with it") is better than trying to accommodate the losers,

who—remember—defended, and are defending, positions that liberals regard as having no normative pull at all. Trying to be nice to the losers didn't work well after the Civil War, nor after Brown. (And taking a hard line seemed to work reasonably well in Germany and Japan after 1945.) I should note that LGBT activists in particular seem to have settled on the hard-line approach.[249]

The UK-based *Guardian* newspaper picked up a similar line, arguing that the Bible itself is the problem when it comes to acceptance of gay marriage. In an article titled "The Bible Is the True Prejudice in Christian Opposition to Marriage Equality," *Guardian* writer Keith Mascord asserted that "homophobic opposition to same-sex marriage" has its roots in adherence to the Bible and therefore Christians will only learn to support "marriage equality" by leaving aside the biblical text.[250]

Mascord ridiculed believers for clinging to outdated notions, suggesting that acceptance of the moral instruction found in Sacred Scripture is akin to belief that the earth is at the center of the solar system. "We need to acknowledge that the Bible, for all of its beauty, wisdom and on-going relevance, is an ancient text, pregnant with ancient assumptions and beliefs, many of which we no longer reasonably hold," he wrote. These "historic and Bible-based

[249] Mark Tushnet, "Abandoning Defensive Crouch Liberal Constitutionalism," *Balkinization* (blog), May 6, 2016, https://balkin.blogspot.com/2016/05/abandoning-defensive-crouch-liberal.html.

[250] Keith Mascord, "The Bible Is the True Prejudice in Christian Opposition to Marriage Equality," *Guardian*, March 22, 2016, https://www.theguardian.com/commentisfree/2016/mar/22/the-bible-is-the-true-prejudice-in-christian-opposition-to-marriage-equality.

understandings of homosexuality have clearly contributed to homophobia, along with the terrible and inexcusable mistreatment of LGBTI people which continues to this day," and thus "the time has come for this prejudice to be shed," he said.

Christians should "feel free to re-think the assumptions and beliefs which underlie Biblical discomfort with same-sex activity," he asserted. The problem, of course, is that many Christians believe the Bible to be God's Word, with crucial teaching for understanding who the human person is and what sort of behavior is worthy of his unique dignity. Christians, moreover, do not see disapproval of gay sex to be a symptom of an irrational "homophobia" but rather a reasonable and cogent moral evaluation of human behavior shared by the vast majority of humanity throughout history.

Calling Christians bigots or attempting to shame them into abandoning their ethical standards is a vile and unworthy practice, even when carried out under the guise of tolerance and "enlightened" thought. Unfortunately, this practice—as well as the others we have examined—is growing more prevalent, not less.

The "Unsuitability" of Christians for Public Office

Article VI of the U.S. Constitution prohibits the federal government from considering a person's faith when assessing fitness to hold federal office, and this important clause has been a bedrock principle since the founding of the republic. Despite the prohibition on any type of religious "litmus test" for public office, however, members of the U.S. Senate have gotten dangerously close to doing just that.

In 2017, President Donald Trump nominated distinguished Notre Dame law professor Amy Coney Barrett to serve as a circuit judge on the U.S. Court of Appeals for the Seventh Circuit. During her confirmation process, Barrett was subjected to a shameful faith-based hazing by the Senate Judiciary Committee, which probed her religious beliefs and how they would bear on the discharge of her duties as a judge.

Several Democratic senators grilled Barrett on her Catholic faith, suggesting that such closely held religious belief was an obstacle to judicial service. "When you read your speeches, the conclusion one draws is that the dogma lives loudly within you," Sen. Dianne Feinstein said. "And that's of concern when you come to big issues that large numbers of people have fought for for years in this country."

Sen. Dick Durbin, who professes to be a Catholic but rejects many of the Church's moral teachings, criticized Barrett's prior use of the term *orthodox Catholic*, saying it unfairly maligns Catholics who do not hold certain positions about abortion or the death penalty. "Do you consider yourself an orthodox Catholic?" he asked her, before asking her what she thought of Pope Francis.

The attacks on Barrett's faith were so brazen that the United States bishops felt obliged to denounce the faith-based harassment as "anti-Catholic bigotry." "America has a strong and venerable tradition of pluralism that respects all religious views," wrote Baltimore archbishop William E. Lori, chairman of the bishops' Ad Hoc Committee for Religious Liberty. "In this context, this week's hearing before the U.S. Senate Judiciary Committee is deeply disappointing. Rather than simply consider the professional achievements of a nominee for the federal judiciary, multiple senators challenged her fitness to serve due to her Catholic faith."[251] Not only are such questions contrary to the Constitution, which

---

[251] Archbishop William E. Lori, "U.S. Catholic Bishops Chairman Statement in Response to Senate Judiciary Committee Line of Questioning of Nominee," September 8, 2017, United States Council of Catholic Bishops, https://www.usccb.org/news/2017/us-catholic-bishops-chairman-statement-response-senate-judiciary-committee-line.

protects the free exercise of one's faith and rejects religious tests for public office, Lori wrote; they are also offensive to basic human rights and betray a thinly veiled anti-Christian bias. These questions "harken back to a time in our country when anti-Catholic bigotry did distort our laws and civil order," he said, and are "a reminder that we must remain vigilant against latent bigotries that may still infect our national soul."

Archbishop Lori also wondered aloud whether the senators in question—notably Feinstein, Durbin, and Mazie Hirono—intended their hazing of Barrett to intimidate aspiring future justices into keeping their faith to themselves. "Were the comments of the Senators meant as a warning shot to future law students and attorneys, that they should never discuss their faith in a public forum, if they have aspirations to serve in the federal judiciary?" he asked. "In truth, we should be encouraging faithful, ethical attorneys to serve in public office, not discouraging them by subjecting them to inappropriate, unnecessary interrogation based on their religious beliefs."

The redoubtable Archbishop Charles J. Chaput, formerly at the helm of the Archdiocese of Philadelphia, also called out the Left for its rabid attacks on Barrett, whom media were trying to portray as an "extremist."[252]

"Barrett's life story suggests that she actually believes and seeks to live what her Catholic faith teaches," Chaput noted in an essay in *First Things*. "Worse, she has a superb intellect, a deep grasp of the law, and an excellent record as a jurist. In other words, she's a nightmare for a certain kind of political tribe." Some in our political class now view with suspicion "Catholics who are more

[252] Archbishop Charles J. Chaput, "When the Dogma Lives Loudly," *First Things*, September 28, 2020, https://www.firstthings.com/web-exclusives/2020/09/when-the-dogma-lives-loudly.

than merely 'nominal' in their faith," he said. Noting a double standard in media treatment of Barrett and Biden, Chaput wrote that in the eyes of the Democrat Party, it's not being a member of the Catholic Church that's the problem: "If you're photographed piously with your rosary beads at prayer — even better." But if you are a Catholic who believes and tries to practice what the Church teaches, that makes you dangerous.

The archbishop also underscored the hostile, anti-Catholic interrogation that Barrett was subjected to by Sen. Feinstein. While Feinstein's anti-Catholicism is particularly crass, he observed, it is hardly unusual. "Disdain for vigorous religious convictions, especially the Catholic kind, is a virus that's going around," he noted. Painting "dissenting Catholics as 'mainstream Americans' and believing Catholics as 'extremists' — now a common and thoroughly dishonest culture war technique — is a particular affront to the free exercise of religion," Chaput declared.

As egregious as it was, the treatment of Amy Barrett was far from unique. In 2018, President Trump nominated another believing Catholic, Brian C. Buescher, to the U.S. District Court for the District of Nebraska. Democrats from the Senate Judiciary Committee questioned Buescher on his membership in the Knights of Columbus, a Catholic charitable organization, suggesting that this affiliation might disqualify him for judgeship. Notably, Sen. Hirono and Sen. Kamala Harris asked whether belonging to the Knights of Columbus could prevent Mr. Buescher from hearing cases "fairly and impartially."[253]

[253] Ed Condon, "Judicial Nominee Faces Senate Scrutiny over Knights of Columbus Membership," Catholic News Agency, December 21, 2018, https://www.catholicnewsagency.com/news/40188/judicial-nominee-faces-senate-scrutiny-over-knights-of-columbus-membership.

The senators suggested that the Knights' opposition to abortion and same-sex "marriage" could cloud the candidate's vision and impair his judgment. The Knights of Columbus have taken "a number of extreme positions," Sen. Hirono stated in written questions sent to Buescher on December 5, such as contributing "to California's Proposition 8 campaign to ban same-sex marriage." Sen. Harris asked Buescher whether he was aware, when he joined the organization, that the Knights of Columbus "opposed a woman's right to choose" and were against "marriage equality."

"The Knights of Columbus does not have the authority to take personal political positions on behalf of all of its approximately two million members," Buescher said in his response. Observers noted that the questions smelled oddly of a religious litmus test, since the positions under examination are held and taught by the Catholic Church herself and are not unique to the Knights of Columbus.

A spokesperson for the Knights of Columbus, Kathleen Blomquist, decried the anti-Catholic bias implicit in the senators' questions. "Our country's sad history of anti-Catholic bigotry contributed to the founding of the Knights of Columbus, and we are proud of the many Catholics who overcame this hurdle to contribute so greatly to our country," Blomquist told the Catholic News Agency.

"We were extremely disappointed to see that one's commitment to Catholic principles through membership in the Knights of Columbus—a charitable organization that adheres to and promotes Catholic teachings—would be viewed as a disqualifier from public service in this day and age," she said.

In the ongoing examination, Sen. Cory Booker underscored Buescher's vocal opposition to abortion when he was running for Nebraska attorney general in the Republican primary. "Why should a litigant in your courtroom expect to get a fair hearing from an impartial judge in a case involving abortion rights?" Sen. Booker asked. "As a candidate for Nebraska Attorney General in 2014," Buescher responded, "I did what candidates for any major state or federal office do, which is to take political positions on a variety of issues of the day."

In his answer, Buescher noted that there is an important difference between taking political positions as a candidate for office and serving as a federal judge. "I believe a judge's role and obligation is to apply the law without regard to any personal beliefs regarding the law," Buescher wrote. "If confirmed, I will faithfully apply all United States Supreme Court and Eighth Circuit Court of Appeals precedent on all issues, including *Roe v. Wade*."

In his questioning, Booker failed to acknowledge that *every* judge has personal opinions—whether favorable or unfavorable—regarding moral questions such as abortion and homosexuality, and he seemed to imply that being in favor of these issues is not an obstacle to judicial impartiality, whereas opposition to them is.

Not long afterward, the Rev. Eugene Rivers, an African American Pentecostal minister and a leader of the black Christian community, published an op-ed in the *Wall Street Journal* decrying the "anti-Catholic bigotry" shown by the senators in their examination of Buescher.[254] "As a leader of black Christians, I feel particularly strongly about the Knights of Columbus. For more than a century they bravely defended minorities," Rev. Rivers wrote. "If Catholics like the Knights can be targeted, what should members of my Pentecostal church expect?"

---

[254] Eugene F. Rivers III, "Another Religious Test in the Senate," *Wall Street Journal*, January 3, 2019, https://www.wsj.com/articles/another-religious-test-in-the-senate-11546559559.

"We share traditional views on abortion and marriage," Rivers continued. "What about Orthodox Jews, Muslims, Mormons and evangelical Christians? Even the Rev. Martin Luther King's biblical beliefs would be anathema to Sens. Harris, Feinstein and Hirono. JFK, himself a proud Knight of Columbus, would be unacceptable too."

Ken Blackwell, a former U.S. ambassador to the United Nations Human Rights Commission, joined in condemning the attacks on Buescher. "This is the kind of thuggish behavior we expect from third world dictators, not United States Senators," Blackwell said in a statement. "That this attack on Catholics comes from the party of John F. Kennedy, who was proudly a Knight of Columbus, is particularly shocking and egregious."[255]

[255] Matt Richardson, "Dems Accused of 'Religious Bigotry' for Questioning Trump Court Pick's Knights of Columbus Ties," Fox News, December 24, 2018, https://www.foxnews.com/politics/dems-accused-of-religious-bigotry-for-questioning-trump-court-picks-knights-of-columbus-ties.

7

Why Things Will Get Worse
Before They Get Better

Although Christian persecution has existed in the world since the first century, a confluence of circumstances suggests that today's assaults against Christians and the Christian faith will get much worse before they get better. As the number of those who hate Christians or hold them in contempt is growing, Christianity in the West is flagging and the will to speak out against Christian persecution or even acknowledge its existence is waning. And though the enemies of Christ — radical Islam, virulent secularism, atheistic communism — grow stronger every day, the determination to resist them is flagging. Meanwhile, Christian morality, the backbone of Western culture, appears more and more foreign to many. Indeed, what once was held to be time-tested common sense is now rejected as bigotry and ignorance.

At the end of his parable of the importunate widow in St. Luke's Gospel, Jesus asks a challenging question: "When the Son of Man comes, will he find faith on earth?" (Luke 18:8). While Christians are confident in final victory, won by Christ's Passion, death, and Resurrection, the unfolding of human history is marked by many setbacks. Jesus phrases His challenge in the form of a question, not a statement, but the mere prospect of the possible disappearance of all Christian faith from the earth is unsettling to contemplate.

With the grace of God, believers are entrusted with the mission of making sure this never happens.

Widespread Ignorance and Denial of the Problem

Many people, particularly in the West, have no idea of the extent and the vehemence of Christian persecution around the world. Aside from reports by Christian-persecution watchdog groups, the mistreatment of Christians receives almost no coverage from mainstream media, and most people have no access to information regarding how Christians are harassed, imprisoned, attacked, and killed across the globe. The less people know about the magnitude and the intensity of the problem, the less they are moved to do anything about it. A vicious circle ensues in which ignorance begets inaction and indifference.

In chapter 1, we discussed the 2019 report *Persecuted and Forgotten?* by Aid to the Church in Need (ACN) in examining the scope of Christian persecution in the world today. Now we turn to the second part of the report's title—the way the persecution of Christians is being *forgotten* or simply disregarded in the world. As the report states, "the extent of this persecution is largely ignored by our media." By whitewashing the fact that the situation of Christians worldwide is worsening, the mainstream media aggravates the problem.[256] As Pakistani Fr. Emmanuel Yousaf wrote in the foreword to a subsequent ACN report: "The more the world knows about acts of religious hatred and neglect, the more the world will be able to do something about them."[257] Conversely, the less the world knows about violations of religious freedom, the less it will be able to do anything in response.

---

[256] ACN, *Persecuted and Forgotten?*
[257] ACN, *Religious Freedom in the World Report 2021*, 5.

Even in places where Christians have been undergoing a systematic genocide, virtually no help has been forthcoming from Western (predominantly Christian) countries or from the United Nations. "Governments in the West and the UN failed to offer Christians in countries such as Iraq and Syria the emergency help they needed as genocide got underway," ACN's website related. "If Christian organizations and other institutions had not filled the gap, the Christian presence could already have disappeared in Iraq and other parts of the Middle East."

In the foreword to *Persecuted and Forgotten?*, Melkite Greek Catholic archbishop Issam John Darwish of Lebanon noted that up to the present, "the UN and other humanitarian organizations have provided no aid," leaving the oppressed Christians to fend for themselves.[258] John Pontifex, the report's editor, said that the "pc agenda" among Western governments and mainstream media is preventing the attention that the Christian community requires. Direct assistance to persecuted Christians is often deemed inappropriate to a secular mindset, especially one with latent anti-Christian bias.

"The UN and western governments send strong messages of support—but that's not matched by action," Pontifex said. "To date, the response of the UN has been too little too late. For example, Iraqi Christians from Mosul and Nineveh who ended up in Erbil were just given tarpaulins; people need homes, medicines and pastoral support."

Compounding the damage done by widespread *ignorance* of the problem is outright *denial* of global Christian persecution along with attempts either to relativize it or dilute it as just one dimension of the larger problem of religious persecution. Despite

---

[258] Archbishop Issam John Darwish, *Persecuted and Forgotten?*, 7.

the irrefutable evidence of ongoing persecution of Christians on a global scale, some insist that complaints of such persecution are nothing more than whiny Christians looking for attention or, worse, evidence of a "Christian persecution complex."

Wikipedia has an entry on "Christian persecution complex," defining it as "a belief, attitude or world view that Christian values and Christians are being oppressed by social groups and governments." Oddly, the article never bothers to ask whether this oppression is *actually occurring* (it is) but starts from the uncorroborated presupposition that such a belief must represent an irrational "complex."[259] Wikipedia goes on to assert that this belief "is promoted by certain American Protestant churches, and some Christian- or Bible-based cults in Europe. It has been called the 'Evangelical,' 'American Christian,' or 'Christian right' persecution complex." The entry cites Candida Moss, an author who has made a career out of attempting to debunk the idea of Christian persecution and martyrdom from the early Church up to the present day.[260]

Curiously, Wikipedia has no entry titled "Black racism complex" and no entry titled "Jewish anti-Semitism complex," whereas it feels justified in including such an entry for Christians. In its biased choice to single out Christians as delusional, Wikipedia confirms and perpetuates the impunity with which Christians can be attacked in the post-Christian West.

---

[259] Wikipedia, s.v. "Christian persecution complex," last updated October 7, 2022, https://en.wikipedia.org/wiki/Christian_persecution_complex#:~:text=Christian%20persecution%20complex%20is%20a,Bible%2Dbased%20cults%20in%20Europe.

[260] See Candida Moss, *The Myth of Persecution: How Early Christians Invented a Story of Martyrdom*, New York: HarperOne, 2013.

Wikipedia is just the tip of the iceberg where mass media are concerned. In 2014, the *Atlantic* published an article titled "The Evangelical Persecution Complex" that asserted that persecution has an "allure" for many Evangelicals but that narratives of "political, cultural, and theological oppression," while popular in evangelical communities, are "rarely accurate."[261] Traditional accounts of Christian martyrs were intended to inspire and strengthen Christians, the article claims, but have devolved into "aspirational fantasy" so that now many persecution narratives in Christian culture "fetishize suffering." The fact that most Evangelical Christians do not face very public and dramatic persecution, the article suggests, "creates an incentive to interpret personal experiences and news events as signs of oppression, which are ostensibly validations of our commitment to Christ." The article writes off growing pressures on Christians to conform to the reigning progressive Zeitgeist as nothing more than the slightest of inconveniences.

The *Washington Post* published a similar piece in 2017, titled "No, Christians Do Not Face Looming Persecution in America."[262] The article cites a survey by the Public Religion Research Institute that found that a majority of white Evangelicals believe that Christians face discrimination in the United States. Yet Christians

---

[261] Alan Noble, "The Evangelical Persecution Complex: The Theological and Cultural Roots of a Damaging Attitude in the Christian Community," *Atlantic*. August 4, 2014, https://www.theatlantic.com/national/archive/2014/08/the-evangelical-persecution-complex/375506/.

[262] Bethany Allen-Ebrahimian, "No, Christians Do Not Face Looming Persecution in America," *Washington Post*, December 12, 2017, https://www.washingtonpost.com/news/democracy-post/wp/2017/12/12/no-christians-do-not-face-looming-persecution-in-america/

cannot be persecuted in the United States, the article contends, because they are "vastly over-represented in national politics." Whereas roughly 70 percent of the U.S. population identifies as Christian, 91 percent of Congress identifies as such, the essay states, so clearly Christians are *privileged*, not persecuted. Because of their numerical majority, it is impossible "that Christians as a group experience formal marginalization or informal scorn," the essay contends. "American Christians who say they are being persecuted are simply, fortunately wrong," it concludes.

The fundamental error in this analysis lies in the author's understanding of Christian persecution and its manifestations in the West. While simply bearing the name "Christian" can be grounds for hatred and violent attacks in certain parts of the world, this is rarely the case in the United States and the rest of the West. American Christians are persecuted not for bearing the *name* of Christian but for taking their faith seriously and endeavoring to live by its moral demands. For this reason, serious Christians are persecuted not only by those outside the faith but by nominal, assimilated Christians as well. Meanwhile, such assimilated Christians are welcomed by the worldly since their faith does not impinge upon the world's conduct or values.

A perfect example of this public acceptance of a certain type of tame Christianity versus intolerance of more committed Christian practice came to the fore during the lead-up to the 2020 U.S. presidential election. Two prominent U.S. Catholics received radically different treatment by mainstream media and even by their co-religionists in Congress because of the different ways they conceive of and live out their faith.

During his candidacy and in the first months of his presidency, Joe Biden was lionized by mainstream media, which repeatedly praised him as a "devout Catholic," noting that he carried a rosary in his pocket and frequently attended Sunday Mass.[263] In the case of Joe Biden—who was able to parade his Catholic devotion before the nation while publicly supporting abortion on demand, officiating at a gay "marriage," and repealing the Mexico City policy, which protected taxpayers from having to finance abortions abroad—being a "devout Catholic" could only be seen as a good thing, since it clearly did not restrain him from embracing a progressive agenda.

On the other hand, Amy Coney Barrett was raked over the coals by the media for being a different sort of devout Catholic: the type who takes his or her faith seriously and upholds its teaching. In Barrett's case, the Catholic faith became a dangerous liability because she took it "too seriously," as if its moral teachings were meant to be understood, espoused, and lived by. As Bill Donohue, president of the Catholic League for Religious and Civil Rights, noted in a searing essay, the mainstream media fawn over Joe Biden's "devout" Catholic faith while pillorying those who actually embrace Church teaching.[264] It is okay "for Catholics to bludgeon the Little Sisters of the Poor provided they carry a rosary," Donohue noted, pointing out that for mainstream media, the only *good* Catholic is a *bad* Catholic.

"CNN ran a piece December 13 noting that Joe Biden goes to church, prays, and carries a rosary," Donohue observed, joining other puff pieces on Biden's Catholicism by *America* magazine, NPR, and the *Washington Post*. What all the left-wing media love about Biden's particular strain of Catholicism is his unapologetic rejection of the Church's core moral teachings about life and marriage

---

[263] See William Donohue, "Media Enamored of Biden's Faith," December 14, 2020, https://www.catholicleague.org/media -enamored-of-bidens-faith/.

[264] Ibid.

and religious freedom while maintaining all the external trappings of the faith, Donohue said.

Donohue underscored the sharp contrast between the media's sycophantic treatment of Biden's faith with their harsh attacks on Barrett's faith. In dealing with Justice Barrett, the media were "anything but kind," Donohue noted. "Indeed, her 'devoutness' was a source of discontent, even rage in some quarters." The difference was that Barrett actually believes and affirms what her Church teaches, while Biden only accepts Catholic teachings that coincide with the platform of the Democrat Party. Thus, the Catholic faith is a liability only when a public figure takes it seriously; if someone plays fast and loose with the faith's moral teaching, that person will have the full support of the establishment Left. "The moral of the story is plain: It is perfectly fine to be a Catholic public official just so long as he or she rejects the teachings of the Church on matters of public policy, even when those policies are life and death issues," Donohue concluded.

Unfortunately, all these tactics seem to be on the rise, not in decline, especially as more and more Americans disassociate themselves from organized religion. Anti-Christian bias has been rightly called "the last acceptable prejudice," one that few bother condemning. "No one much cares about offending Christians," wrote the Coalition of African American Pastors in a 2019 essay.[265] "In fact, mocking, belittling, and blaspheming Christianity is becoming a bit of a trend in our culture. Anti-Christian bigotry truly is the last acceptable prejudice."

[265] Coalition of African American Pastors, "Anti-Christian Bigotry Is the Last Acceptable Prejudice," Coalition of Americans for Action and Principles, March 12, 2019, https://caapusa.org/2019/03/anti-christian-bigotry-is-the-last-acceptable-prejudice/.

"The hypocrisy on display is astounding," the pastors continued. "Christianity is the dominant religion of our country. It is the foundation of our government and morality. And yet, Christians are treated as fair game for mockery and insult."

Media Silence Surrounding Christian Persecution

Perhaps more than any other cause, the pervasive ignorance of the extent to which Christians are persecuted around the world stems from the remarkable degree to which the mainstream media choose not to report on it. A tragic case in point is the media silence surrounding the Nigerian Christian genocide, a phenomenon nearly as alarming as the massacres themselves. To appreciate this, it is sufficient to examine two parallel incidents of religiously motivated mass killings in March 2019 and the media coverage each attracted—or didn't.

On March 15, 2019, a twenty-eight-year-old Australian named Brenton Tarrant went on a rampage in Christchurch, New Zealand, opening fire in two mosques and killing fifty-one people. Political leaders and public figures fell over themselves to condemn the attacks, and the media gave the atrocity around-the-clock coverage. Presidents, prime ministers, royalty, and religious leaders rushed to extend their condolences to the victims and their families—as well they should have—while decrying the hate that motivated the shootings. Without exception, the mainstream media gave top billing to the shootings, with newspapers carrying the story on their front pages and television news channels leading off their broadcasts with the story.

The bizarre aspect of the coverage was not, in fact, the tremendous attention paid to a heinous crime committed in New Zealand but the absolute silence surrounding the massacre of scores of Christians by Muslim militants in Africa during *exactly the same period*. Fulani jihadists racked up a death toll of more than 120 Christians in central Nigeria in just the first three weeks of March 2019, employing machetes and gunfire to slaughter men, women, and children, burning down more than 140 houses, destroying property, and spreading terror.[266]

The *New York Times* did not place the story of the slaughter of Christians on its front page; in fact, the paper did not cover it at all. Apparently, when assessing "all the news that's fit to print," the massacre of dozens of African Christians did not measure up. The same can be said for the *Washington Post*, the *Chicago Tribune*, the *Detroit Free Press*, the *LA Times*, and every other major paper in the United States. On television, the news shows from the three major networks did not mention the story, nor did CNN or MSNBC.

Two weeks later, the Vatican's secretary of state Cardinal Pietro Parolin decried the "appalling number of innocent persons that suffer persecution because of their beliefs, including many Christians," noting that these violations "often occur with impunity and at times receiving little, if any, attention in the media."[267] In an address at a symposium on international religious freedom organized by the U.S. Embassy to the Holy See in Rome, the Vatican's number-two man said that this persecution constitutes

---

[266] Samuel Smith, "120 People Killed, 140 Homes Destroyed by Nigeria Fulani since February," *Christian Post*, March 15, 2019, https://www.christianpost.com/news/120-people-killed-140-homes-destroyed-by-nigeria-fulani-since-february.html.

[267] Cardinal Pietro Parolin, "Intervento del Cardinale Segretario di Stato al Simposio 'Stand Together to Defend International Religious Freedom,'" Vatican website, April 03, 2019, https://press.vatican.va/content/salastampa/it/bollettino/pubblico/2019/04/03/0285/00578.html.

"an aggressive attack that strikes at the very core of the enjoyment of fundamental human rights."

In his address, Cardinal Parolin said that "those involved in the area of media and social communications must bring to light those realities that threaten the common good of the human family. Crass violations of the freedom of religion should be numbered among such threats."

There are several possible explanations for the striking media silence surrounding the killing of Christians, none of which is good. On the one hand, Muslim radicals massacring Christians might not seem like news to many in the media, since it happens with startling regularity, and one more slaughter might not have caught the attention of media decision makers. If this were the motive, it would suggest that media managers have at least tacitly accepted Islamic violence against Christians as a fact of life, one that does not rise to the level of *news*. The shooting of Muslims, on the other hand, may have struck many as newsworthy precisely because it is so *unusual*.

A second motive for the media silence over the massacre of Christians in Nigeria may be geopolitical and racial. New Zealand is a first-world country where such things are not supposed to happen, whereas many people still consider Africa to be a backward place where brutal killings are considered somewhat normal. Furthermore, the slaughter of black Christians in Africa may not enkindle rage among Westerners, as the murder of white and brown Muslims in New Zealand would. It is, after all, an "internal affair." The acceptance of the slaughter of Africans as unworthy of coverage smacks of a racism and first-world elitism that the Left takes pains to criticize in others.

Finally, the story simply does not play to the political agenda that many mainstream media would like to advance. How much mileage can be gained from reporting on Muslims murdering Christians, when Christians in America are often seen as an obstacle to the "progress" desired by so-called liberals? The radical Left—of which the mainstream media are a part—sees Christians in the West as obstacles to their agenda and thus seeks to undermine their credibility and influence. Shining a light on Christian martyrs, victims of radical Islam, simply does not advance the narrative that progressives wish to promote.

The Decline of Christianity in the West

Religious practice has been dwindling for many years in formerly Christian Europe, now notorious for its empty churches and nominal religious affiliation. The United States, by contrast, has stood out as a singularly religious country among the nations of the first world, with consistently high figures of belief, prayer, and religious practice over decades. In the past fifteen years, however, America has experienced a staggering drop in both belief and practice, the steepest decline of its entire history.

A 2020 study in *Foreign Affairs* underscored the incredible scale and speed of this change. "From 1981 to 2007, the United States ranked as one of the world's more religious countries, with religiosity levels changing very little," the authors noted. "Since then, the United States has shown one of the largest moves away from religion of any country for which we have data."[268]

---

[268] Ronald F. Inglehart, "Giving Up on God: The Global Decline of Religion," *Foreign Affairs*, September/October 2020, https://www.foreignaffairs.com/articles/world/2020-08-11/religion-giving-god?utm_medium=social&fbclid=IwAR0TAtl7Xk_HJpbG-CTovsUeu5Km-5Dh8UyoLtM0IYWcXQvr7X3xcVVQMJM.

In early 2021, the Pew Research Center reported that the Christian population in the United States had fallen to just 63 percent of the population, the lowest figure in American history.[269] In fewer than fifteen years, Christianity had plummeted from 78.4 percent of the population in 2007, a drop of a 15.4 percentage points, or more than one point per year.[270] The denominations taking the biggest hit have been mainline Protestant churches and Catholicism, whereas Evangelicalism has experienced more modest losses. Some of the smaller groups, such as Mormons and Jehovah's Witnesses, have remained virtually unchanged, while the larger denominations have seen significant decreases. Although the United States is still a statistically "Christian nation," with nearly two-thirds of Americans identifying as Christian, it is markedly less so than even a generation ago, when it was more than three-quarters Christian. If loss of Christian affiliation continues at this pace, the United States will be less than 50 percent Christian in another fifteen years.

As more Americans have shed their religious attachments, the ranks of the unaffiliated or "nones"—people describing themselves as atheist, agnostic, or "nothing in particular"—have swollen correspondingly, moving from just 16.1 percent of the U.S. population in 2007 to more than a quarter of the adult population (28 percent) in 2021. Outright atheists have more than doubled, growing from a slim 1.6 percent of the population in 2007 to 4 percent in 2021,

---

[269] "Measuring Religion in Pew Research Center's American Trends Panel," Pew Research Center, January 14, 2021, https://www.pewforum.org/2021/01/14/measuring-religion-in-pew-research-centers-american-trends-panel/.

[270] Pew Research Center, "America's Changing Religious Landscape," May 12, 2015, https://www.pewforum.org/2015/05/12/americas-changing-religious-landscape/.

while those espousing "nothing in particular" experienced a 5.9 percent growth, from 12.1 to 18 percent of the nation.

Of the 63 percent of U.S. adults currently identifying as Christians, 43 percent described themselves as Protestant, 19 percent as Catholic, and 2 percent as Mormon. Conversely, of the 28 percent of unaffiliated "nones," 4 percent identified as atheists, 5 percent as agnostics, and 18 percent as "nothing in particular." During this period, the only religions to grow in America were Islam, Hinduism, and the nebulous category of "other religions," comprising everything from Baha'i to Wicca to Satanism.

The United States still remains home to more Christians than any other country in the world, but the accelerating downward spiral of traditional Christianity seems to bode even more significant losses in the future.

A contributing factor to the downward trend is the age difference between religious and nonreligious Americans. The members of traditional Christian faiths are getting older, while the unaffiliated are comparatively young and are getting younger on average over time. In 2014, the median age of unaffiliated adults was 36, down from 38 in 2007 and significantly lower than the general adult population's median age of 46.4. Mainline Protestant adults, on the other hand, now average 52 years of age (up from 50 in 2007), while Catholic adults are 49 years old on average, up from 45 seven years earlier.

In its American Worldview Inventory 2021, the Cultural Research Center at Arizona Christian University found that while 57 percent of millennials (born between 1984 and 2002) consider themselves to be Christian, 43 percent "don't know, care, or believe that God exists."[271] The study also revealed that millennials support

---

[271] Susan Berry, "Survey: 43% of Millennials 'Don't Know, Care, or Believe God Exists,'" Breitbart, May 20, 2021, https://www.

expansion of government to facilitate a better life and are seeking "fewer formal marriages," due, in part, to "the reduced appeal of raising children."

The United States is a perfect example of a country where waning Christian faith is accompanied by a corresponding drop in appreciation for religious liberty. In March 2021, Archbishop Chaput noted precisely this: that religious liberty is in peril in the United States due to declining awareness of the importance of faith. "The United States was founded by Europeans seeking religious liberty," he noted. "It was a very important issue for them, even though they didn't really recognize the liberty of Catholics at first, or the liberty of slaves, in the first decades of our country."[272]

"It seems there is real danger to religious freedom now and in our country—mostly because people aren't serious about religion or religious freedom," the archbishop observed. Recognizing and defending religious liberty goes hand in hand with recognizing the dignity of every single person, he suggested, as well as the order of God's creation. "Today, we don't have any respect for the dignity of the unborn as a country. When you don't do that, you begin to embrace ideologies that enable us to interfere with the order of creation, like gender theory. Likewise, if we don't respect the elderly, which we don't, then we embrace things like euthanasia," he added. "Things can turn pretty bad pretty quickly and I worry about that."

breitbart.com/politics/2021/05/20/survey-43-millennials-dont
-know-care-believe-god-exists/.

[272] Pablo Kay, " 'The Holy Spirit Always Wins in the End': An Interview with Archbishop Chaput," Angelus News, March 26,
2021, https://angelusnews.com/arts-culture/the-holy-spirit-always
-wins-in-the-end-an-interview-with-archbishop-chaput/.

This decline in support for religious freedom has accelerated over the past several years, leading the archbishop to declare: "I would say that I worry about the future of our country in a way that I didn't worry about 10 years ago." He developed an interest in our country's roots "because I began to worry about religious freedom and the loss of commitment to our founding principles," he said. "And I thought that my contributions might help change that. I don't know that they have, but we'll see."

The West's Growing Hostility to Its Christian Roots

The Western world is not only abdicating its former role as a defender of the rights of Christians around the world; it is fast becoming one of the foremost *opponents* of Christian thought and practice. Christian teachings on human nature, marriage, human sexuality, and human life—once taken for granted as self-evident in the West—are increasingly condemned as fanatical, sectarian, and prejudiced.

The late Cardinal Francis George, archbishop of Chicago, had some sobering words to describe the state of Christian persecution in our day and the trend it is following: "I expect to die in bed, my successor will die in prison and his successor will die a martyr in the public square. His successor will pick up the shards of a ruined society and slowly help rebuild civilization, as the church has done so often in human history."[273] In the cardinal's view, antipathy toward Christianity is growing fiercer by the day and will eventually erupt in more violent expressions. As Western nations drift

---

[273] Tim Drake, "Cardinal George: The Myth and Reality of 'I'll Die in My Bed,'" *National Catholic Register*, April 17, 2015, https://www.ncregister.com/blog/tim-drake/the-myth-and-the-reality-of-ill-die-in-my-bed.

ever further away from their Christian roots, those who uphold Christian morality will find themselves isolated, misjudged, and punished for their "unacceptable" views.

On February 25, 2021, the U.S. House of Representatives passed legislation known as the Equality Act by a vote of 224 to 206. Ostensibly a law about equal rights and nondiscrimination, the act would radically redefine what it means to be a male or a female, abandoning the notion of biological sex in favor of gender identity, a move that even secular feminist groups have condemned. Prominent Evangelical pastor Franklin Graham wrote on Twitter that the Equality Act "has nothing to do with equality" but is, in fact, a "smokescreen to force Americans to accept the LGBTQ agenda."[274]

With their understanding of human beings as created male and female in the image of God, Christians are the most visible adversaries to this revolution in Western political thought. Bill Donohue warned that the Equality Act would "promote the most comprehensive assault on Christianity ever written into law" because of its re-envisioning of the human person.[275]

The Act would also undermine the Religious Freedom Restoration Act by conferring special status on gay rights, prioritizing them over religious freedom and conscience rights, Donohue added.

The Equality Act would require healthcare providers to provide "hormone therapies and surgical procedures that are required to change the physical characteristics associated with sex changes,"

---

[274] Franklin Graham (@Franklin_Graham), Twitter, February 22, 2021, 9:36 p.m., https://twitter.com/Franklin_Graham/status/1364041311175778304.

[275] Bill Donohue, "Equality Act Is Anti-Christian," Catholic League for Religious and Civil Rights, February 22, 2021, https://www.catholicleague.org/equality-act-is-anti-christian/.

Donohue said, without regard for the beliefs of healthcare workers. "It has become increasingly clear that the expansion of rights
to transgender women—really biological males who identify as
female—has come at the expense of rights for biological females,"
Donohue added.

This would also mean that "Catholics, evangelicals, Orthodox
Jews, Mormons, Muslims, and many other religious communities
could not raise religious liberty objections to any of the aforemen-
tioned rights of transgender women," Donohue insisted.

The U.S. Catholic Bishops' Conference warned that the Equality Act would "discriminate against people of faith" and "punish
faith-based organizations, such as charities and schools who serve
everyone in their communities, simply because of their beliefs."
The proposed legislation would also "force girls and women to
compete against boys and men for limited opportunities in sports,
and to share locker rooms and shower spaces with biological males
who identify as women," the bishops said.[276]

The Equality Act is just one example of a trend in Western society away from the Christian understanding of the human person
and human society, and consequently away from the traditional
undergirding of human dignity. Christians are increasingly seen
as the enemies of an inevitable "progress" toward a redefining of
human beings independent of their biological makeup toward a
subjective, gender-based identity.

As we noted in the last chapter, then-Cardinal Ratzinger noted
in 2004 that for centuries in the Western world, basic moral

[276] Catholic News Service, "Catholic Bishops: Stop Biden-Backed
Equality Act That Would 'Force Girls … to Share … Shower
Spaces with Biological Males,'" CNS, February 21, 2021, https://
www.cnsnews.com/article/washington/cnsnewscom-staff/catholic
-bishops-stop-biden-backed-equality-act-would-force.

insights revealed by Christianity were so obvious to all that they have often been regarded as insights that every rational man took for granted. "But what seemed a compelling, God-given insight of reason retained its evidential character only for so long as the entire culture, the entire existential context, bore the imprint of Christian tradition," he concluded. In the United States and elsewhere in the West, this cultural imprint is fading by the day, not just by neglect but by design. More and more, Christians who stand up to the trend will be accused of closed-mindedness, bigotry, discrimination, and tribal chauvinism.

Christian opposition to gay marriage, gender fluidity, sexual libertinism, and abortion is already being depicted as obscurantist vestiges of a medieval worldview that has been definitively superseded. The American tendency to conflate legality with morality aggravates this situation: as practices that Christians understand to be *immoral* become *legal*, Christians' failure to embrace the new morality looks more and more like obstinacy and bigotry rather than fidelity to Christ and His message.

The Rise of Big-Tech Censorship

Government is not the only or even necessarily the primary mover of Christian persecution in the West. Being treated as bigots because of Christian moral beliefs takes many forms, one of which is ostracization and banning by large, private organizations, especially Big Tech, which increasing holds the reins of social communications. As Big Tech has assumed the role of de facto arbiter of acceptable and unacceptable ideas — a real-life version of Orwell's Thought Police — it has begun flexing its digital muscles by rooting out purveyors of dangerous notions. Many large tech companies that operate virtual monopolies on books, videos, and social communications have been clamping down on religious expression with jarring regularity, notably targeting texts espousing Christian morality. Any expression of opposition to the new, progressive mindset can be sufficient cause for censorship and silencing.

According to a *Wall Street Journal* report in late March 2021, during the first three months of the year, religious groups and figures had been silenced by tech companies at a rate of about one a week.[277] The popular Christian news website LifeSiteNews, for example, had its YouTube channel permanently banned by Google in February 2021; this included the deleting of all its videos and the removal of its 314,000 subscribers.[278] According to the *Journal*, YouTube had flagged LifeSiteNews for a video of an American Catholic bishop criticizing vaccines developed with fetal cells. The website's editor in chief, John-Henry Westen, said, "Our best guess is that the channel was taken down for our frank and factual discussion of the controversy around abortion-tainted medicines and vaccines."

In January 2021, Twitter banned the Irish Catholic bishop Kevin Doran for tweeting against a government plan to legalize assisted suicide. "There is dignity in dying. As a priest, I am privileged to witness it often. Assisted suicide, where it is practiced, is not an expression of freedom or dignity," he wrote. Twitter removed this message and banned Bishop Doran from posting further, even turning him down on appeal, and reversed its decision only after

---

[277] Josh Holdenried, "Big Tech Censors Religion, Too," *Wall Street Journal*, March 28, 2021, https://www.wsj.com/articles/big-tech-censors-religion-too-11616959164?mod=hp_opin_pos_2.

[278] "YouTube's Permanent Ban on LifeSiteNews Prompts Censorship Concerns," *National Catholic Register*, February 13, 2021, https://www.ncregister.com/cna/youtube-s-permanent-ban-on-lifesite-news-prompts-censorship-concerns.

a public outcry. Similarly, tech giants had interfered in Ireland's 2018 constitutional referendum on abortion, banning ads from pro-life groups on the run-up to the referendum.[279]

In February 2021, Amazon erased a bestselling book by Dr. Ryan T. Anderson titled *When Harry Became Sally: Responding to the Transgender Moment*. Amazon canceled the meticulously researched book not because of any factual errors or incendiary language but because it countered the transgender ideology popular in certain circles. Renowned experts in the field, including the former psychiatrist in chief at Johns Hopkins Hospital, Dr. Paul McHugh, had heaped praise on the book, and yet Amazon deemed the book's ideas too dangerous to continue making it available. Anderson had made the mistake of advancing the heretical notion that boys are boys and girls are girls, and therefore boys who think they are girls need counseling, not surgery.

Anderson's book was released in 2018, but Amazon decided to erase the book from its website just days before a Congressional vote on the Equality Act, which Anderson vocally opposed. Not long afterward, Amazon doubled down on its move, reiterating its intent to continue banning books that argue against the reigning progressive narrative on LGBT issues. In a March 11 letter to four Republican senators who had questioned the censorship, Amazon said that while "we provide our customers with access to a variety of viewpoints, including books that some customers may find objectionable," they draw the line at those that see gender dysphoria or other LGBT issues as pathologies. We "have chosen

---

[279] Kevin Hay, "Twitter Bans Irish Bishop Because He Criticised Euthanasia," Catholic Arena, February 20, 2021, https://www. catholicarena.com/latest/irishbishopbanned.

not to sell books that frame LGBTQ+ identity as a mental illness," they declared.[280]

A *Wall Street Journal* op-ed noted that just when tech censorship had reached unprecedented levels, two Congressional Democrats wrote to Amazon CEO Jeff Bezos requesting more—not less—ideological suppression of uncomfortable ideas. "Our country's public discourse is plagued by misinformation, disinformation, conspiracy theories, and lies," wrote Reps. Anna Eshoo and Jerry McNerney in their letter to Bezos, echoing claims that right-wing media are "much more susceptible" to such misinformation. "Corporate media censorship, such as Amazon's scrubbing of a heretical book, is accelerating," the *Journal*'s editors observed. "And government is right alongside, pushing for censorship with increasing force."

Acting in lockstep with Amazon's agenda, Twitter blocked a post from the *Daily Citizen*, which is run by Focus on the Family, an Evangelical Christian nonprofit, and suspended its account. The reason Twitter gave was a tweet that (respectfully) challenged the underlying premise of transgenderism.

The *Wall Street Journal* further noted that books from specific Christian publishers are often targeted, such as the Catholic publisher TAN Books. TAN Books is banned from advertising the work of its writer Paul Kengor, author of an anticommunist tract called *The Devil and Karl Marx*. Facebook banned ads promoting the work of Catholic scholar Dr. Carrie Gress, whose book *The Anti-Mary Exposed: Rescuing the Culture from Toxic Femininity* criticized the ideological underpinnings of radical feminism as well

---

[280] Brian Huseman to the Hons. Marco Rubio, Josh Hawley, Mike Braun, and Mike Lee, March 11, 2021, https://s.wsj.net/public/resources/documents/Amazonletter0311.pdf.

as the tactics of the LGBT lobby.[281] Facebook also banned ads for *Motherhood Redeemed: How Radical Feminism Betrayed Maternal Love* by Catholic author Kimberly Cook, whose offending ad described the text as "a book that challenges feminism in the modern world."

"It seems likely that religious groups and individuals will face mounting threats from tech companies," the *Journal* concluded. "Their views on marriage, sexuality, life and other moral issues are unpopular among the Silicon Valley set."

The addition of Big Tech to the growing list of powerful forces attacking Christianity does not augur well for a lessening of anti-Christian hostility. While the traditional drivers of Christian persecution are gaining strength and momentum around the world, new agents of repression in the West are joining them in an unholy alliance. Coupled with the anemic will to oppose such persecution, all indicators point to an acceleration of anti-Christian hostility with no end in sight.

---

[281] Claire Anderson, "Facebook Censors Catholic Professor's Book on 'Toxic Femininity,'" *The College Fix*, February 5, 2021, https://www.thecollegefix.com/facebook-censors-catholic-professors-book-on-toxic-femininity/.

8

The Christian Response to Persecution

Given the manifold forces that are driving Christian persecution and given that Christians can expect to face new and old forms of persecution in the future, how should we prepare ourselves as individuals and as a community? What can we learn from Jesus Himself and from the faithful Christians who have developed distinctive responses to hostility over the centuries?

Let's begin with Our Lord, since loyalty to Christ entails identifying with His way of dealing with the abuse that often accompanies faithfulness to the mission.

As we have seen, Jesus was not merely "resigned" to the violent opposition that awaited Him. His act of surrender to the Father's will was fully free. Even in His darkest hour, Jesus prayed, "Not my will but your will be done." When one of His disciples drew a sword to defend Him, Jesus responded: "Do you think that I cannot appeal to my Father, and he will at once send me more than twelve legions of angels? But how then should the scriptures be fulfilled, that it must be so?" (Matt. 26:53–54).

There was never a sense of fatalism in Christ's foretelling of His Passion, except as an inevitable consequence of His love for the Father. "For this reason the Father loves me, because I lay down my life, that I may take it again," he exclaimed. "No one takes it

227

from me, but I lay it down of my own accord. I have power to lay it down, and I have power to take it again; this charge I have received from my Father" (John 10:17–19). In the same way, Christians are called to embrace whatever share of persecution befalls them as a consequence of their free choice to follow in their Master's footsteps. In choosing to be His disciples, we choose to accept the cross that unfailingly accompanies it.

Indeed, Jesus describes His self-offering as an act of love: "Greater love has no man than this, that a man lay down his life for his friends" (John 15:13). His Passion is His gift to the Church, His gift to His friends. Christians are invited to embrace their own crosses with the same sentiments. As Paul declared, "Now I rejoice in my sufferings for your sake, and in my flesh I complete what is lacking in Christ's afflictions for the sake of his body, that is, the church" (Col. 1:24).

As we followers of Christ strive to discern appropriate responses to the forms of persecution or threats of persecution that come our way, we should also be aware of the many paths that are *not* open to us. While fear of pain, torture, harassment, and ridicule is a perfectly rational human response, we are invited to beg the grace of God to endure whatever He asks of us without compromising our loyalty to the truth.

In today's world, the greatest temptation for many of us is not apostasy per se but rather assimilation. It is so much easier to shade the truth of the gospel in order to be well liked, to advance in our careers, and to be accepted by "the world" than to stand firm and expose ourselves to ridicule and ostracization for our fidelity to Christ. Today, the Roman emperors' invitation to "save ourselves" by burning a little incense to them, a "harmless" act of external compliance, often takes the form of pressure to "go along to get along" — to adapt to the moral trends of our times rather than stand as a sign of contradiction.

What, then, are the key attitudes and virtues that the true Christian should cultivate in response to persecution? In this chapter, we will explore the qualities of mind and heart that have enabled Christians throughout the ages to develop responses characterized by the gifts and fruits of the Holy Spirit (see Gal. 5:22-23)—the very qualities exemplified by Christ's own response to suffering. They are remembrance, love, joy, prayer, serenity, courage, patience, docility, and hope. We will conclude with an appeal for all Christians not only to face the persecution that comes their way with an awareness of the role of suffering in evangelization but to do their part in actively defending religious freedom, one of the most important components of a Christian response to persecution in today's world.

Remembrance

Since the earliest centuries, the Christian Church has been proud of and grateful for her martyrs. They are "Heaven's athletes," who, in Paul's words, have fought the good fight and finished the race. Shortly before his own martyrdom, Paul wrote these memorable words from prison to his disciple Timothy, describing his final witness to Christ:

> I am already on the point of being sacrificed; the time of my departure has come. I have fought the good fight, I have finished the race, I have kept the faith. Henceforth there is laid up for me the crown of righteousness, which the Lord, the righteous judge, will award to me on that Day, and not only to me but also to all who have loved his appearing. (2 Tim. 4:6-8)

No one seeks persecution for its own sake; it is unpleasant, painful, and repulsive to our human nature. No one wants to be mistreated, misunderstood, or ridiculed—much less punished, tortured, or put to death. And yet a willingness to endure such things out of fidelity to Jesus points to the truth of the faith and the sustaining power of God's grace even in the most trying ordeals.

In 2001, St. John Paul II urged his fellow Christians to preserve the memory of the martyrs. "Their witness must not be forgotten," he said. "They are the most eloquent proof of the truth of the faith, which can give a human face even to the most violent death and show its beauty even in the midst of atrocious sufferings."[282]

The Church is called to live a new springtime of Christianity, "since she has been watered and fertilized by the blood of so many martyrs," John Paul said at the beginning of the third millennium. "*Sanguis martyrum, semen christianorum!* The blood of martyrs is the seed of Christians! Today these words, coined during the persecutions of the first centuries, must instill hope in your apostolic initiatives and pastoral efforts in the often difficult task of the new evangelization. For this you can rely on the incomparable help of your martyrs. Remember their valor."

Christians are encouraged to remember their martyrs and the clear witness they left for future generations. They continue to inspire us today, reminding us that we are not alone—that we belong to a glorious history of heroes who shed their blood for Christ.

For a Christian, remembrance is not bitterness. We don't remember in order to keep old wounds aliveor to stir up anger or pain or to point fingers at our persecutors. We remember in order to draw strength from the powerful witness of love and loyalty left to us as a precious inheritance from our elder brothers and sisters.

---

[282] Pope John Paul II, Homily for the Beatification of the Servants of God José Aparicio Sanz and 232 Companions, Sunday, 11 March 2001.

Love

Jesus Himself provides the quintessential Christian response to persecution in His Sermon on the Mount, in which He calls on His followers to fight hatred with love. By refusing to succumb to hate and loving instead, Christians imitate the Heavenly Father, who treats the ungrateful and insolent in this very way. Sunshine is not reserved for the pure of heart, and rain and snow fall on good and bad people alike, Jesus observes. Similarly, a Christian's response to others should not be dictated by their kindness or unkindness but by a higher principle.

> You have heard that it was said, "You shall love your neighbor and hate your enemy." But I say to you, Love your enemies and pray for those who persecute you, so that you may be sons of your Father who is in heaven; for he makes his sun rise on the evil and on the good, and sends rain on the just and on the unjust. (Matt. 5:43–45)

Christian virtue calls us to something more than a natural human response to people's kindness or hostility. On a natural level, people spontaneously respond to love with love, to affection with affection. On the other hand, when people are unkind to us, we spontaneously react with anger, indignation, and even retaliation and vengeance. It is divine to forgive, to return love for hate, a blessing for a curse.

> For if you love those who love you, what reward have you? Do not even the tax collectors do the same? And if you salute only your brethren, what more are you doing than others? Do not even the Gentiles do the same? You, therefore, must be perfect, as your heavenly Father is perfect. (Matt 5:46–48)

Christian charity cannot be reduced to a quid pro quo: "I receive good, I give good back; I receive evil, I respond with evil." My treatment of others cannot simply be a conditioned response to their treatment of me and a strict meting out of what others "deserve." This would be nothing more than an eye-for-an-eye, tooth-for-a-tooth, Old Testament–style justice. This is, as Jesus said, what comes naturally to tax collectors and pagans. Jesus invites us to go beyond this and reminds us that the measure we use for others will be measured back to us (Mark 4:24–25; Luke 6:37–38). The model for Christians is the Father, who is good to all people: the good, the bad, and the indifferent. There is always a chance for conversion while life lasts, and after that comes judgment.

St. Paul echoes Christ's counsel in his Letter to the Romans, urging the early Christians to take a higher road in responding to the world's hate. "Bless those who persecute you; bless and do not curse them," Paul tells the Christians of the Church in Rome. A little later he adds: "Repay no one evil for evil, but take thought for what is noble in the sight of all," insisting that they never avenge themselves but rather that they leave all punishment to God. "Do not be overcome by evil, but overcome evil with good," he concludes (Rom. 12:14, 17, 21). If persecution makes Christians bitter and vindictive, then the devil has won. Victory is to be found in resisting the natural inclination to hate and, with God's grace, to forgive, to excuse, and to love, no matter what.

Joy

One of the quintessential Christian responses to persecution is also the most counterintuitive: *joy*. "In the world you have tribulation," Jesus tells His followers, "but be of good cheer, I have overcome the world" (John 16:33). Knowledge that our ordeals are temporary while Christ's victory is eternal leads to cheerfulness in the face of trials, Christ suggests. Yes, we must suffer, but the cross leads to the resurrection, the ultimate joy.

As Pope John Paul II told the sick and the suffering at the beginning of his pontificate:

> May the glorious wounds of the risen Christ serve to illuminate and heal your wounds, physical and moral, which are still open and aching. Remember the ascetic maxim: "*Per crucem ad lucem,*" [through the cross to the light,] that is: through the sufferings of the Cross we reach the beatitude of light. Know that with his Resurrection Christ ransomed and redeemed pain, which thus acquired its dignity, having been called to come out of its uselessness and to become a positive source of good and a luminous sign of hope that does not disappoint.[283]

In the Acts of the Apostles, we read how the apostles were hauled before the Sanhedrin for continuing to preach about Jesus in the temple despite strict orders not to do so. Peter and the other apostles famously responded to the high priest, "We must obey God rather than men." Eventually, the tribunal had the apostles flogged, ordered them not to speak any more in the name of Jesus, and released them. "Then they left the presence of the council, *rejoicing* that they were counted worthy to suffer dishonor for the name," Acts recounts. "And every day in the temple and at home they did not cease teaching and preaching Jesus as the Christ" (Acts 5:29, 41–42, emphasis added).

After being whipped, the apostles *rejoiced* because they were found *worthy* of suffering for the sake of Jesus. This is not the response one would ordinarily expect. After being unjustly punished,

---

[283] Pope John Paul II, General Audience, April 18, 1979.

many people naturally become indignant. They grow angry. They demand their rights. They seek redress. But the apostles instead *rejoice* because they have been found worthy of suffering for the sake of the Name.

In his first epistle, the apostle Peter reflects on this: "Beloved, do not be surprised at the fiery ordeal which comes upon you to prove you, as though something strange were happening to you," he writes. "But rejoice in so far as you share Christ's sufferings, that you may also rejoice and be glad when his glory is revealed."

"If you are reproached for the name of Christ, you are blessed, because the spirit of glory and of God rests upon you," he continues. "But let none of you suffer as a murderer, or a thief, or a wrongdoer, or a mischief-maker; yet if one suffers as a Christian, let him not be ashamed, but under that name let him glorify God" (1 Pet. 4:12–16).

In the Sermon on the Mount, Jesus counsels joy in the face of persecution, proclaiming His followers blest when they suffer for His sake. "Blessed are those who are persecuted for righteousness' sake, for theirs is the kingdom of heaven," Jesus declares in Matthew's account. "Blessed are you when men revile you and persecute you and utter all kinds of evil against you falsely on my account. Rejoice and be glad, for your reward is great in heaven, for so men persecuted the prophets who were before you" (Matt. 5:10–12). Here, Jesus enumerates insults, persecution, and malicious lies as sufferings that His disciples will experience. But He also gives two motivations for rejoicing when faced with these trials. First, Christians are urged to rejoice because the heavenly rewards for faithfulness are "great," far greater than the ordeals themselves. Second, Jesus reminds His hearers that in bearing such tests, they resemble the prophets who went before them and who suffered similarly.

In Luke's account of the Beatitudes, Jesus' description of Christian persecution varies slightly from Matthew's: "Blessed are you when men hate you, and when they exclude you and revile you, and cast out your name as evil, on account of the Son of man!" (6:22). Here, Jesus specifically includes the *hatred* that many Christians will experience because of their beliefs and adds that many will be *excluded*, an experience with which many Christians are familiar. The upshot, however, is the same. Whatever the nature of the persecution, Jesus declares His followers blest when they undergo it and urges them to rejoice because of it.

In April 2020, Pope Francis explored this final beatitude, noting that in the midst of vehement persecution, Christians are still able to rejoice, even though they are rejected by the world, because they have discovered a pearl of great price. "What makes those who are rejected by the world because of Christ rejoice?" the pope asked. "They rejoice at having found something that has more value than the entire world. Indeed: 'For what does it profit a man, to gain the whole world and forfeit his life?' What is the advantage there?"[284] This last beatitude "proclaims the eschatological joy of those persecuted for righteousness' sake," the pope stated, adding that "the Kingdom of Heaven belongs to the persecuted."

Prayer

On the night of the Last Supper, Jesus told His disciples to "watch and pray" and warned them: "You will all fall away because of me this night; for it is written, 'I will strike the shepherd, and the sheep of the flock will be scattered.'" Sure of himself, Peter responds: "Though they all fall away because of you, I will never fall away," for which Jesus must gently reprove him: "Truly, I say to you, this

---

[284] Pope Francis, General Audience, April 29, 2020.

very night, before the cock crows, you will deny me three times." Peter replies: "Even if I must die with you, I will not deny you" (Matt. 26:31, 33–35). We know what follows.

The Christian counsel to "watch and pray" is especially relevant for those who are experiencing persecution. We are aware of our weakness, our frailty, our potential to succumb rather than to hold firm. In this awareness, we ask for grace and strength to endure whatever comes. Indeed, if we are honest, we recognize that "the spirit indeed is willing, but the flesh is weak" (Matt. 26:41). Even if, like Saint Peter, we believe we are strong, that we will not falter in the face of trials and tribulations, humility teaches us that we cannot do this by our own strength. We "watch and pray" to avail ourselves of the infinite stores of strength and fortitude in the heart of Christ. The old saying "pride goeth before a fall," taken from the book of Proverbs (16:18), reminds us that overconfidence in our own resources is a recipe for disaster.

"The strength of Christ's martyrs, both men and women, is Christ," wrote St. Augustine.[285] No one should presume to have this strength within himself but should humbly ask for it. During Decius's persecution in AD 250, the Christians Castus and Aemilius failed during their first encounter with martyrdom and burned the incense required by the imperial cult. Later, however, they were arrested again, and this time remained faithful and were martyred.[286] Preaching on their feast day in 397, Augustine declared: "Perhaps they too, to begin with, relied presumptuously on their own powers, and that's why they fell away. He showed them who they really were, in themselves, and who he really was."[287]

---

[285] Augustine, Serm. 299E.1 (PLS 2:625).

[286] Cyprian, De lapsis 13.

[287] Augustine, Serm. 285.4 (PL38:1295).

In this, as in all things, Jesus is our model. The day before His Passion and death, Jesus withdrew with His closest disciples to pray in the Garden of Gethsemane. "My Father," he said, "if it be possible, let this cup pass from me; nevertheless, not as I will, but as thou wilt" (Matt. 26:39). Jesus knew what was approaching, and He recoiled from the pain, asking God to intervene to take the chalice away. God did not take away His Passion, but He did give Jesus the strength He needed to carry it out perfectly, according to the Father's will.

But Christian prayer in the face of persecution is not directed only to our own situation. For most of us, this prayer will primarily take the form of *intercession* for our persecuted brothers and sisters. As the Body of Christ, the communion of saints, we are summoned to intercede on behalf of the persecuted members of this Body, that they may have the courage and grace to withstand whatever comes.

"It is painful to remember that, at this moment, there are many Christians who suffer persecution in various areas of the world," Pope Francis has said, "and we must hope and pray that their tribulation will be stopped as soon as possible."[288]

As Christians, we have the duty to entrust our suffering brothers and sisters to God in prayer. One of the seven spiritual works of mercy is to comfort the sorrowing and the afflicted. Sometimes we can comfort them in person but many times this is not possible. By commending them to the mercy of God, we lend them a comfort and strength that far exceeds what we could offer ourselves.

Serenity

A great danger involved in encountering opposition is that it can make us think we are on the wrong path. Success in our endeavors

---

[288] Pope Francis, General Audience, April 29, 2020.

is a normal sign that we are doing things the right way, and failure often indicates that we messed up somewhere. It would make sense for persecuted Christians—beaten, imprisoned, ostracized—to feel as if they are doing something very wrong and to want to correct it.

Fortunately, Jesus foresaw this danger and warned His disciples over and over that persecution is to be expected. As we saw in chapter 2, opposition and resistance were an integral part of Christ's mission and are also a mark of anyone who follows Him. This awareness changes everything. Knowing that persecution has always been part of the plan, we can more easily persevere when people oppose us. Rather than assuming that this means we are on the wrong path, it becomes an assurance that we are on the *right path*. In fact, if a Christian faces no resistance at all, he should probably examine the intensity of his engagement with the faith.

"Martyrdom is the life's breath of a Christians and Christian communities," Pope Francis has declared.[289] "There will always be martyrs among us: this is the sign that we are traveling on the path of Jesus." As painful as it is, persecution is not a curse for Christians, the pontiff insisted, since it conforms them to Christ and testifies to the authenticity of their witness. "It is a blessing from the Lord that among the people of God there is someone who gives the witness of martyrdom."

This awareness, in turn, gives rise to serenity and peace of heart. There is no reason to anguish if we are where we should be, doing what we should be doing. It may be difficult, it may be painful, but there is no reason to second-guess our choices. Serenity does

---

[289] Pope Francis, General Audience in the Vatican's Paul VI Hall, December 11, 2019.

not mean an absence of suffering, but it allows us to face suffering peacefully, and that changes everything.

After promising His apostles a share in His suffering and persecution, Jesus also promises them a share in His peace, and the two promises are not contradictory. "Peace I leave with you; my peace I give to you; not as the world gives do I give to you," he states. "Let not your hearts be troubled, neither let them be afraid" (Matt. 14:27). Again, this serenity of spirit, this lack of anxiety and fear, stems not from a smooth, easy road but from the knowledge that God holds us in the palm of His hand. "I have said this to you, that in me you may have peace. In the world you have tribulation; but be of good cheer, I have overcome the world," Christ assures His apostles (John 16:33).

This serenity is, finally, a "fruit of the Spirit" under the name of peace: "The fruit of the Spirit is love, joy, peace, patience, kindness, goodness, faithfulness, gentleness, self-control" (Gal. 5:22–23). These are the marks of a soul that has given himself or herself over to the Spirit, who lives by the Spirit of Christ. It is unsurprising that this list reads like a description of the Christian response to persecution or like a litany of Christ's own virtues in the face of His Passion.

Courage

Philosophers of the ancient Greek and Roman civilizations, along with the book of Wisdom, held up four virtues as cardinal—or pivotal—namely, prudence, justice, fortitude, and temperance. Fortitude, or courage, is the moral virtue that enables us to be steadfast in trials and constant in the pursuit of the good. It strengthens our resolve to resist temptations and to overcome obstacles in the moral life. The virtue of fortitude enables us to conquer fear, even the fear of death, and to face trials and persecutions.

The Coming Christian Persecution

As a virtue, courage has somewhat fallen out of favor in our age, since, to some, it smacks of "toxic masculinity," of warriors setting out to battle, unsure whether they will return alive. Our age prefers to speak of the "feminine" virtues of compassion, tenderness, care, empathy, and understanding. Although these undoubtedly have their place, courage is no less central to the Christian life than it was in ages past, and men and women are meant to practice it equally.

St. Thomas Aquinas said that courage is especially necessary for two things: to undertake difficult enterprises and to be patient in bearing suffering. It is for this reason that we rightly associate courage with the witness of the martyrs. It took extreme courage for the martyrs to accept death rather than to betray God and their faith in Him. We gaze with admiration at the courage of even little children—such as St. Agnes, St. Tarcisius, and St. Maria Goretti—who showed such astonishing courage in the face of torment and death. But courage is necessary for every Christian heart. It is not an easy, well-trodden path that we are called to travel: "The gate is narrow and the way is hard, that leads to life, and those who find it are few" (Matt. 7:14).

A Christian's courage in the face of antagonism is not simply stoicism or raw toughness. While Christianity undoubtedly has its heroes, men and women of exceptional valor, the real source of Christian fortitude is the grace of God Himself. As St. Paul exclaimed, "I can do all things in him who strengthens me" (Phil. 4:13).

As we saw in the cases of Sts. Perpetua and Felicity, the saints themselves were often aware that, in themselves, they did not have the courage required to face martyrdom, but they trusted in God to give them that strength when it became necessary. Felicity famously cried out in pain during the birth of her baby in prison, and it prompted one of the servants to taunt her, saying that if she could not bear the pain of childbirth, how was she going to endure being thrown to the beasts? As we have seen, Felicity replied that in childbirth, it was she who was suffering, but in the arena, it would be Christ who suffered in her and for her.

In the history of the Church, there have been exceptional martyrs who longed to be able to give their lives for Christ. St. Ignatius of Antioch left a bracing witness of such a desire in his *Letter to the Romans*, composed as he traveled in chains to Rome for execution. "What a thrill I shall have from the wild beasts that are ready for me! I hope they will make short work of me," Ignatius wrote. "I shall coax them on to eat me up at once and not to hold off, as sometimes happens, through fear. And if they are reluctant, I shall force them to it. Forgive me—I know what is good for me."

"Now is the moment I am beginning to be a disciple," Ignatius continued. "May nothing seen or unseen begrudge me making my way to Jesus Christ. Come fire, cross, battling with wild beasts, wrenching of bones, mangling of limbs, crushing of my whole body, cruel tortures of the devil—only let me get to Jesus Christ!"

In that same letter, Ignatius begged the Christian community at Rome not to intervene on his behalf out of a false compassion, insisting that his chance for martyrdom was a rare opportunity that he did not want to miss: "I am corresponding with all the churches and bidding them all realize that I am voluntarily dying for God —if, that is, you do not interfere. I plead with you, do not do me an unseasonable kindness," he wrote. "Let me be fodder for wild beasts —that is how I can get to God."

"I am God's wheat and I am being ground by the teeth of wild beasts to make a pure loaf for Christ," he continued. "I would rather that you fawn on the beasts so that they may be my tomb and no scrap of my body be left. Thus, when I have fallen asleep, I shall be a burden to no one. Then I shall be a real disciple of Jesus Christ when the world sees my body no more. Pray Christ for me that by these means I may become God's sacrifice."[290]

Although most of us are not called to yearn for persecution and martyrdom the way Ignatius did, his heroism and radiant faith stand as a beacon of courage for all generations. It is difficult to read those words and not feel emboldened to confront our own small part in the Church's sufferings with greater bravery and valor.

Patience

Patience—the ability to suffer and bear sorrows—is the quintessential virtue for facing persecution. Among all the possible attributes of Christian charity, St. Paul places patience at the head of the list. Charity is patient; that is, charity knows how to suffer.

In the *Summa theologica*, St. Thomas Aquinas insists it is necessary "for a virtue to safeguard the good of reason against sorrow, lest reason give way to sorrow, and this patience does."[291] In other words, patience is the virtue that enables a person to stay on the right path despite the sufferings and sorrows required. Without this patience, Christians would abandon the mission as soon as persecution reared its head.

Similarly, the great African Doctor of the Church, St. Augustine of Hippo, wrote that "properly speaking, those are patient who would rather bear evils without inflicting them, than inflict them without bearing them."[292] Patience is not, therefore, just a stoic

---

[290] St. Ignatius of Antioch, *Letter to the Romans*, trans. Cyril C. Richardson, in *Early Christian Fathers* (Philadelphia: Westminster Press, 1953), 104–105.

[291] St. Thomas Aquinas, *Summa theologica* II-II.136.1.

[292] St. Augustine, *De patientia* II.V.

ability to bear pain in indifference but rather the virtuous ability to suffer for goodness.

Augustine further noted that "sorrow and pain are of themselves displeasing to the soul, wherefore one would never choose to suffer them for their own sake, but only for the sake of an end. Hence it follows that the good for [whose sake] one is willing to endure evils is more desired and loved than the good [whose privation] causes the sorrow that we bear patiently."[293] By this Augustine means that the patient person loves God more than he fears the sorrow occasioned by the loss of other goods, even that of one's life. This, Augustine says, is why patience is considered by St. Paul as the first quality of charity.

Looking at the lives of the martyrs, the heroes of Christian persecution, one cannot help but notice how they excelled in patience. Threatened with the most horrifying pains, separated from friends and family, tempted to believe that their sufferings were for naught, they nonetheless remained firm in the faith. Their battle was not against "flesh and blood" but against their own inclinations and against the powers of evil that would have them deny their Lord and Savior.

In describing the Last Judgment, Thomas à Kempis underscored the eternal value of patience and how it will be prized by those who practiced it:

> In that day every trial borne in patience will be pleasing and the voice of iniquity will be stilled; the devout will be glad; the irreligious will mourn; and the mortified body will rejoice far more than if it had been pampered with every pleasure. Then the cheap garment will shine with

---

[293] Ibid., IV.

splendor and the rich one become faded and worn; the poor cottage will be more praised than the gilded palace. In that day persevering patience will count more than all the power in this world; simple obedience will be exalted above all worldly cleverness; a good and clean conscience will gladden the heart of man far more than the philosophy of the learned; and contempt for riches will be of more weight than every treasure on earth.[294]

The author adds another consideration that is helpful for understanding patience in the face of persecution, whatever form it may take, remembering that we do not choose our crosses:

The man who will suffer only as much as seems good to him, who will accept suffering only from those from whom he is pleased to accept it, is not truly patient. For the truly patient man does not consider from whom the suffering comes, whether from a superior, an equal, or an inferior, whether from a good and holy person or from a perverse and unworthy one; but no matter how great an adversity befalls him, no matter how often it comes or from whom it comes, he accepts it gratefully from the hand of God, and counts it a great gain.

For with God nothing that is suffered for His sake, no matter how small, can pass without reward. Be prepared for the fight, then, if you wish to gain the victory. Without struggle you cannot obtain the crown of patience, and if you refuse to suffer you are refusing the crown. But if you desire to be crowned, fight bravely and bear up patiently. Without labor there is no rest, and without fighting, no victory.[295]

---

[294] Thomas à Kempis, *The Imitation of Christ* I.24.
[295] Ibid., III.19.

The medieval author offers great spiritual wisdom, even though it sounds harsh to our modern ears. "If you were but worthy to suffer something for the name of Jesus, what great glory would be in store for you, what great joy to all the saints of God, what great edification to those about you! For all men praise patience though there are few who wish to practice it."

"With good reason, then, ought you to be willing to suffer a little for Christ since many suffer much more for the world," he observes.[296]

Docility

A key Christian conviction is that God is actively working in each of our lives to mold us into saints. Sometimes we cooperate with this divine action, sometimes we ignore it, and sometimes we resist it. God has myriad ways of accomplishing this sanctification in every life; He does not apply a one-size-fits-all approach to bringing us to holiness. This is why St. Thérèse of Lisieux compared souls to flowers, each with its own perfection and each contributing to the harmony and beauty of the whole of the garden:

> Jesus deigned to teach me this mystery. He set before me the book of nature; I understood how all the flowers He has created are beautiful, how the splendor of the rose and the whiteness of the lily do not take away the perfume of the little violet or the delightful simplicity of the daisy. I understood that if all flowers wanted to be roses, nature would lose her springtime beauty, and the fields would no longer be decked out with little wild flowers. And so it is in the world of souls, Jesus' garden. He willed to create great

[296] Ibid., II.12.

souls comparable to lilies and roses, but He has created smaller ones and these must be content to be daisies or violets destined to give joy to God's glances when He looks down at His feet. Perfection consists in doing His will, in being what He wills us to be.[297]

We Christians are called to see the divine hand in everything and to unite ourselves to the divine pedagogy. The knowledge that nothing befalls us without God's allowing it can encourage us to accept and embrace all things from His loving hand, even things that cause pain and sorrow. In persecution and incomprehension, God shapes Christians in virtue, fashioning them into more perfect replicas of His divine Son.

As a virtue, docility is not the same as passive resignation. Docility requires active cooperation and action. God does not put us under anesthesia and operate on us, making us saints despite ourselves. Instead, He respects our freedom, inspiring us, encouraging us, emboldening us, and engaging our memory, intellect, and will and all our faculties. This is true in times of peace and in times of crisis. When we are called to suffer for the faith, God is with us, and our job is to cooperate with Him and to allow ourselves to be led and *taught* by Him.

Docility is the virtue of the apprentice, the good student, the disciple. It comes from the Latin word *docere*, meaning "to teach." Docility is a willingness to learn and to be fashioned into a vessel of God's choosing. For some, this path may be arduous and painful; for others, it may be less so. Each of us is called to embrace the path that God has lovingly chosen for us. As St. Paul so wisely said: "Will what is molded say to its molder, 'Why have you made

---

[297] St. Thérèse of Lisieux, *The Story of a Soul*, chap. 1.

me thus?' Has the potter no right over the clay, to make out of the same lump one vessel for beauty and another for menial use?" (Rom. 9:20-21). The divine Potter's fingers may seem gentle in times of consolation and hard in times of persecution, but it is always the same love behind them.

Hope

St. Paul famously said that if Christians' hope is in this world alone, we are the most pitiful of people and our faith has been "in vain" (see 1 Cor. 15:16-19). Following Jesus rarely brings steady consolations in this world; this is why Christians are urged to "seek the things that are above" (Col. 3:1) rather than the things of this earth. This is nowhere clearer than in persecution and martyrdom, in which Christians bear aggression, abuse, and even death for the sake of Jesus. If this life were all there is, such Christians would indeed have squandered the one thing of value they had.

Persecution is a constant reminder that Christians are in exile and that our home is not in this world. It urges us to look elsewhere, to place our aspirations in eternity rather than in earthly comfort and success. In times of prosperity, when everything is going well, it is tempting for us to become complacent, to allow ourselves to be attached to this world and its pleasures. In times of trial, however, our gaze naturally turns upward, hoping—and trusting—that there is something better to come.

It is significant that the first pope, St. Peter, told Christians they must be prepared to give reasons for their hope (see 1 Pet. 3:15). These reasons are founded in God's goodness and faithfulness, not in a sunny optimism that things will necessarily get better or that people will have a change of heart. Maybe they will, and maybe they won't. Theological hope ultimately concerns eternal life rather than temporal well-being, and true hope does not wax and wane with the times—good or bad. Hope shines most truly, indeed, when the times are darkest. Hope is the stuff of gulags and cancer wards, not of cruise ships and cotillions.

In 2007, Pope Benedict XVI published an encyclical letter on the Christian virtue of hope called *Spe salvi* (*Saved in Hope*). In it, he raised a troubling question: whether people today even desire eternal life, the goal of Christian hope. "Faith is the substance of hope. But then the question arises: do we really want this—to live eternally?" Benedict asked. "Perhaps many people reject the faith today simply because they do not find the prospect of eternal life attractive. What they desire is not eternal life at all, but this present life, for which faith in eternal life seems something of an impediment." To continue living forever, the pope noted, "appears more like a curse than a gift."

On the other hand, the love that people crave can never be fully satisfied in this world, Benedict contended, because it is a love that "remains fragile," and it can be "destroyed by death" and thus cries out for eternity.

> The human being needs unconditional love. He needs the certainty which makes him say: "neither death, nor life, nor angels, nor principalities, nor things present, nor things to come, nor powers, nor height, nor depth, nor anything else in all creation, will be able to separate us from the love of God in Christ Jesus our Lord" (Rom 8:38–39). If this absolute love exists, with its absolute certainty, then—only then—is man "redeemed," whatever should happen to him in his particular circumstances.[298]

---

[298] Pope Benedict XVI, encyclical letter *Spe salvi* (November 30, 2007), no. 26.

This is indeed the love that St. Paul found that enabled him to face his own martyrdom with serenity.

The Vietnamese martyr Paul Le-Bao-Tinh († 1857) wrote a letter from the concentration camp where he was held, a "letter from hell," but filled with hope and even joy:

> The prison here is a true image of everlasting Hell: to cruel tortures of every kind—shackles, iron chains, manacles—are added hatred, vengeance, calumnies, obscene speech, quarrels, evil acts, swearing, curses, as well as anguish and grief. But the God who once freed the three children from the fiery furnace is with me always; he has delivered me from these tribulations and made them sweet, for his mercy is forever.

Le-Bao-Tinh found courage and solace in the companionship of Christ, in the assurance that he was not alone in his suffering. Knowledge of this companionship filled him with hope, hope that he already shared in the final victory achieved by Christ in His Passion:

> In the midst of these torments, which usually terrify others, I am, by the grace of God, full of joy and gladness, because I am not alone—Christ is with me.... How am I to bear with the spectacle, as each day I see emperors, mandarins, and their retinue blaspheming your holy name, O Lord, who are enthroned above the Cherubim and Seraphim? Behold, the pagans have trodden your Cross underfoot! Where is your glory?

And thus he was able not only to bear the sorrows and sufferings of the prison but even to encourage and inspire his brethren:

> As I see all this, I would, in the ardent love I have for you, prefer to be torn limb from limb and to die as a witness to

your love. O Lord, show your power, save me, sustain me, that in my infirmity your power may be shown and may be glorified before the nations.... Beloved brothers, as you hear all these things may you give endless thanks in joy to God, from whom every good proceeds; bless the Lord with me, for his mercy is forever.... I write these things to you in order that your faith and mine may be united. In the midst of this storm I cast my anchor towards the throne of God, the anchor that is the lively hope in my heart.[299]

Imitatio Christi

For the Christian, hostility and persecution offer a unique opportunity to identify with Jesus and follow His shining example. This *imitatio Christi*—the imitation of Christ—that is central to Christian spirituality reaches its culmination in martyrdom: "Greater love has no man than this, that a man lay down his life for his friends" (John 15:13).

Christians are called to imitate Jesus in everything. We are called to learn from Him, who is meek and humble of heart (see Matt. 11:29). Like Jesus, we are called to be generous, single-hearted, resolute, compassionate, and prayerful. Yet nowhere is the disciple's imitation of Christ more tested than in persecution.

Thomas à Kempis notes with searing acuity the tendency for Christians to follow Christ at a distance, drawing the line at accompanying Him to His Passion:

Jesus has always many who love His heavenly kingdom, but few who bear His cross. He has many who desire consolation, but few who care for trial. He finds many to share His

---

[299] *The Liturgy of the Hours*, Office of Readings, November 24.

table, but few to take part in His fasting. All desire to be happy with Him; few wish to suffer anything for Him. Many follow Him to the breaking of bread, but few to the drinking of the chalice of His passion. Many revere His miracles; few approach the shame of the Cross. Many love Him as long as they encounter no hardship; many praise and bless Him as long as they receive some comfort from Him. But if Jesus hides Himself and leaves them for a while, they fall either into complaints or into deep dejection. Those, on the contrary, who love Him for His own sake and not for any comfort of their own, bless Him in all trial and anguish of heart as well as in the bliss of consolation.[300]

"The whole life of Christ was a cross and a martyrdom, and do you seek rest and enjoyment for yourself?" Kempis continued. "You deceive yourself, you are mistaken if you seek anything but to suffer, for this mortal life is full of miseries and marked with crosses on all sides. Indeed, the more spiritual progress a person makes, so much heavier will he frequently find the cross, because as his love increases, the pain of his exile also increases.[301]

Jesus Christ is not only our Savior; He is also our *model*. As well as being God, He is the perfect man and exemplifies for us what humanity is meant to look like. When we face persecution, we are offered a privileged opportunity to imitate Christ in His redemptive act and in His perfect obedience to the Father. "Although he was a Son, he learned obedience through what he suffered; and being made perfect he became the source of eternal salvation to all who obey him" (Heb. 5:8–9).

---

[300] Thomas à Kempis, *The Imitation of Christ* II.11.
[301] Ibid., II.12.

The Coming Christian Persecution

Evangelization through Suffering

We have seen that Tertullian famously declared that the blood of the martyrs is the seed of Christians (*sanguis martyrum, semen Christianorum*).[302] Just from a historical point of view, this was indisputably the case. The more Christians were persecuted, the more others wanted to join their ranks. When the Romans thought they could extinguish the fledgling Christian community by making life miserable for it, they found the opposite was true: it flourished all the more. This phenomenon goes hand in hand with another apparent paradox: when Christians' lives get too comfortable, the Church stops growing, and witness becomes less convincing.

The growth of the persecuted Church lends itself to two explanations. One certain cause for such growth is the blessing of God upon the faithfulness of His servants. If, indeed, "you will know them by their fruits" (Matt. 7:16), then who can doubt that God will reward the witness of His holy martyrs with a superabundance of grace and the conversion of many souls to the faith? God is trustworthy and crowns faithfulness with fruitfulness.

A second explanation for such growth is closely related to the first. Evangelization is empowered by witness, and the greatest witness is martyrdom. Words and clever arguments rarely convince, especially when we are talking about something as central to our identity as the meaning of human existence. It is sanctity—the witness of a holy life—that people find compelling. We can ask ourselves, "What is it that led me to embrace, or continue embracing, the faith?" In most cases, we can trace our own faith convictions to the witness of a holy life.

Thus, years before becoming pope, Cardinal Joseph Ratzinger could write that art and the witness of a holy life are the most

---

[302] Tertullian, *Apology* 50.13: CCL 1, 171.

compelling tools of evangelization. "The only really effective apologia for Christianity comes down to two arguments, namely, the saints the Church has produced and the art which has grown in her womb," he said in his 1985 interview book, *The Ratzinger Report*. "Better witness is borne to the Lord by the splendor of holiness and art which have arisen in the community of believers than by the clever excuses which apologetics has come up with to justify the dark sides which, sadly, are so frequent in the Church's human history."[303]

Christian steadfastness, even joy, in the midst of injustice and suffering is a powerful witness to the truth of the gospel and the sustaining power of God's grace. Martyrs evangelize with their bloodshed in a way more eloquent than mere words or argument. Persecution, therefore, must be recognized as a means of drawing others to Christ. Jesus said that when He was lifted up from the earth, He would draw all people to Himself (John 12:32). When Christians, like their Master, are lifted up from the earth, when they faithfully, even joyfully, share in the cross of Christ, they, too, draw all people to Him.

Jesus also proclaimed that His disciples were destined to be salt and light—salt that seasons and preserves, light that illuminates. A light is not meant to be put under a bushel basket, He insisted, but upon a lampstand (Matt. 5:13–16). There it will be seen and provide light for many, but there it will also be a target. The very distinctiveness of a true Christian makes him both beacon and prey.

The Battle for Religious Freedom

The foregoing virtues characterizing a Christian response to persecution speak much of peaceful acceptance, patience, and even

---

[303] Joseph Ratzinger and Vittorio Messori, *The Ratzinger Report* (San Francisco: Ignatius Press, 1985), 129.

joy. It would be a mistake, however, to conclude that Christians are called to allow persecution to go on unchecked. Religious freedom and the defense of basic human rights are central to the mission of the Church in the world since they stand at the core of the common good. Where rights are violated with impunity, the common good cannot flourish. Christians must insist on their right to carry out their mission of living and preaching their faith without undue interference.

When writing to the bishop Timothy, St. Paul urges "that supplications, prayers, intercessions, and thanksgivings be made for all men, for kings and all who are in high positions, that we may lead a quiet and peaceable life, godly and respectful in every way. This is good, and it is acceptable in the sight of God our Savior, who desires all men to be saved and to come to the knowledge of the truth" (1 Tim. 2:1–4). Here, Paul is not asking for a lot from government—merely that it defend the common good and secure for all a "quiet and peaceable life" without undue interference or oppression. But the common good has religious freedom at its core.

As the *Catechism of the Catholic Church* teaches, the common good resides particularly "in the conditions for the exercise of the natural freedoms indispensable for the development of the human vocation, such as 'the right to act according to a sound norm of conscience and to safeguard ... privacy, and rightful freedom also in matters of religion.'"[304] In this regard, Christians do well to work to make known their plight and to push vigorously for greater religious freedom in the world. As Pope Benedict wrote, "the deliberate promotion of religious indifference or practical atheism on the part of many countries obstructs the requirements

[304] CCC 1907, quoting GS 26 § 2.

for the development of peoples, depriving them of spiritual and human resources."[305]

St. John Paul II, a champion of religious liberty, insisted that respect for the dignity of the person

> demands the recognition of the religious dimension of the individual. This is not simply a requirement "concerning matters of faith," but a requirement that finds itself inextricably bound up with the very reality of the individual. In fact, the individual's relation to God is a constitutive element of the very "being" and "existence" of an individual.[306]

Since the religious dimension stands at the core of what it means to be human, John Paul did not hesitate to assert that the "source and synthesis" of all human rights is "religious freedom, understood as the right to live in the truth of one's faith and in conformity with one's transcendent dignity as a person."[307] As the pinnacle of human rights, religious liberty demands the very highest protection. It is not just another human right among many but the source of all other rights.

Thus, John Paul continued, the effective acknowledgment of the right of freedom of conscience and religious freedom

> is among the highest goods and the most serious duties of every people that truly wishes to assure the good of the person and society. Religious freedom, an essential

---

[305] Pope Benedict XVI, encyclical letter *Caritas in veritate* (August 15, 2009), no. 29.

[306] Pope John Paul II, post-synodal apostolic exhortation *Christifideles laici* (December 30, 1988), no. 39.

[307] Pope John Paul II, encyclical letter *Centesimus annus* (May 1, 1991), no. 47.

requirement of the dignity of every person, is a cornerstone of the structure of human rights, and for this reason an irreplaceable factor in the good of individuals and of the whole of society, as well as of the personal fulfilment of each individual.[308]

It follows, he wrote, that "the freedom of individuals and of communities to profess and practice their religion is an essential element for peaceful human coexistence," and therefore the "civil and social right to religious freedom, inasmuch as it touches the most intimate sphere of the spirit, is a point of reference for the other fundamental rights and in some way becomes a measure of them."[309]

In July 2018, the U.S. State Department launched its first-ever Religious Freedom Ministerial under the direction of Secretary of State Mike Pompeo, whose stated purpose was "to advance religious freedom around the world." This hugely significant endeavor brought together more than eighty national delegations, including more than forty foreign ministers. At the time, Pompeo told Vatican Radio that the State Department under President Trump had "made religious freedom a true priority for this administration," adding that the mission of the ministerial was "to spread the word of the importance of religious freedom for every individual around the world."

"We want to press for that," he said. "There are countries that share America's understanding of that and there are those who don't and we want to move each of them in the right direction, toward increasing religious freedom," he said.[310]

---

[308] Pope John Paul II, *Christifideles laici* 39.

[309] Ibid.

[310] Devin Watkins, "US SecState Pompeo: Religious Freedom a Fundamental Human Right," Vatican News, July 23, 2018, https://

A year later, the State Department held its second ministerial, to which the U.S. invited more than a hundred foreign delegations and more than a thousand civil and religious leaders from all faiths as well as representatives from persecuted ethno-religious minorities. "This is the largest human rights event ever hosted at the State Department and the largest religious freedom event ever done in the world," Ambassador at Large for International Religious Freedom Sam Brownback declared at the time.

The following year, President Donald Trump issued an executive order on advancing international religious freedom, insisting on its importance for national security and human rights. "Religious freedom, America's first freedom, is a moral and national security imperative," the order declared. "Religious freedom for all people worldwide is a foreign policy priority of the United States, and the United States will respect and vigorously promote this freedom." The order said that the U.S. would "prioritize" international religious freedom, noting that the American Founders "understood religious freedom not as a creation of the state, but as a gift of God to every person and a right that is fundamental for the flourishing of our society."[311]

This tremendously hopeful and important initiative was brought down with a crash by the Biden administration, which explicitly repudiated the centrality of religious freedom in the edifice of human rights, insisting that no hierarchy of rights exists. Human rights are "co-equal," Secretary of State Antony Blinken

---

www.vaticannews.va/en/world/news/2018-07/us-secstate-pompeo-religious-freedom.html.

[311] President Donald Trump, "Executive Order on Advancing International Religious Freedom," June 2, 2020, sect. 1, https://trump whitehouse.archives.gov/presidential-actions/executive-order -advancing-international-religious-freedom/.

said at the rollout of the 2020 Country Reports on Human Rights Practices, adding that "there is no hierarchy that makes some rights more important than others."[312] In so saying, the secretary ignored the fact that the International Covenant on Civil and Political Rights, to which the United States is a party, makes certain rights, including religious freedom "non-derogable," which means that they cannot be suspended even in times of national emergency.

"Past unbalanced statements that suggest such a hierarchy, including those offered by a recently disbanded State Department advisory committee, do not represent a guiding document for this administration," Blinken stated. "At my confirmation hearing, I promised that the Biden-Harris administration would repudiate those unbalanced views." Rather than emphasize the importance of religious liberty, Blinken insisted that other new rights, such as abortion and gender identity, be added to the list and that they have equal status with other, more foundational rights.

These threats to religious freedom in a country that long prided itself on its championship of human rights manifest the importance of Christian watchdog groups in their endeavor to promote religious freedom and make known the sufferings of believers around the world. We have spoken at length of the heroic witness of the Christian martyrs, who shed their blood in fidelity to Christ. Those who defend religious freedom and fight Christian persecution are also heroes. Open Doors, Christian Solidarity Worldwide, the Becket Fund for Religious Liberty, Aid to the Church in Need, Voice of the Martyrs, ChinaAid, the Barnabas Fund, the Observatory on

---

[312] "Secretary Antony J. Blinken on Release of the 2020 Country Reports on Human Rights Practices," March 30, 2021, U.S. Department of State, https://www.state.gov/secretary-antony-j-blinken-on-release-of-the-2020-country-reports-on-human-rights-practices/.

Intolerance and Discrimination against Christians in Europe, the Alliance Defending Freedom, the Hudson Institute's Center for Religious Freedom, and many others are doing invaluable work to make known the plight of persecuted Christians, advance the cause of religious freedom, and assist our suffering brethren. Many of their founders and members have left lucrative careers in order to put their lives at the service of the suffering Church and to ensure that religious liberty is everywhere defended. They deserve our gratitude, our prayers, and our active support.

Jesus famously told His followers to turn the other cheek, yet the one time He is struck in the face by an officer of the Sanhedrin, He does *not* turn the other cheek. Instead, He objects, saying, "If I have spoken wrongly, bear witness to the wrong; but if I have spoken rightly, why do you strike me?" (John 18:21–23). This suggests that there are times when Christians are called to exercise discernment, which will often mean standing up for the truth rather than passively resigning themselves to lies and abuse.

Christian persecution is wrong and must be opposed. It is evil to persecute people because of their beliefs, and it creates unjust situations of pressure in which many may end up betraying or hiding their beliefs out of fear of reprisals. But Christians are not the only ones harmed by Christian persecution. The perpetrators of such actions also do damage to their own souls. The words of Christ are powerful: "Woe to the world for temptations to sin! For it is necessary that temptations come, but woe to the man by whom the temptation comes!" (Matt. 18:7).

Jesus Himself bears witness to this in speaking of Judas Iscariot and his betrayal. Even though Judas ends up serving the plan of God by his evil actions, those actions are still evil and worthy of punishment. "The Son of man goes as it is written of him, but woe to that man by whom the Son of man is betrayed! It would have been better for that man if he had not been born" (Matt. 26:24). These are terrible words indeed. In the same way, Christians may ultimately benefit from being persecuted since God makes use of this for good, but the evil action does not for that become less evil.

Awareness of the widespread persecution that afflicts the followers of Christ should give us pause, but in the end, it should embolden rather than intimidate us. When I was growing up, my parents had hung on the wall of our home a small plaque that read: "The will of God will never lead you where the grace of God cannot keep you." If His will includes suffering for us, His grace will be sufficient for us to bear it.

Jesus' words must be a light for our path: "In the world you have tribulation, but be of good cheer, I have overcome the world."

About the Author

Dr. Thomas D. Williams, a 2018 visiting research fellow for the Center for Ethics and Culture at the University of Notre Dame, has written widely on theology, philosophy, ethics, and spirituality. He teaches theology at St. John's University's Rome campus and has done extensive media work, including serving as consultant and commentator on faith, ethics, and religion for NBC, CBS, and Sky News in the UK. He was appointed by the Holy See as spokesman for the synod of bishops in 1997 and again in 2001. Williams's books include *Who Is My Neighbor? Personalism and the Foundations of Human Rights* and *The World as It Could Be: Catholic Social Thought for a New Generation*. He is also the author of the children's book *The First Christmas* (Sophia Institute Press, 2022).

CRISIS Publications

Sophia Institute Press awards the privileged title "CRISIS Publications" to a select few of our books that address contemporary issues at the intersection of politics, culture, and the Church with clarity, cogency, and force and that are also destined to become all-time classics.

CRISIS Publications are *direct*, explaining their principles briefly, simply, and clearly to Catholics in the pews, on whom the future of the Church depends. The time for ambiguity or confusion is long past.

CRISIS Publications are *contemporary*, born of our own time and circumstances and intended to become significant statements in current debates, statements that serious Catholics cannot ignore, regardless of their prior views.

CRISIS Publications are *classical*, addressing themes and enunciating principles that are valid for all ages and cultures. Readers will turn to them time and again for guidance in other days and different circumstances.

CRISIS Publications are *spirited*, entering contemporary debates with gusto to clarify issues and demonstrate how those issues can be resolved in a way that enlivens souls and the Church.

We welcome engagement with our readers on current and future CRISIS Publications. Please pray that this imprint may help to resolve the crises embroiling our Church and society today.

Sophia Institute Press® is a registered trademark of Sophia Institute.
Sophia Institute is a tax-exempt institution as defined by the
Internal Revenue Code, Section 501(c)(3). Tax I.D. 22-2548708.